MW01146112

WATER MUSIC

*Adventures
of a
journeyman surfer*

WATER MUSIC

Adventures
of a
journeyman surfer

David Rearwin

MONTEREY BOOKS

Copyright © 2021 David Rearwin

All rights reserved.
Except for brief citations in reviews, no part of this work may be used or
reproduced in any form.

Email all communications to:
watermusic808@gmail.com

ISBN: 978-1-7366477-2-1

DEDICATION

I owe so many things to so many people who have helped me get this far that it's impossible to include them all here, but here's a partial list.

First and foremost, to my long-suffering wife: for putting up with me during my long and moody enforced absence from surfing and tolerating – even encouraging – all my aging-surfer-dude nonsense after my comeback, not to mention my intermittent aging-would-be-writer-dude nonsense.

To Tami and Maia for their suggestions and encouragement.

To the tight-knit crew in Santa Barbara – Kemp Aaberg, Bob Perko, Frank Suttner, Sam Webster, Glenn Vargen – who welcomed me into their lineup and provided the motivation and encouragement that made my comeback possible.

To the many Bird Rock area surfers who shared waves and friendship. Among them (random order) Andy Yuen, Mike Norman, Jake Grosz, Rick Farley, Steve Johnson, Jerry Catarius, Mike Newlee, Rawli Davis, Richard Miller, Jonathan Gumbert, Scott Darran, Bruce Herridge, Jay Mickelsen, Pete Robson, Mikhail Alexseev, Doug Bodenstab, Hiroshi Takahashi, Misa Takahashi, Mike Cairns, Chris Lundgren, David Susi, Eric Kay, Fred Marchal, James McGrew, John Law, Mark Arthurs, Mike Donnelly and many others.

To my SUP mentors Andy Yuen, Richard Rios and Sean McGee.

To Hawaiian waterman, surfer and videographer Elliott Wong, for all the aloha in the lineup and on shore.

To Dr. Jeffrey Tash of Honolulu for sewing me up and fixing my dings on several occasions.

To Pat and Bryce for saving my life or at least my leg.

Posthumously to Steve "Sealbite" Fujii, Michael "Biker" Sherlock, Roy Eder, and John "Wheels" Williams – your passing left a gap.

Finally, in memory of the old Windansea crew:

Wayne Land, for introducing me to karate and Japan.

Ronald Patterson, for sharing his love of slack key guitar.

Butch Van Artsdalen, for showing me that the best way to learn something is to try it.

To dance with the waves
You must learn to hear
the music of the sea.

BAJA CALIFORNIA PENINSULA
&
MAINLAND MEXICO

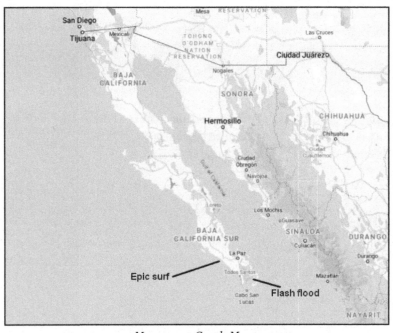

Map source: Google Maps

Cardón cactus with eagles' nest, Baja California - Stephen Marlett photo
A cardón can be 30-60ft. high and weigh up to 25 tons.

WAIKĪKĪ & DIAMOND HEAD
Relative locations of selected spots

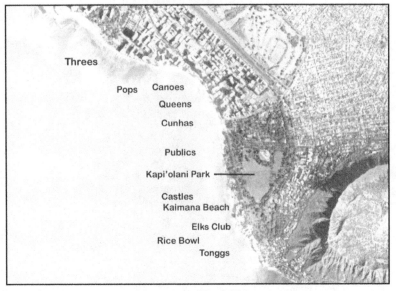

Map source: Google Maps

Table of Contents

Windansea: summer, 1950s
Balsa longboards and old-style planks

NOTES TO THE READER

1. In the context of this book, the term Older Guy (capitalized) refers to any surfer over the age of about twenty or so, as perceived by young surfers. An Older Guy retains this status as he and those younger surfers age.

2. Bob Simmons was a pioneer in several aspects of surfboard design.

3. For surf breaks I use the names – like Boomer (no –s) and the Middle (no –s) – that were used at the time.

4. haole: In Hawai'i, a white person whether local or mainlander. The word itself is fairly neutral but it is often used in a derogatory context. For some reason people of Portuguese descent are not normally included in this category.

5. The Mexico I once knew has been completely transformed. Many roads, towns, and developments that are major landmarks today simply didn't exist, at least in anything like their present form. Other places have been abandoned. Place names have changed and roads have been altered and re-routed to pass through entirely different places than before. I do have the events right, but please bear with me if some locations appear to be "off" related to what you yourself may have experienced.

6. The Great Malibu Surf Contest Bus Trip has inspired a number of fanciful accounts by people who weren't there. The eye-witness description in this book is accurate.

7. The green flash, caused by atmospheric refraction, can be seen best in clear, dry weather at sunset. When the sun is almost entirely below the horizon with the upper edge still visible it will appear green in color for a second or two.

8. Some seabirds (alcids) use their short wings to "fly" underwater.

1970s: 7'6" Canyon by Rusty
This board saw me through some serious adventures.

PREFACE

After a certain age all you have left is your story – and if you don't write it down somewhere it disappears forever, taking with it the world you knew and the lessons you've learned. So here is mine.

I'm a journeyman – a surfer who has some standout moments but will never be a star. I've been content to enjoy the endless magic and beauty of the sea without riding monster waves or entering contests. But I've had a lot of fun and some uniquely challenging experiences and adventures.

I think you'll find the incidents in this book interesting and entertaining. All of them actually happened and I've tried to present them as accurately as possible. Luckily I wrote some of them down years ago before they could sink beneath the waves of forgetfulness or fade into hazy recollections. Others are still as vivid to me today as they were the day they happened, and will stay with me forever.

• • •

This book is about the sea and the magic it creates. A big part of that magic is surf and surfing, but this isn't just a surf book. It's also the story of my love affair with the sea in all its myriad aspects: ups and downs, triumphs and disasters, closeness and separation. It deals with the adventures that seem to happen naturally whenever people and waves – or indeed, moving water – interact. Finally, it's about lessons learned.

If there's a message in the book, it is this: magic is all around us, waiting for us to recognize it and let it become part of our lives. The key is freshness of approach: the beginner's mind sought by Zen practitioners, in which everything is always new. You might think of it as a child's mind, say that of an inquisitive ten-year-old. Everyone has an inner ten-year-old; the sea may help you stay in touch with yours.

I have changed or omitted some names to avoid embarrassment to those concerned.

Cunha's 2013

Prologue

I'm floating, cradled by warm water. Above me rises an enormous liquid wall, a towering ridge of water, the base still shrouded in predawn gloom. As the peak rises up, it touches the first rays of the sun. The entire length of the crest is transformed, turned to a sheet of rainbows as the offshore wind blows the spray from the top.

I've pushed my board away to keep it from hitting me if we're caught by the breaking wave, pushed it parallel to the wave in the hope that it won't be broken in half. It floats away gently, then begins to rise up the face.

Unexpectedly, caught by the offshore wind, my board lifts off the water, points its nose upward, and launches vertically up and through the rainbow crest, trailing a shower of sparkling diamonds in all the colors of the universe.

It's the most beautiful thing I've ever seen. How lucky I am to be able to witness this! Next time I really must bring a camera.

Underneath these thoughts, I'm only dimly aware that my mind is wandering.

Am I dreaming? It occurs to me that I'm falling asleep. Why? This ocean is not cold. I actually fell asleep in the ocean once, from hypothermia. But this ocean is warm, and this sleep feels different.

If I fall asleep, my face will slump into the water. I will take a breath. And I will drown. I regard the thought with detachment; mild interest is all I can muster. I don't really care.

Then another set appears, a huge dark line building on the pre-dawn horizon. This, I care about.

How did I get here? And what is going to happen next?

LA JOLLA
Relative locations of selected spots

Image source: Wiki Commons

Part I: Learning Curve

All at once, the boundary between me and the rest of the world disappeared; a sudden weightlessness took hold of me, as though I were no longer a body...For some unidentifiable period of time, I lost track of who and where I was.
—Description of a first kiss (*Joe College* by Tom Perrott)

1951: First wave, first love

I caught my first unbroken wave on a surfboard at the age of ten. The board I used was a massive slab of thick balsa timbers at least ten feet long, glued together and covered with fiberglass for a total weight of around forty pounds. One of my little buddies had access to it, and with some struggle the two of us managed to carry it the two or three blocks from his house to the long sand beach at La Jolla Shores without dropping it.

We started out trying to catch waves by launching the board into the soup of a wave that had already broken, one of us lying on the board and paddling by flailing his arms frantically, the other standing on the bottom in the shallow water and pushing the board from behind to generate momentum. The waves were small – maybe knee high – and we weren't having much success.

After a few minutes of taking turns pushing and being pushed in order to ride the white water of broken waves, my pal went off to get a drink of water and left me and the board to our own devices.

Somehow it occurred to me to try something more ambitious, so I pushed the board out past the tiny breaking ripples, lay down on it and

3

awkwardly paddled out through the slight rolls of swell. When I judged that I was far enough out, with great effort I got it turned around to point toward shore. Then I sat on the board and waited, looking over my shoulder toward the horizon, just as I had seen surfers do on occasion. It was a perfect Southern California morning: clear blue skies, no wind, warm summer sea.

I see the wave long before it arrives: a slender line rolling down off the horizon and sliding toward the beach, growing as it approaches. It's a small swell, really little more than a large ripple, but smooth and round and perfect. Focused in anticipation, I see everything with enhanced vision. The water is like a thick layer of blue-green glass of crystalline clarity, so perfectly transparent that it's hard to distinguish the approaching swell from the sky behind it.

At what I think is the right moment I begin to paddle. In my heightened state of awareness, I feel everything around me. The warmth of sun on my back, the coolness of the summer water on my arms and stomach, the cawing of a gull. I'm paddling with a butterfly stroke, both arms at the same time like oars.

Two strokes, three... Beneath the board the water magnifies the sandy bottom, meticulously decorated with scalloped ripples. A pair of small fish eye my shadow suspiciously, then dart away. Four strokes, five... I feel the tail of the board lift ever so slightly. The small swell rolls under the tail toward the center of the board, lifting and pushing at the same time.

Then the energy reaches me and the board is moving on its own. I stop paddling, and I am suspended in time and space. Just a smooth, silent gliding, the crystalline water rendered invisible, so that it's impossible to tell where the air and the sea and the sand are separated. I'm so enthralled that I forget to breathe. The board is moving as if by magic. The rest of the world disappears.

I was ten years old, I had just been kissed by my first unbroken wave, and I was hopelessly and irrevocably in love. The entire experience lasted only a few seconds, and yet it has stayed with me – wonder and surprise and pure joy, indelibly engraved on my brain and fused into my soul – for seventy years.

I have no idea what happened after the initial burst of awe. If I stood up, if I got more waves, how long I stayed out, how we got the board home. All I remember is the magic of that first kiss.

1950s: Surfing scared

I was soon to find that my new love had another, darker side. The 1950s was a tough decade for a skinny, athletically challenged late bloomer who was just getting into surfing, for in those years the ocean unleashed some seriously heavy waves on the West Coast. In Southern California the winter surf was ranging from big to huge. Film maker and Surfer magazine founder John Severson called the winter of 1952-53 – my first year in junior high and just a year or so after I caught my first unbroken wave – "a great winter for surfing," and noted that during that winter the waves at Rincon were running twenty feet. La Jolla wasn't getting much surf that extreme, but there were a lot of double overhead days during that decade. That may have been great surf for some but for me it was frightening.

I was attending La Jolla Jr.-Sr. High School, just up the street from the reefs at Windansea. Since that was now the most convenient break – I had gotten my own board, which I stashed at a classmate's house – that is where I surfed. It was quite a step up from what I was used to, and I spent a lot of time surfing scared.

Most of my fear was, of course, due to the sheer size of the waves. Surf like this might not have been much for a kid raised someplace like Mākaha or the North Shore of O'ahu – I had heard tales of Hawaiian kids "surfing their age": twelve-foot waves at age twelve, fifteen-foot waves at age fifteen – or maybe even for some of my local contemporaries. But for me, who had learned on gentle chest-high waves at a sheltered summer beach break, it was beyond intimidating. I remember sitting in class and hearing

5

the rumbling thunder of a big swell – in the classroom the windows would tremble and vibrate on the biggest sets – as the waves jacked up and crashed on the reefs. I trembled right along with the windows.

My anxiety was amplified by an early childhood episode, when I had gotten knocked down and dragged around by the shorebreak on a steep beach at night – an incident that took me a long time to get over. That childhood memory tended to make big waves seem even more ominous and threatening than they already were.

As if all this weren't enough, on a big day in 1954 an Older Guy named Bob Simmons drowned while surfing at Windansea, right down the street from the school. The drowning itself had troubling implications – Simmons was an accomplished surfer, so if he couldn't handle the waves how could I hope to? – and the aftermath was even worse. For Simmons didn't just drown, he drowned and failed to come up. For days there were rumored sightings of the body, and at one point someone actually came in contact with it. Finally the body was recovered, but the macabre mental image of a corpse washing around beneath the waves kept me spooked for months.

Big surf and psychodrama notwithstanding, I knew that at some point – if not today, tomorrow; if not tomorrow, some other day but sooner or later, no getting around it – I would have to go out and surf. Everyone else was going to and if I didn't, I was going to lose whatever tenuous hold I had on inclusion in the group. At that age that's the most intolerable concept in the world. I feared the waves – and, for a time, the lurking specter of Simmons – but I feared ostracism and ridicule even more. So I went.

I went, and more often than not I got my lunch. Losing my board pushing through. Going over the falls backwards. Getting smashed down by the lip just as I was getting to my feet. Hold-downs. Running out of air. Struggling to get to the beach and getting blitzed by the shorebreak. The amazing thing is that I never once had to be rescued; somehow I always managed to survive and get to shore on my own.

On big days getting wiped out was like being caught in a washing machine. Rag-dolled, tossed up, pushed down, spun around. Even worse than a wipeout was losing your big, cumbersome longboard while trying to push through a wave (what is now called a turtle roll). It was the worst of both worlds – you under the water dealing with the swirling turbulence of the wave, your board above you dealing with the full onslaught of the roiling white water hitting like a speeding freight train.

The absolute worst spot to be caught in was just shoreward of the impact point of the breaking wave. Tons of water hurtling down from a height of ten feet or more would drive into the trough of the wave, then rebound. If the rebound was under your board, you were in for a very rough time. Sometimes the rebounding water blasting upward against your board would drive the nose straight up and fling you into a sort of reverse pole vault with your board as the pole. You were thrown upward and vaulted over the soup, backwards, then hurled down again for a crushing impact and a lengthy, violent hold-down. Even in less extreme cases you were pretty much guaranteed to lose your board – in my case the guarantee was absolute and iron-clad – and get churned and held down for what seemed like an eternity.

On a big day the hold-downs at Windansea presented some serious problems. First – at least in the summer – was the brightness. The water on the Windansea reef was very clear, and when a wave broke it seemed like the millions of tiny bubbles created by the impact had captured light from above and were releasing it all around you. It was like being submerged amidst millions of swirling, scintillating beads of light. This uniform brilliance made it impossible to see which way was up – you couldn't just go toward the light, because it was all around you.

Not that it mattered, because due to so much air in the water, you couldn't swim. It was weird – the water had plenty of force to hold you down and throw you around, but not enough density to allow you to swim to the surface. And boy, did it throw you around. Washing machine, threshing machine, good old-fashioned pounding. And it seemed to go on forever. Nothing you tried – relax, try to float, try to swim, go with the flow – had any effect. All you could do was wait and stay calm and at some point you would come up.

When finally you were allowed to surface, on a big day you were not coming up into open air, but rather a dense layer of foam. So before you could take a breath, which by at this point you sorely needed, you had to thrash your arms around to clear a hole in the foam so you could breathe. By this time the next wave would be about to arrive and pound you some more.

Even after I had become more or less adapted to all this, well into high school there were days when my old fears were triggered by conditions and I was surfing – if not scared, certainly very apprehensive. For example:

I'm surfing with a kid named John Pettit, a big north swell before school in the morning. There's no wind, but the water is frigid and a winter fog makes the air cold and heavy and ominous. The break is the Middle at Windansea. The sand has washed out, as it does every winter, forcing us to pick our way among the huge lithified sandstone outcroppings that have been exposed along the beach.

Paddling out with Pettit, I'm a little more to the north of the peak. A set comes with a little more north in it, putting him right in the line of fire. Pettit's a good paddler, but it becomes a real race to see if he'll make it out or not. I'm lined up perfectly to see the wave from the side as it jacks up, pitches and breaks. Pettit makes a heroic effort to get to the top and punch through, but comes up short and rolls over at the last second. The lip – tons of cold, angry water – drives straight down onto the bottom of his board. The board, a thick ten-footer with three redwood stringers, snaps like a matchstick.

I get out to the lineup alone, turn and watch Pettit recede into the distance as he swims to shore with long, quick strokes. Occasionally I get a glimpse of half his board as it is bounced and tossed by the foam. There is a cluster of guys in the parking lot atop the bluff, cheering him on. They look very small, but I catch bits of their cheers as the rumble of the last wave of the set dies away.

I scan the horizon for the next set. I'm alone in the water. It's cold. I put my feet up on the board, legs stretched out in front of me, to conserve heat. It doesn't help much.

When a set comes I let the first wave pass, then get on my knees and stroke for the second one. I feel the surge of water beneath the board, the rush of water and wind coming up the face of the wave. I pop up early, almost too early. Looking down, I feel like I'm perched on a narrow ledge high on the front of a building. The water below me is black and unforgiving. The shore seems a mile away. I see the shiny-wet, dark, ominous shapes of the rocks on the shore and the cars in the lot. The cars look tiny.

I make the drop, but I get caught at the bottom of it and I can't get the round-railed balsa board to climb back up the face to the fastest part of the wave. As I'm struggling to move up the face, the peak explodes behind me. I can hear the curl grinding and roaring behind me, feel the powerful shoulder boiling and tugging at the tail of my board. I'm actually talking to the board: "*Please, go faster!*" If I fall or get knocked off, the board will be smashed on the rocks before I can swim to the beach. I'm not enjoying the ride at all; I just want it to be over. Get me out of here.

Somehow I get out in front of the shoulder, finish the ride, get back to the beach and up into the parking lot, dry off and dress for school.

This pretty much sums up a lot of the '50s for me.

1950s: Saved by a wave

The big surf of the '50s did provide one unexpected benefit, however. There was a bully at the beach who loved to target me and, ironically, my fear of big surf helped me neutralize him.

It was a big day by my standards, a solid eight feet inside with bigger sets approaching double overhead. Somehow everyone got caught inside when a cleanup set appeared. I started paddling for the edge, then realized that I wasn't going to make it. The old dread came bubbling up and the one thing I knew was that I didn't want to lose my board, which would surely happen if I got caught sideways to the wave. So I changed course and paddled directly at the approaching swell, with the desperate hope that I could somehow make it over the top before it broke.

Since everyone else in the lineup was a faster paddler than I was, I could see them in front of me and off to the side. They all made it up over the first wave, and the second; somehow I managed to do the same. But the third wave was a monster, standing up farther out than the first two. When it broke, a couple of guys were caught by the bounce and tossed into the air, boards and all, then buried by the white water. Then I only had time to get a death grip on the rails, take a deep breath, roll over and pray.

Never in my life have I put such effort into anything. They say that human muscles can exert superhuman force in times of crisis; people have been known to pick up the end of a car to save someone being crushed underneath. I can only surmise that something like that happened to me.

The wave tried to snatch the board away from me and on a normal day it would have succeeded, but I was a man-kid possessed. I was jerked and tossed and tumbled and pounded but finally I came out into daylight behind the wave, still hanging onto my board. I was gripping it so hard that if it had been a foam board, instead of balsa, I'm sure I would have left pressure dings in the rails.

I looked across the foam trail of the wave and saw that it was littered with heads bobbing in the water. Almost everyone else – Older Guys and bigger guys and tougher guys – had lost their boards and were going to have to swim all the way in.

Once everyone's amazement that I still had my board died down, the bully – who had lost his board – started swimming toward me.

"Hey, Rearwin, lemme rest on your board for a minute."

I knew this game because I'd been through it before. He would swim over, get a hold of my board, push me off and then surf in to recover his own board, leaving mine on the beach to get beaten up by the shorebreak, and leaving me to swim in. This time, instead of allowing it to happen yet again, I paddled away from him.

"You scrawny shit, if you don't lemme rest on your board I'm gonna kick your ass when we get to the beach."

I knew he was as good as his word, but today I didn't care. Better a pounding later, than a drowning now. I wasn't going to give up my board in this surf.

When the bully finally swam in and got back out to the lineup on his own board, he made a few intimidating comments but made no attempt to catch me, which he easily could have. Luckily he preferred to surf. But later, even back on shore he seemed less interested in picking on me than before. Somehow my act of self-preservation had been interpreted as an act of defiance, which had bought me a measure of respect, however small. He never knew I was acting out of pure, raw fear.

That one wave didn't get me permanent respect, by any means. After all, you're only as good as your record, and mine was pretty weak. But my situation improved considerably.

1957: Part of the crew

By the time I was sixteen, I was part of the Windansea crew. I still was way behind everyone else, but at least I could stay close enough to keep them in sight some of the time.

The better surfers, Graham and Butch and Diff and others, would invent all sorts of little tricks and stunts, things to make surfing more interesting.

On big days they would wait on the beach for an approaching lull. When the last wave of a set came crashing onto the shore, they would time it, run down the sloping sand toward the water holding their boards in both hands out to the side, leap over the onrushing surge of whitewater rushing up the beach, and throw themselves atop the board in a standing position, riding the backwash out and up over the next wave.

On steep sections they would run to the nose of the board, then do some sort of tip and twist to lift the tail and make the skeg come out of the water. This would make the board sideslip down the wave at an angle, tail first. Then they shifted their weight to change the angle so that the skeg made contact with the water again. At that point they would allow the board to return to normal trim and keep riding.

At the end of a ride, when the wave was closing out, they would kick the board out vertically, simultaneously spinning their body upright, parallel to the upright board, in a tight rotation like a figure skater, doing a 360, catching the board in the air, and coming down with it, on the deck and ready to paddle.

I couldn't do any of that stuff. I still can't. All I could do was watch and admire, and realize that I was never going to be a high-level surfer.

And that didn't really matter to me. What mattered was the sea, and the waves, and the joy of being among them and occasionally riding one. Feeling the power, the raw energy pulsing beneath me. Gliding like magic. Hurtling down a face, or skimming across a wall.

1957: Paipos rule!

There were other ways to have fun in the waves. At one point Rick Naish – who went on to ride epic waves at Waimea and later was the founder of Naish sails – got the idea to make paipo bodyboards. This was before foam was widely available, so we used wood. Besides, real paipos were made of wood. For some reason – artistic purity? – we didn't even consider using plywood, which would have been simple. Instead, using furniture clamps, we each glued up two wide strips of redwood with a spruce stringer, which contrasted nicely against the dark redwood.

The template and bottom were simplicity itself: round nose, parallel rails, square tail, no rocker. The only refinement of the rails was to sand them upward close to the nose and rounded on the tail and the sides of the board. We glassed them, with small glassed-on fins made by hand from wood. The boards were a bit over three feet long, and maybe eighteen inches wide; about the size of a very small coffee table.

Those things were rockets! They weren't suitable for small waves, so we rode Boomer, South Boomer, and Windansea when the swells were good.

Getting out through the surf on a big day was a piece of cake, even easier than today's duck diving with a shortboard. Our heavy wood paipos had virtually no flotation, so all you had to do to when caught inside was tip the board down and kick your fins to quickly get a few feet below the surface. It you were still in the path of the wave underwater, the force of the incoming foam would drive the inclined board, and you, down to the bottom. Then, after the main force of the wave had passed, just tip the nose of the board upward and the remaining energy of the wave would plane you to the surface behind the white water. On big days we could actually get out to the lineup faster than a surfboard could.

When you rode bigger waves you would be airborne half the time as you skipped over the chop, but you would easily pass surfers on longboards. The only downside was getting wiped out: if you lost your grip on the board – which was easy to do – you would be caught in the foam ball with the board chopping and hacking at you underwater. It was like being trapped in a washing machine with a dull meat cleaver.

The funny thing is that in the midst of all our surf-related creativity, none of us was smart enough to think of using a comb – just an ordinary comb – to rough up the paraffin wax on our boards. And none of us was smart enough to realize that the wax would adhere much better and last a lot longer if we had roughed up the deck itself with a little coarse sandpaper prior to putting on the first coat of wax. Nope. Surfboard or paipo, we wanted the whole board to be glossy and shiny, even though we were going to cover the deck with wax.

1950s: The good ol' days

Old Guys – including me – love to talk about how uncrowded it was in the good old days, and they're right. Well, no wonder. Half the time you were swimming for your board and the other half the time you were freezing. Or, to put it into a simple formula: no wetsuits, no leashes, no crowds. Most people – normal people – just weren't that crazy or desperate or driven. True, our small numbers and shared self-inflicted discomfort did create a sense of camaraderie up and down the coast. We were brothers in hardship.

To see what it was like in the good old days, take a board out on a foggy winter morning – slight wind optional. Water must be mid 50s. No wetsuit, no leash. The board must be a fat-railed heavy balsa log with little rocker, single fin glassed on so far back that it protrudes past the tail, difficult to turn. Lug the big, heavy board to the beach and wax it with paraffin. Then into the ocean. You're wearing only trunks, no wetsuit, so in the winter the water is cramp-inducing cold.

Paddle out, preferably on your knees to stay as dry as possible for as long as possible. If a set catches you inside, there's no way to duck dive with this monster, so you roll over and try to hang on. Those thick rails are slippery and paraffin doesn't give much grip, so on big days this will be as far as you get on your first attempt.

Swim back to the beach – swimming fast so you can save your board from destruction on the rocks. I did so much gotta-save-my-board swimming that when I got to college they wanted me to try out for the swimming team. As the swimming coach put it, "Your stroke is a mess, but we can fix that, and somehow you've learned how to move through the water pretty fast." You bet I did – surfboards were expensive.

The total immersion from your swim in will leave you a bit clumsy and your fingers unresponsive, which in turn makes it even harder to hang onto your board on the next go-around. And harder to surf well when you do catch a wave.

By the time you get back out to the lineup, you're tired and half-frozen. Then freeze some more while waiting for a set. If there's any wind, you freeze faster due to the wind chill factor.

When you come out of the water you are staggering with a stiff, awkward gait and the soles of your feet are so numb with cold that you feel like you're walking on pillows.

And you do this day after day. The good news was that if you started young you think this is normal.

1950s: Island magic

On the other hand, there was Hawai'i.

My first exposure to Hawai'i was in the mid-1950s, before commercial jet travel and before I was old enough to drive. It was on a family trip to O'ahu and it was like going to paradise. Eternally warm water and crisp, clean waves, held up by the offshore trade wind, peeling left and right above coral reefs in crystalline water.

In the coral-tinted O'ahu dawn, I would walk beneath coconut palms through the gentle burbling and cooing of the tiny Hawaiian doves, my homemade balsa board under one arm, coarse sand golden and already warm beneath my feet, and paddle out at Canoes or Queens.

Sitting there on my board, floating on the gentle swells, I was ecstatic. Warm air, warm water and no people until the sun was already high! I could go out at Queens on a head high day and have it to myself until what seemed to me to be late in the morning.

Waves were so available that it took a really good swell to entice surfers into the water early, or indeed at all. Why get up early to surf? The wind would still be offshore, tidal changes were minimal, there would be plenty of waves all day. Lots of breaks to choose from. Later today was fine. Or maybe tomorrow. Maybe bigger tomorrow. Anyway, no hurry.

On the beach a then-famous professional wrestler named Gorgeous George would arrive to snooze in the sun on the golden sand, tanning his massive beefy body and sun-bleaching his long blond hair to look better for his fans. The biggest hotels were still the Moana and the Royal Hawaiian, where from late afternoon you could hear the music of Don Ho wafting out across the water. The Outrigger Club was still on the beach near the Royal Hawaiian.

The beauty of that phase of my existence was an absolute lack of any sense of history. To paraphrase Gertrude Stein, there wasn't any then, then. There was only now. Life could not have been better or more beautiful. And being on the water made it even more so.

Wave after wave after wave after wave – and you never got cold! This was the life! Finally some local kids came paddling out from the Outrigger Club to check me out. Since they knew all the local *haole* kids who normally surfed the area, they were curious. La Jolla? Where's that? Near Los Angeles? Their knowledge of California geography was similar to my knowledge of the Islands. We hit it off and they couldn't have been nicer.

We surfed together and they invited me to parties. They gave me advice on local breaks, and took me out to surf when a big southern hemi swell came through.

"Gotta get out there – you're not gonna get another chance like this!"

We paddled out to a distant break named Steamers, so called because it seemed like it was almost in the shipping lanes. It was weird being that far off shore. The waves were big and had a lot of punch, but there was no worry – even in those pre-leash days – of your board going all the way to the beach if you fell off. Like many outer reef breaks in Waikīkī, the wave would back off when it got to one of the deeper trenches that crisscrossed the bottom between the reefs. And swimming for your board was never going to make you cold. I didn't set the world on fire that day, but I didn't embarrass myself too badly.

They were right about the rare opportunity: in my twelve years of surfing Waikīkī from 2004, including some very large south swells, I never saw the surf break that far out again. Or maybe it just seemed farther at the time.

I'm sure none of those people has any memory of me at all; to them I was just a short-term mainland visitor passing through their island world. But to me it was all like a dream. Warm water, warm air, gentle offshore breezes, surf every day, magic upon magic.

That time and that Hawai'i is gone forever. Except when I look out over the ocean on a clear sunlit morning and the steady, reassuring motion of the waves brings it back like the image on a long-dormant photographic film. It's all one ocean, and it touches every place I've ever loved.

1950s: More island magic

A year or so later I was back, with Rick Naish and a kid named Randy Sweeney. Three eager but clueless high-school kids on an ultra-low-budget airborne surf safari. What could possibly go wrong?

Our first taste of low-budget flying was at the San Diego Airport. We were through the gate and about to board the plane when out came the baggage carts. We looked for our boards but only saw two of them. Then Naish's board appeared, not on a cart, but handled by a lone baggage guy.

In those days there were no board bags and he was dragging it across the tarmac by the skeg! Luckily in those days there also was no airport security, so Naish dashed out onto the tarmac and ran over shouting and waving his arms to stop the guy, and luckily he had a good glass job so that the damage was minimal. But then the first order of business when we got to Waikīkī was to get the rail patched.

After nearly twelve hours of eardrum-numbing, bone-vibrating propeller-plane travel, we landed. It was raining. On the way in, our airport "limo," boards strapped to the roof luggage rack, stopped at a red light. On the left, nondescript commercial buildings and a cracked, weed-filled sidewalk. On the right, a huge Samoan was engaged in throwing an unconscious US Navy sailor, in uniform, against the exterior wall of a seedy-looking bar. Throw him. *Splat.* He slid limply down the wall like a cartoon character. Pick him up. Throw him again. *Splat...*

We looked at each other, wordlessly. Had we made a mistake?

We had rented a small, rundown house a couple of blocks in from Queens, in the area affectionately known as "the Jungle" – possibly due to the predatory nature of the locals. In those days the vast majority of the hotels and condos that tower above the streets today did not yet exist, and the area was a warren of small, dilapidated houses seeded with cheap bars and the occasional eatery. Violence was in the air at night, and *haole* kids like us were better off indoors after dark.

Daytime was surfing and more surfing. We surfed Queens until our arms were ready to fall off. We paddled from one break to the next, reveling in the warm water. Since there was no chance of getting cold, we would stay out most of the day. Paddle to Pops, catch a few waves, then continue toward Ewa, riding Paradise, Fours, Threes, Kaisers. One day we surfed and paddled all the way past Ala Moana, then realized that we had to work our way back.

With dusk falling, I caught a small wave and popped up to see a shark crossing my path. Too scared to think, much less take evasive action, I ran over the shark. I don't remember if I was jolted from my board by the impact or if I simply fell off in a panic. What I do remember is swimming to my board in record time and somehow swimming and slithering straight over the tail and right up onto the board without even slowing down. I'm sure the shark was more upset than I was, but my imagination was working on me all the way back to Queens.

One moonlit night with a nice head-high swell running we braved the Jungle to try night surfing at Queens. We had it to ourselves. After a couple of waves, Sweeney lost his board and went swimming after it. Just as he went to heave himself back onto it he let out a yelp of surprise.

"Whoa! My foot just hit something big!"

"Probably just a big kelp ball."

Moment of silence.

"They don't have kelp over here."

That was the end of our night surfing.

We bought a $40 car, an old De Soto four-door with a leaky muffler that heated the floorboards to a temperature just hot enough to burn your feet but not enough to melt the soles of our rubber sandals, and with brakes that only worked if you pumped them at least three or four times. We discovered this quirk at the first traffic light out of the used car lot – Naish put the brake pedal to the floor and we sailed right through the red light without even slowing down.

We drove all over the island, surfing the breaks we could handle and marveling at the ones we had the good sense to avoid. We hadn't thought to bring fins, but when we got to the famous bodysurfing break at Makapu'u we gave it a shot anyway. Even in that pre-crowded era, we were not welcome. We had barely made it through the nasty outside shorebreak when a couple of local heavies swam out to let us know that they didn't want us at "their" beach.

"What you doin' here, stupid haole kids, go away or we drown you."

We left. There were plenty of other breaks to enjoy, and tomorrow would be full of waves no matter where we were.

1950s: Not ready for prime time

Back on the mainland, we might have been used to cold water but that didn't mean we liked it. At least I didn't. And finally I got the chance to do something about it.

Not long after my introduction to Hawai'i, the word got out that a small dive shop in La Jolla was selling something called a wetsuit, to keep you warm in the water. Since my natural clumsiness was magnified by prolonged exposure to cold water, I wanted one. So I got one.

The way it worked was this: you went to the shop and they took your measurements, just like a tailor would. Arms and body only; full suits were still in the future. A week or so later, they called and said my wetsuit had arrived. Excitement! Comfort would be mine! When I went in to pick it up, they handed me a box. Inside, sheets of neoprene, cut into various shapes, strips of rubber tape and a small bottle of glue. The customer was supposed to take this kit home and construct his own suit from the pre-cut parts.

No worries – I loved building things and this would be easy.

I got the suit glued up, gave it twenty-four hours to set up solid, and hit the waves at Windansea. It was a perfect day for a trial run: clear skies, head-high waves and water temperature in the high fifties. A bit of wind, but my wetsuit would neutralize any wind chill. I felt invincible.

Paddling out, I had to roll through a wave. When I got to the lineup, I felt a cold spot on my arm and realized that a shoulder seam had developed a leak. No problem; I could re-glue it later on. Meanwhile, except for that one flaw, I was all warm and toasty and the wetsuit was really well tailored.

My first wave felt great. Being warm seemed to make me surf better! Took off, stalled, dropped under the peak, made a couple of shallow turns, and rode to the inside reef where I got blasted by the soup. Fell onto my board, got to the shoulder, and started to paddle back out. After a few strokes one sleeve of my brand-new wetsuit started flopping down over my hand. I stopped to investigate and found that the entire sleeve had detached at the shoulder.

Distracted by this discovery, I sat up on the board and tugged the sleeve upward, trying to get it higher so that it would stop sliding down toward my hand with each stroke. The next thing I knew, I was caught inside by the set of the day. I had to roll through several waves, and as I got churned by each one, more pieces of my new wetsuit abandoned ship. By the time the set passed, I was left sitting on my board, suitless, surrounded by a swarm of floating pieces of neoprene and rubber tape.

It would be years before I owned another wetsuit.

Late 1950s: Party time

Of course, there was more to life than surfing.

Sometime after our Hawai'i trip, Naish had a brilliant idea. Since we were still way under the legal drinking age of twenty-one, getting beer or booze was always a problem. You could go the fake ID route, and you could get some sailor to buy you a six-pack in exchange for a couple of cans of beer, but these tactics were risky and unreliable.

My family's house had a walkout basement that had been converted into a small rental unit. The tenant had moved on and the space was empty. It was only a single room with no kitchen, but it did have a bathroom. With a bathtub.

Seeing this resource sitting idle, Naish had an inspiration: why not use the bathtub to make beer? No more sneaking around to find a source. We would become the source.

Somehow we found the fixings and supplies: hops, malt, yeast, sugar, whatever else you need to make beer with. We got bottles, bottle caps and a bottle capping device. We got a little floating thing that looked like a thermometer and measured the alcohol content by how high it floated in the beer.

The rest was pretty simple: dump all the stuff in the bathtub with some water, stir, and wait. And wait. As the days passed, a scummy foam formed on top, which was good: it meant something was happening. The liquid beneath the foam was a murky brown, but we figured the murk would settle over time. Using our floating alcohol density meter, we monitored the progress of the brew. After a little discussion – start bottling early, or hold out for the strongest possible brew? – we went for high alcohol content. The resulting concoction – brown, evil-smelling and clouded with sediment despite our attempts at filtering through cloth – was at least twenty proof. It had the appearance of swamp water, but you could smell the alcohol wafting up through the scum. We called it the Brown Death due to the wild high and wickedly head-piercing hangovers it produced. We quickly learned to avoid it ourselves, but it made us very popular. We were like drug dealers who never use the stuff themselves. Of course it never occurred to us to sell it; we gave it away to others in the Windansea crew. Share and share alike.

Windansea parking lot
The author is on the left, then Del Cannon, Butch Van Artsdalen, Danny Prall,
PG Bent (holding board), Pat Curren (waxing board), Dean Perry
Note that the wall in the background looks tilted. Some days were like that.

A goodly amount of Brown Death was consumed in the Windansea parking lot. The lot also served as a hangout, meeting place and launch point for activities ranging from night tennis at the rec center – sharing racquets because not everyone had one – to coast trips or expeditions to Tijuana for bullfights or the Long Bar. It was like an outdoor pub. On rainy days, some of us would congregate in a VW camper or other van to play cards or chess.

At night, one of the frustrating things was to arrive at the lot to find it fairly full of cars but empty of people, meaning that everyone had piled into two or three cars and headed out for an evening of adventure while you were left to try to guess where they might have gone. Sometimes you might find them in a bunker.

During the Second World War, La Jolla's Mount Soledad – at over 800 feet, the highest point for miles and strategically overlooking the coast – was taken over by the military and fortified against any possible Japanese attack. Strategic positions overlooking the sea were honeycombed with installations carved into the hillsides, bunkers lined and topped with thick concrete, the only openings the entry hatch and the menacing slits for coastal artillery to fire at hostile ships offshore.

Inside the bunkers was another world, a dry-land version of Nemo's Nautilus, filled with the ghosts of history. You entered through a hinged steel hatch on the top, like the one on a tank or a submarine. Each bunker was on several levels connected by vertical metal ladders consisting of bent steel bars embedded in the concrete walls. The cave-like interiors were always cool. On the uppermost level, where the gun slits were, rusting iron tracks curved in a smooth arc where the massive guns had swiveled back and forth to cover a broad field of fire, and hinged steel plates provided protection against incoming rounds. Here the light was dim and secretive; on lower levels the darkness was as profound and absolute as in a coal mine or at the center of the earth. If you closed the top hatch and the gun slits, using the hinged steel plates and turning the latching mechanism, you were sealed off from the outside, free to create a world of your own choosing.

As kids we had played in the bunkers on our hiking expeditions. As we got older, we discovered another use.

HOW TO HAVE A BUNKER PARTY

1. Take one abandoned World War II bunker (must be concrete, underground, with gun ports and hatches that can be sealed from the inside).

2. Add a dozen or so kids, both sexes, ages 16 to 20ish (approximate measure), a few candles and flashlights, maybe a grotty pillow or two and a couple of towels or a ratty old army surplus blanket from the back of someone's car; alcoholic beverages.

3. Optional: music.

4. Enter bunker, carrying ingredients, and seal bunker from inside. Sweep all trash (if any) to lowest level. Ingest beverages. Mix sexes. Allow to ferment until fatigue sets in.

5. Unseal bunker, attempt to climb back down hill to road and return home by car.

The great thing about the bunkers was privacy and security. Once the hatches were closed, even if the cops knew we were in there – the cars parked off the road at the bottom of the dirt path up to the bunker were a dead giveaway – there was no way they could get in. After all, these installations were meant to withstand assault by Japanese marines! And in reality, why would the cops even want to get in? They had us right where they wanted us: isolated from civil society and free to indulge our worst impulses on each other. Knock yourselves out! It was a win-win situation.

This recipe worked for several years, until some idiot (not anyone we knew) fell down a ladder, broke a leg, and created such a community uproar that the bunkers were all sealed shut. It was the end of an era.

1958: Nautical pheromones

Suddenly it was 1958 and I was going to graduate from high school. I had found an activity I loved and a group of people to enjoy it with. But I was more than just a surf bum in the making. I was going to go to college.

My dad had spent my high school years nagging and pressuring and threatening about school and grades and it must have done some good. I got a scholarship valid for four years at the school of my choice. And I got admitted to Pomona College. So off I went.

My parents were overjoyed that I would be a long way from the ocean. They had never approved of my infatuation with surfing and they weren't really sure what it was. My dad called surfing "rafting," perhaps because as kids we had played in the waves with a Navy surplus life raft. Being from the Midwest they didn't have much use for the ocean – it was just something to look at – and they really didn't trust it. To them it was like a desert, with salt water instead of sand. Death Valley with waves.

I think the distance between Pomona and the ocean had almost as much to do with their excitement as the quality of the education I would receive, although the two were interrelated. Surf's up, final exam tomorrow, what would I do? In pre-freeway California, they figured a forty- or fifty-mile buffer of surface streets and traffic lights should be enough to keep me hitting the books instead of the beach. (Actually, there were a few freeways in California in those days – the first one dated from 1940 – but none of them led to anywhere I wanted to go. Obviously freeway builders did not put surf safaris high on the list of essential transportation needs.)

I knew nothing of these ulterior motives in September 1958. All I knew was that I was finally through with high school and off to college. The excited, nervous anticipation temporarily overcame any intuitive misgivings I might have had.

I had barely gotten my things put away at Pomona when I began to feel the pangs of separation. Not homesickness but something more elemental:

what I missed was the ocean. I was forty miles inland, and it might as well have been a thousand. I missed the almost imperceptible feel of salt in the air, the sound of sea lions barking at night, the distant rumble and hiss of surf, the knowledge that the sea was there in all its restless majesty.

Living in La Jolla you became programmed to recognize the scent, the energy, the feeling in the air when there were waves. Here the air was different: the odor was new-mown hay and orange blossoms and the sweet chemical tang of smog blown eastward from L.A., overpowering any marine air that might have been with it at the beginning. The area was still so undeveloped that the major event on Friday and Saturday nights was to go down to the soft ice cream drive-in and watch truck drivers holding impromptu drag races, using the cabs of their big rigs for dragsters. What a thrill.

I missed the ocean. God, did I miss the ocean! Paradoxically, I missed it more because even at this distance I could still feel it. It was a primal ability. Certain types of moth have an olfactory sensitivity that verges on the supernatural, able to detect a single molecule of the female sex hormone from miles away. I was something like that with surf, only better. On warm, hazy autumn days at Pomona, forty smog-filled miles inland, I could feel the sea. And even though I was forty miles from the coast, I could still get the surf's-up vibe if there was a swell. Even when I didn't feel the distant energy of surf I would go to the beach anyway, but on some days I felt an overpowering need to go, and sure enough there would be waves.

I would stick my board in the back of my car – rear seat removed for the purpose – and make the arduous pre-freeway journey through all the towns and cities between Pomona and the coast, all the stop signs and traffic signals. It didn't matter what beach, as long as there was a way to get into the water and catch a wave. I would drive all the way out to someplace like Huntington Beach or Long Beach and ride nondescript beach break for an hour or so, then drive all the way back. This took most of a day.

I went to Huntington Beach a lot because it was the closest. My memory of Huntington Beach in the late '50s is lots of vacant land and weedy sand dunes and oil wells which added a generous hydrocarbon film to the surface of the waves. It might have even kept the chop down on windy days.

Huntington Beach, late 1950s

This was hardly the ocean I grew up with, and in retrospect I'm amazed that I didn't just bag it and stay inland at Pomona and study and watch the big-rig-cab drag races. Maybe the surf bug is connected to a dormant gene, one that's triggered by just the right combination of environmental factors. Whatever it is, once it's activated it's hard to shut down. Like trying to plug a gushing oil well or make a river run uphill.

1958, Winter: Ocean Beach 1, Me 0

Meanwhile, there was life outside of Southern California. My parents had moved to San Francisco. I wasn't too keen on going home for winter break but my mom was nagging me and guilt-tripping me about it, and she made my dad's homework-and-chores-nagging look very mild by comparison. There was also a nostalgia element – I had been to San Francisco when I visited my older brother at Stanford a couple of years earlier, and my high-school self had thought North Beach was beyond cool – plus there was some stuff of mine at my parents' house, so I went up for a quick visit. Naturally I took my board, just in case.

Their house was on the west side of town, not far from the beach. The beach in this case was Ocean Beach, a three-mile-long stretch of sand and surf along the Great Highway, which extends from the cliffs near the foot of Sloat on the south end, all the way to the Cliff House and Seal Rock on the north. This was the sometime haunt of the likes of big-wave rider and waterman Jim Fisher, and there was a hardy crew of local surfers who hung out at the beach or in the parking lot of Playland, the scruffy amusement park that existed across the street from the north end of Ocean Beach until it was demolished in 1972.

Ocean Beach is noted for frigid water, powerful waves, nasty rip currents and great white sharks attracted by the large seal and sea lion population. When you're a great white shark, nothing beats a fat, tasty seal on a cold day. But none on this was on my mind. I saw only the glistening glassy sea and sunshine and inviting waves on blue water.

San Francisco is famous for fog, but I happened to hit it during a spell of perfect weather. Blue skies, not a wisp of fog to be seen, sun, glassy ocean. And there was surf! So I threw my 9'6" fat-railed balsa board into the car, drove down to the parking area at the beach below the zoo, got out a piece of paraffin and waxed up. I was truly excited to have caught such perfect timing. The surf was about four feet, breaking fairly far out.

When I hit the water it was cold, but that was to be expected. I waded out a few yards, then hopped on the board and started toward the surf line, knee paddling to stay as dry as possible. After a few hundred feet, when I looked out toward the horizon and saw some very dark lines far away I realized that what I had seen from the shore wasn't four-foot surf, but a big outside shorebreak, maybe six feet or so, impacting on a sand bank.

The actual break was far beyond that. And it was bigger. To get there meant a paddle of what looked like another couple of hundred yards or more beyond the inner break, and there were no channels and no consistent, well-defined peaks. Everything was shifting around. The deep sand banks and bars where the waves broke seemed to be in constant motion, pushed this way and that by the massive swirls of water moving in and out of San Francisco Bay with the changing tides. Each wave was picture-perfect beautiful, peeling lefts and zipping rights, but there was no lineup, no way to guess where the next wave would break.

Well, I hadn't come all this way to turn around, and after all I had ridden some fairly solid waves in my time. Nothing epic, but certainly double overhead and more. So I paddled around inside the "shorebreak" on the inside bar until the set passed, then turned on the gas and went full speed toward the lineup.

When I got to the inside bar things started to go south. The waves were much more powerful than they appeared, and the bar they were breaking on was so shallow that they were pitching and crunching on it with great force and turbulence. At the same time the water was too deep to touch bottom and still have my head above the surface. And the waves were constant – no lulls, just an endless succession of real grinders. I would roll through a wave, pull myself back onto my board, take half a dozen increasingly desperate strokes – no thought of knee paddling now; it was all about speed – and then roll through the next one.

After what seemed like a very long time of getting thrashed, I finally got past the inside surf zone, mostly due to having been swept sideways into a minor rip and pulled out through a temporary channel. I kept paddling like a madman until I was sure I was clear of the set zone. I was cold, and I was feeling some fatigue from all the pushing through waves. Then I sat up to find a lineup point and assess the situation.

I was shocked to find that while I was busy getting beaten up by the waves, the current had carried me hundreds of yards to the south, below the cliffs. I could see the meandering foam tracks in the water that indicated the path of the current.

I was used to winter ocean temperatures in the mid 50s in San Diego but this water was far colder, and this far north the sun seemed devoid of heat. And for the first time I started thinking of sharks – in particular an incident I had read about, in which some kid had his arm ripped off by a great white at Ocean Beach. That had been at other end of the beach, to be sure, but a trifling distance to a shark. There was no one in sight – not on the beach, certainly not in the water. If anything happened to me, there would be no one to tell the tale, let alone help me out. I enjoyed solitude, but given the context this was a bit much.

I put my feet up on the board, legs outstretched – the standard move that gives the illusion of safety in sharky waters. In reality, great whites have been known to bite right through surfboards and even the occasional kayak, so putting your legs up doesn't really put you out of danger. But it makes you feel better, so you do it. I would have put my legs up anyway, since my feet were getting numb from the cold and I wanted to conserve all the body heat I could.

But I couldn't just sit there; the current was still dragging me south along the cliffs. I faced north and paddled against the current sitting down, but an occasional glance at the shore told me that I was losing ground. My butt and thighs were still awash in frigid water and my hands – which probably looked like tasty little tidbits to any shark – were losing heat with every stroke.

I was already prepared to make this a one-wave session. Get the first one I could, and get the hell out of here. But I was getting cold and clumsy.

Catching a wave and falling off would be fatal, and with numb legs and only rock-hard paraffin wax for traction, falling off was almost a sure thing.

I changed strategy. My only option, I decided, was to take advantage of this lull and head for the beach. I would get in as far as possible and then, since I probably couldn't make it to shore before a set came, I would catch a broken wave and soup it out prone, all the way to the shore. I took one last look toward the horizon to be sure that no set was in sight, then got on my knees, put my head down, and started paddling as hard as I could for the beach. I didn't want to lose precious time and energy by trying to look over my shoulder for any set waves, but I did look forward. I could see that I was moving sideways at least as fast as any progress I was making toward the beach. I could only hope that I wouldn't be pulled laterally into an outward bound rip current; if that happened I was done.

By now my imagination was running riot. If I survived the cold and the sharks, losing my board in these currents meant that I would never make it to the beach. If they found my body, it would be miles to the south. If they found it.

Then I heard the distant crack and rumble of a wave breaking somewhere out there behind me. I had used up too much valuable time making up my mind.

Above me, a bright but heatless sun stares down from the indifferent cloudless sky. In front of me, two-hundred-foot cliffs and miles of deserted beach. Behind me, the first wave of the set. I don't have to turn around to see how close it is; I can hear it approaching with the thundering roar of an avalanche.

I paddle as hard as I have ever paddled, both to match my speed even slightly closer to the speed of the onrushing white water, and to decrease by even the slightest bit the distance to the shore and the force remaining in the wave. Just before the avalanche reaches me, I use all my remaining energy to take a few fast strokes to get up as much speed as possible, then hurl myself prone, get a death grip on the rails of my board and hang on as if my life depends on it. Which it probably does. I flatten myself against the board, pressing myself to the deck like a limpet on a rock.

The impact is shocking – like getting smashed from behind by a ton of crushed ice blasted from a gigantic water cannon. The raw energy is almost overpowering. I get bounced and tossed and nearly lose my board, but I manage to make it in, hanging on until the skeg is scraping on the sand. By the time I drag my numb body onto dry land, I'm somewhere below Fort Funston. After that it's a long and miserable slog back up the beach to the car.

I never considered surfing Ocean Beach again.

1959: Sorry, Dave

Back at Pomona College, I was soon to face an even bigger problem than Ocean Beach. P.E. was required, and in those days the college believed that every young man should learn the manly art of self defense, so the course opened with several weeks of boxing. Once we got gloves and headgear on the coach lined everyone up according to size and weight. Everyone, that is, except me and a kid named Cody, one of the linebackers from the football team. He was perhaps an inch shorter than I was, and outweighed me by at least thirty pounds, all of it muscle.

While the others paired up and began shuffling around, the coach came over to us. I noticed that he was looking at me strangely, with a gleam in his eye that might have been...what – hostility? Sadistic anticipation?

Something seemed to be amiss, but I was trained to believe that resistance was both misguided and futile. Do as we say and you will not be harmed. Trusting in this line of reasoning, I awaited further instructions.

"Okay. Cody, you're on offense. Rearwin, you're on defense. Get going."

I stood there awkwardly the way you do when you're in a new physical situation, the gloves like enormous heavy cushions dangling at the end of my spindly pipe-stem arms.

"Defense? What do I..."

"Cody tries to hit you. You try to prevent him. Get going!" His irritation was starting to show.

I raised the gloves in front of my face, trying to imitate some boxing movie I'd seen somewhere. They felt heavy. I had no idea of how to stand or where to put my feet or how to move. In front of me, Cody lowered himself into a coiled crouch, one glove slightly advanced. The white mouthpiece showing between his lips shaped his mouth into a sinister, snarling leer. His biceps and pecs and shoulders bulged. He looked like a tiger ready to pounce, except more menacing.

Cody was a nice guy, and he may even have liked me. But a guy's gotta do what he's gotta do. Coach says so.

"Sorry, Dave."

The smack of leather, a sudden numb feeling on the side of my face, the clumsy flopping slap of a body – mine – hitting the canvas. I never saw it coming. The coach, bless his heart, was right there to help.

"C'mon, don't just lie there, get up. Defense, defense."

He pronounced it DEE-fense like they do in football.

I clambered to my feet. Once more into the breach. Cody was there waiting, swaying lightly on the balls of his feet. There may have been a hint of pity, even guilt in his expression, but it didn't affect his technique.

"Sorry, Dave."

This time I did see it coming – the glove growing bigger and bigger like in a cartoon, until it filled my field of vision. Blackness. A thick splat, a sharp pain in my nose. The quick, sweet rush of blood in my mouth. I open my eyes. In front of me is the ceiling; I'm on my back on the canvas again. There's a sign on the ceiling, put there for the benefit of the wrestling team:

33

IF YOU CAN READ THIS, YOU ARE IN TROUBLE

The words glared down at me from above. Far more than an ironic warning to motivate some hapless wrestler at risk of being pinned, they described my entire life at this point in time. I didn't have time to ponder this, though; Cody was waiting and the coach was hovering right behind him. I got to my feet, which of course did not mean that I was no longer in trouble.

And so it went. I lost count of the knockdowns. My nose stopped bleeding. Cody gave me a break and started aiming at spots where his punches would do less damage while still putting me on the mat. The only additional damage was a lip which felt the size of an overinflated inner tube but bravely refused to split, and countless welts and scuffs. From time to time the coach came by to observe the carnage. He would nod, as if satisfied with some abstruse athletic concept, and go back to the rest of the class.

Boxing class was three days a week. After the second day I was getting used to the pounding and I had started to flinch away from the punches but I still had nothing remotely resembling DEE-fense. This wasn't *From Here to Eternity*, with the plucky target learning through experience until he finally bests his biggest tormentor. This was real life, and there was no way I was going to stop Cody. Or the coach.

Other guys noticed what was going on, and some of them suggested that I do something. But what? Complain to the school? Who at the school? They would contact the coach, and that would just invite retaliation. Phone my parents? First, I just didn't want to. Second, I knew what their response would be. My mom would tell me to bear up and surely something good would come of it; my dad would say that I probably had it coming. Besides, to me the coach was just another bully, on a higher level, using someone else to do his bullying for him. In my experience, from this there was no escape.

Finally the coach came over and stopped us in the middle of a session.

"Got some of it sweated out of you yet?"

He was looking at me, he must have been asking me, and I had no idea what he was talking about. Too tired and intimidated to ask what he meant, I managed a sort of gurgling grunt through the sweat and soreness and fatigue. Apparently it was enough.

"Okay, that's it. Get back in the group."

And thereafter the two of us rejoined the regular class, paired with more appropriate partners.

I didn't know what it all meant, but as the academic year ground on, I realized that my future at this particular school was nonexistent. Next year I would have to take P.E. again, and the coach would find a way to get me. The reason for his attitude was a total mystery but what difference did it make? He was out to get me, and that was enough. I was stranded in the boonies, cut off from my true love and subject to the whims of a demented autocrat. Who knew what the coach would come up with next?

At Easter break I immediately headed to La Jolla and spent all the time I could at the beach and in the water. Predictably, when I returned, the campus seemed like more of a prison and I felt increasingly deprived. Sometimes depression would not have been too strong a word. Something had to change.

1959, Summer: Decision time

Back at the beach after the end of the academic year, I moved with a couple of surf buddies into a slum-like dwelling near a welding shop in Pacific Beach and got a job as a day laborer.

The work was repetitive but it was nice to be outdoors. And I learned some things about life. After a couple of days running a jackhammer – we were demo'ing some virtually indestructible concrete steps that some genius had decided would be unsafe in case of an earthquake – I could barely open my fingers when it was time to take a break, and I would wake up in the night with stabbing pains in my wrists. Then I noticed that the old guys – for me, anyone over about forty – had permanently swollen wrists and fingers. I made a mental note: after this summer, I wasn't going to do this type of work again.

There was other, more dramatic stuff. Rival lunch wagon companies had a turf war that led to threats and at least one stock-car-circuit type of crash when two trucks tried to race each other into a job site and collided at the gate. A plumber dropped a tool or something into a pot of molten lead, instinctively reached to grab it, and melted the ends of his fingers off. Once a guy backed a truck into a power pole and a line broke, snaking in a shower of sparks to the ground, where it snapped and sputtered and wriggled around. Motivated either by a death wish or an inexplicable and fatally flawed decision-making process (didn't want to get in trouble?) he jumped out of his truck, rushed over to move it, picked it up, and was electrocuted on the spot. Unable to let go, he stood there shuddering and then fell over. They had to let him lie twitching until the power had been shut off by someone somewhere. By then, of course, he was beyond saving. Construction, I learned, could be a very dangerous occupation.

But mostly it was routine; good hard physical labor. At the end of the day, I would go back out to the beach and hurl myself into the shorebreak to cool off, clean off the dirt and grime, and revel in the fresh briny tang of the ocean. I started wearing my swim shorts under my work clothes, to save the time and bother of changing my clothes in my car at the beach. Just peel off the dirty layer and jump into the water. I had a simple, clean life: work, ocean, work, ocean. But it wasn't something I really wanted to continue forever.

The problem of boxing and the coach and Cody festered in my brain all summer. The only time it left me was while I was riding a wave. Even sitting on my board between sets, I could see Cody's mouthguard-enhanced leer in the whiteness of a breaking wave, and sometimes when I was being churned by an especially violent wipeout it seemed as if enormous boxing gloves were pummeling my entire body.

I had never been a quitter, but no matter how I looked at it, I could see nothing but misery if I went back to Pomona College. The smog had been bad, the nightlife worse. It was too far from the ocean. And my beating at the hands of Cody had been the last straw.

I made my decision: I wasn't going back.

1959-60: Salt water or fresh?

By the time I had made up my mind to abandon Pomona it was too late to register for college anywhere else. What to do? Two options presented themselves.

In the fall of 1959, a group from Windansea was getting ready to hit the north shore of O'ahu to ride the big surf at Waimea. It sounded exciting – like being churned in a cement mixer full of salt water while going over Niagara Falls – but, based on my experience being held down by ten- to twelve-foot waves on the West Coast, I wouldn't be able to hold my breath long enough to survive a twenty-foot wave. Cody was bad, but drowning was worse. Even at eighteen a guy has to know his limits, and keep his priorities straight. I had a fairly high tolerance for a certain degree of risk, but I wasn't crazy. For me, Waimea wasn't risky or even high risk; it was more like all-risk, 100% probability of failure, AKA death by drowning. Or maybe it was that little voice of childhood fear, whispering to me from the shorebreak that nearly got me when I was six.

But what was I going to do? I could get another laborer job – this time, no jackhammers! – or something similar. But there was another, more attractive possibility.

Back when Mammoth was rope tows and Squaw Valley was still virgin forest, I had done a fair bit of skiing at Southern California ski areas and even a trip or two to Mammoth. From Pomona, I had often skied Mount Baldy – a wind-blasted, weather-beaten peak of ten thousand feet, covered in spots with sheets of thick, blue, glacier-like ice, only twelve miles from campus. It had give me some interesting experiences in involuntary extreme skiing, like the time I slipped on an icy traverse and slid several hundred feet down an almost vertical ravine, shedding most of my equipment on the way but somehow missing the jagged rocks protruding from the ice. It took me most of the day to climb back out, using the point of the one ski pole I had managed to hang onto, to chip footholds in the ice.

Mount Baldy was no Alpine paradise and neither were its surroundings. In those days the air in the eastern Los Angeles basin was so foul with automotive and industrial pollution that the snow-covered peak was invisible from the surrounding area, and vice versa. Standing atop the summit on a glorious clear day, the sky a brilliant blue, all below you was a dirty brown carpet of smog penetrated by occasional plumes from a smelter. It looked thick enough to ski on.

The rich blend of toxic chemicals created sulfuric acid smog, tiny droplets so potent that they would burn tiny black pinholes in the paint on a car. And it worked on humans, too: one year sulfuric acid smog in London caused the death of thousands of people and put tens of thousands in the hospital. Like many kids in those days, I wasn't overly concerned with air quality or with health, but I did notice that on smoggy days my lungs hurt and I wheezed like an emphysemic smoker for several hours after any kind of extended exertion. And even worse, the paint on my car was getting trashed.

During all this I was bombarded with enthusiastic letters from a surfing buddy who had gone to Colorado and tormented me with graphic narratives of clear blue skies over crisp feathery powder, craggy peaks towering over miles of uncrowded runs. A number of Windansea surfers, including some Older Guys, had gotten heavily into skiing, and some of them would spend the entire season working in a ski resort. They would go to the mountains, get a job on the slopes or in a bar at night, and ski during the day.

So: Pomona was untenable and Waimea was out, but maybe Colorado was the answer.

Remember again about surfing in 1959: no leashes, no wetsuits. Missing mid-winter surf wasn't as much of a loss as it would be later. At that time a thirty-minute session – in fifty-something degree water – was a long one, and if you lost your board the swim in would leave you so hypothermic that you might be through for the day. In contrast, with warm clothes and gloves you could ski all day without getting cold. Besides, snow was just frozen water, and a ski run – moguls and chutes and drop-offs and the occasional boulder – was like an enormous frozen wave with steep spots and sections and boils and reefs. So I made arrangements to put my scholarship on hold, and off I went.

1959-1960, Aspen: Frozen waves

As the 1959 ski season opened, I was in Aspen. Arriving with five dollars in my pocket, I was lucky enough to run into some Older Guys from the beach who let me sleep on their floor until I got a job and a place to stay.

Aspen was a very different place in the winter of 1959. It could best be described as charming or picturesque, sometimes tending toward grungy and rundown. The burning civic issue that season was whether or not the pharmacy should be allowed to ruin the atmosphere by installing a neon "Rx" sign to identify itself at night. A guy named Ed, who ran a cheap skiers' bunkhouse called Ed's Beds, used to drive around town in an old troop carrier truck decorated with paper lanterns and a sign advertising his place. The town was still full of old Victorian homes, most of which could probably have been purchased for about five thousand dollars apiece. Of course, I wasn't thinking in those terms and I didn't have five thousand dollars, so it was a moot point.

That season in Aspen was more a series of vignettes than a coherent narrative. After a couple of false starts on the employment front, I ended up with two jobs that covered all the basics. In the morning, drive to the brand-new Aspen Highlands ski area and work for a few hours in the ski shop fitting rental skis and doing miscellaneous stuff. This gave me a free lift ticket and 50% off on all food, clothing and equipment.

I would ski for the rest of the day, then show up at the Red Onion by 4 pm to work as a back waiter, substitute waiter (if a real waiter didn't show up), and occasional bartender's assistant. This job paid a pittance plus a share of tips, but it provided a free employee meal – cooked-up rejects like chicken gizzards and rice, but it was nourishing and stayed with you and there was all you could eat, every night, plus the chance to poach uneaten steak and lobster from the plates of the rich and trendy. I kept a doggie bag in the kitchen.

I liked the setup. Free skiing, free food. The Highlands wasn't as steep or as high as Ajax, but so what? It got me away from the hotshots and the Hollywood vibe of Aspen. In surfing terms, Ajax was Malibu; the Highlands was Windansea. Not famous, not iconic, just fun. The country cousin, the outpost, the frontier. And because it was new and unfamous and unglamorous, it was never crowded. It gave solitude and untracked powder, and I loved it.

In Aspen, as in many other places, there was a pecking order, and I decided that I didn't want to be at the bottom of it. The ability to ski well trumped a lot of other considerations, so I hurled myself into improving. Day after day, regardless of the weather, I skied to exhaustion until it was time to report for work at the Onion. I skied in sun, in snowstorms, in whiteouts, in wind. On powder and on crust and on ice. I worked and practiced with a single-minded, almost grim determination. And I did get better.

Like any resort town throughout history – I'm sure the same phenomenon existed in the Roman Empire or classical Greece or ancient Egypt – there were the owners and the guests, and then there was the underclass that kept the whole thing running. I was in the underclass, and although the owners and the guests had more money, I think we had more fun.

We worked and partied all night and skied all day. We had picnics of bread and wine and cheese above the top of the Highlands, overlooking the backside of Ajax. We had road trips to Alta to visit the kids who had gotten jobs there and who would let us crash with them or sneak us into vacant hotel rooms for free. We had toga parties and beer slaloms. We were in torchlight parades at the Highlands for the free beer.

The torchlight parades were a great deal and a lot of fun, but made hazardous by the circumstances. Participants got a pitcher of beer and a pizza. First you ate the pizza and drank the beer. Then you went out into the freezing night, put on your skis – the surprising difficulty of this simple task revealed the onset of alcohol-related coordination problems – and rode the chair up the mountain in the dark.

There was no off-ramp at the starting point for the parade, so you rode the chair all the way up to a point hundreds of vertical feet above the start and skied back down to the starting point on the icy run, over bumps and hollows, in the dark. If there was a moon it helped, but not much. No poles were used, since they would get in the way during the actual parade. By now the beer and the cold were wreaking havoc with balance and coordination, not to mention mental acuity.

Once the slipping and falling was over and everyone assembled midway down the hill, the "torches" were handed out. They were nothing more than highway flares, the kind where you light one end and try to avoid pointing it at anything close. We'd form a sort of ski train, everyone in a snowplow position with the skis of each person inside the skis of the next one in front, light the flares, hold them aloft like the Statue of Liberty, and go for it. The idea was to ski down in a series of S-curves for the delight of the visiting skiers and tourists drinking in the Bierstube at the bottom of the hill.

The good news was that the flares lit up the hill so you could at least partially see where the group was headed. The bad news was that it was still icy, many of the participants were drunk, and the torches would burn a hole through anything they got close to. In addition, we were in such close formation that if one person fell they would drag down everyone around them. Picture a precision flying team, expanded to a dozen or more aircraft, with all the pilots half in the bag and performing at low altitude at night in a turbulent wind-shear environment, and you are close to understanding the situation.

One night the inevitable happened: the combination of darkness, ice and diminished capacity resulted in a colossal pileup, bodies and skis flailing and crossing and tangling like coat hangers in a crowded closet, the whole scene lit by the eerie reddish-white glow of the flares and punctuated by urgent cries that blended together like the shrieking of agitated baboons:

look-out-my-leg-my-leg-move-the-goddam-flare-don't-don't-move-it-stop-stop-you're-gonna-set-my-ski-on-fire!

Somehow we got through it without casualties. A tribute, I suppose, to youth and instinctive survival skills. From then on, the rules were changed, and participants got the beer and pizza after the parade, not before. Safer, but nowhere near as challenging.

The hill and the snow were the center of everything. It was almost like surfing! Being the first one up the chair with two feet of fresh powder on the ground, so light and cold that when you tossed a ski-full into the air it disappeared in a shower of diamonds, sublimated to vapor before it hit the ground. Blasting down the lift line in the new snow, leaving a string of S-curves to admire on the way back up. If they were good, you could take the credit; if they were ugly – irregular; sloppy turns; even a sitzmark – no one needed to know it was you. Sitting on a boulder under an endless blue sky, surrounded by an undulating sea of white, mountains all around, basking in a penetrating mix of Rocky Mountain sunshine and fatigue and satisfaction. And after hours or in the evenings when I didn't work, there was every sort of live music of the era – bluegrass, jazz, folk, flamenco – to enjoy.

Perhaps the biggest benefit was invisible: although I didn't realize it, I was actually getting good at skiing, which meant that I was no longer a total loss at sports. Other people on skis accepted me as an equal. Progress!

I skied the Highlands for free, but I put in time on Ajax as well. At six dollars a day, lift tickets on Ajax weren't cheap on our wages – the Onion paid $1 a night plus a share of tips – but they came on a beaded keychain which made them easy to use communally. Or you could hang out at the bottom of the chair in the late morning and try to pick up an unwanted ticket from someone who was quitting for the day or a tourist who was leaving town.

There were other bargains. A ski buddy and I rented a room in the Brand Building, a commercial building across from the post office where on warm days a pack of old guys sat on benches in the afternoon sun. The entire downstairs was taken up by an auto repair shop. Upstairs there was a dance studio, an art studio and, inexplicably, our rental room-plus-full-bath. The room was enormous – probably twenty feet by twenty-five feet – and included an upright piano, two steam radiators that kept it toasty warm, two double beds, and fresh sheets and towels twice a week, all for forty dollars a month.

Outside the window was an enormous pillar of an icicle cascading down from the overhanging roof onto a porch roof below. We cut cave-like holes in it and *voilá*! a refrigerator was born. Thanks to the auto shop downstairs, the building was connected to a seemingly limitless supply of hot water that came from the tap just below the boiling point. We had no stove (microwaves were yet to become widespread, probably because they cost more than a car) but we could puncture the lid on a can of food and float it in the sink, heated by a flow of near-boiling water until it was ready to eat. When entertaining in the evening, we could pick the lock at the dance studio (classes were held only during the day), borrow the record player and a stack of records, and have music as a background to whatever activity was occurring in our room. The building had no other night-time tenants, so no one ever complained. Just put the stuff back before morning, and no one was the wiser.

The only drawback was the set of swinging doors at ground level, leading to the sidewalk. A lot of warm air leaked out through those doors, and at night a pack of large dogs – huskies, malamutes, the occasional St. Bernard – would sometimes congregate in a furry pile in front of the door to keep warm. They got very territorial – growling and snarling ominously while baring their wolf-like fangs – if I tried to push past them to go inside, so when I got home, bone-tired after a day of skiing and working until midnight, I had to stand across the street and throw chunks of ice at them until they grudgingly drifted away to find someplace more peaceful to lie down. Then, and only then, could I go up to bed.

By the end of the season, I was feeling pretty good. My skiing had improved dramatically. I'd arrived with five dollars and was leaving town with all new equipment, a hundred bucks in my pocket and a lot of memories. We had never been given a bill for the forty-dollar-a-month rent on our room, but we didn't want the sheriff coming after us so we stopped at the Hotel Jerome (which owned the Brand Building) to pay up. Amazingly, they had no record of the rental. We gave the desk girl a nice tip for having failed to find the bill, and hit the road in our separate cars.

The odd thing about Aspen was this: although I never fell in love with skiing the way I did with surfing, not once in the Rockies did I lament the absence of the sea they way I had in Pomona, and would later in life when I was forced to take a long break from surfing. Maybe there was too much going on, maybe I had lost myself in the pursuit of improvement, maybe I was having too much fun. Maybe a ski hill really is just an oversized frozen wave. But when I got back to the ocean, I was hooked all over again.

When I arrived in La Jolla some twenty hours later, I went straight to the parking lot at Windansea. I had only been gone for a few months, but my mind and eyes had habituated to the jagged starched whiteness of the Rockies. The ocean looked strangely flat, as if a steamroller had gone berserk at the edge of the earth and rolled everything beneath a vast bolt of crumpled blue satin, all the way to the horizon. The surface moved restlessly as waves wriggled shoreward like enormous drunken sideways worms. I was home.

It was 1960. New decade, new directions.

Part II: Riding High

1960: Joe College

Back from Aspen, like many others I applied for a job as a San Diego lifeguard. I passed the tests without difficulty. Nothing outstanding, middle of the pack as always, a solid journeyman performance. So now I was a lifeguard. Today was calm and flat; nothing to rescue anyone from.

Rookie mistake.

A couple of very large women are floating on an inner tube, back to back. Somehow they both manage to fall off at the same time, driving the inner tube out of reach. As they begin thrashing and coughing and yelling, I realize that neither of them can swim.

No time to grab a can or rescue board or put on fins. Besides, they're so close to shore that there's no need. I dive in; when I get close enough I submerge, trying to come up behind them so they can't grab me and pull me down.

Another rookie mistake! I soon discover that it's very difficult to come up behind two people at the same time. One of them somehow spins around and grabs my hair; the other one follows suit. As I'm pushed under, they adjust their survival strategy by climbing onto my shoulders. They drive me down until my feet hit the bottom. Topside, in the world of sunlight and blue sky and life-giving oxygen, I feel them consolidating their grip on my hair.

Okay, no need to panic, let's think. I'm in only about eight feet of water, just a couple of feet over my head. The sandy bottom is moderately steep, and we're close to shore. I should be able to walk back to shallow water before my air runs out. So that's what I do, shuffling my way along the bottom with well over three hundred pounds of panicked human squirming around on my shoulders while clinging to my hair.

When I got my head and shoulders above the water I leaned forward and tipped them off into the shallows where they landed with loud shrieks and squeals and a mighty splash. I never even got a thank you.

Next time I'll use the rescue board.

Later that summer, sitting on the bench with another guard, who had also done the ski bum thing the previous winter, the conversation turned to the end of summer, when we seasonal guards would be laid off.

"What are you gonna do this winter – Aspen again? Sun Valley? Alta?"

His question got me thinking. I had escaped from smog, the coach and the drudgery of higher education, and I was enjoying a simple, physical existence which was much more to my liking than classes and studying and tests and grades. Nevertheless, I suddenly was struck by an image of my life, stretching into the unimaginable reaches of old age (which at that time was anything over about forty): winters on the slopes, summers on the ocean, not much in between, as if these two mirror-image poles were the only alternatives in life. There had to be more.

The deciding factor was a conversation from when I was still in junior high, trying to become a surfer.

I was working after school as a kitchen helper in a retirement home. The manager, Mrs. Hopper, was a Captain Bligh of the kitchen who treated all of us like dirt. It was hell, but it was a job and I needed the money to buy a surfboard.

The people I worked with were two broken-down old guys named John and Pete, who washed pots and stoves and mopped floors and cleaned up the toilets. Pete had even been on the wrong side of World War II, a private in the Italian army who somehow ended up in the US. They were both high school dropouts and stuck in this dead-end job, slaving away in dirt and heat for minimum wage, and they were determined to steer me up the ladder to something better. John made sure I knew the stakes.

"Ya gotta go ta school, kid. Ya don't wanna end up like us."

At fourteen, it was impossible to imagine being their age, much less as decrepit as they were, but their message came back to me now as I sat on my lifeguard bench and pondered the future.

The following Monday I drove out to San Diego State to reactivate my scholarship and register for the fall semester.

The campus was nothing like today. It included a large, untamed canyon of sagebrush and cactus, now filled in for a parking lot, where ex-UDT surfer and waterman Tom Carlin was said to have lived in a cave to save money on rent while getting his degree. It was a commuter college: drive out from the beach, take your classes, drive back to the beach.

The key was to get all your classes close together so that you spent as little time away from the ocean as possible. If you could get all your classes bunched up between ten or eleven in the morning and two in the afternoon, you could surf in the morning and get back to the beach with plenty of daylight to hit the afternoon glass-off. My senior year I even managed to create a schedule that gave me Tuesdays and Thursdays off. It was a surfer's dream.

1960s: Watermen

Consciously or otherwise, most of us aspired to be what was called a "waterman." This meant an individual completely at home with all aspects of the sea, who not only surfed, but bodysurfed, dove for fish and lobster and abalone, and knew tides, currents and bottom configurations.

Many of us had gotten an early start. I had gotten into snorkeling with some kids from the Shores at about the same time I caught my first wave.

There was something otherworldly about snorkeling, cruising face down, wrapped in the slight chill of the summer sea, hearing your own breath amplified in long, rhythmic exhalations through the snorkel, the underwater world slightly distorted by the diving mask and blurred around the edges by condensation inside the glass.

With your head in the water you discover how noisy a reef can be: a cacophony of clicks, grunts, burbles and fizzing noises made by the ocean and its inhabitants. Over the sand and the reef we saw all sorts of sea life, from big spider crabs and rays – stingrays, guitarfish, butterfly rays and bat rays – to leopard sharks, horned sharks, halibut, kelp bass. We were in a world of gliding fish, the crackling of the reefs, the gentle swaying of eelgrass and kelp

Occasionally a jolt of fear: a moray eel, sharp-toothed mouth gaping evilly, gills pulsing. A sudden school of barracuda, like streamlined silver piranhas, reptilian eyes staring without expression, lower jaws thrust belligerently forward, coldly examining a skinny local kid like shoppers in a fish market. Nah, looks like yesterday's catch. And off they would dart into the deep, looking for something more nutritious.

Dominating all of it was the endless throb and pulse of the sea, arriving from beyond the edge of the earth, inexhaustible.

With snorkeling came skin diving. We made pole spears, using round wooden shafts ten feet long, tipped with barbed trident heads. For propulsion, we used a few feet of surgical tubing. These were formidable weapons to hunt bottom fish like halibut and rays. You might also, if you got lucky, spear an unwary reef fish or even a corbina, although the pole spear was so cumbersome and slow that only the most hapless fish would fail to elude it. But the first instinct of halibut and rays was to stay put and hope to avoid detection, which made them a lot more vulnerable.

This was a great foundation to build on. As we got older, we built our basic kit: in addition to a surfboard (rarely more than one, since they cost money and took up a lot of space), swim fins for body surfing and skin diving, a facemask, a snorkel – plain "J" shape, no filters or valves – an abalone iron (usually made from the leaf spring of a car) and a spear.

For most of us, the spear to have was now a Hawaiian three-prong: a steel rod about five feet long with three thinner, shorter rods welded onto one end and filed to sharp points to form a sort of elongated trident. Propulsion was a length of surgical tubing. These light, hand-held spears were easy to handle among the reefs and were very effective at short range. When you hit a fish, the three pointed rods would curve outward as they entered, keeping the fish from wriggling off. Some of us also got Arbaletes (or the smaller Baby Arbalete), lightweight French spearguns powered by elastic bands.

In the pre-leash era, we honed our bodysurfing skills in wipeouts or when we failed to make a wave: when you felt yourself going off the board, you launched your body toward the shore in a flat surface dive, trying to catch the wave and ride it in before your board hit the beach and the rocks. Sometimes you would find yourself bodysurfing the soup next to your board – those old boards had a tendency to flip over and ride the soup upside down and sideways, all the way to the beach. Then you could try to grab it – or evade it, depending on the size of the wave and the situation.

The bottom line was this: no surf, no problem. We enjoyed the ocean no matter what. On it, in it, or under it, there was magic to be found. In the process, you learned to feel the pulsing rhythms of the sea. As a bonus, when the waves were flat, skin diving was a great way to learn the reefs and get some dinner at the same time.

And it was so easy – the abundance of surf spots was matched by the abundance of fish, abalone and lobster. At one point Rick Naish was renting a house right across the street from a great surf break and a reef with excellent diving. Once a group of us were hanging out there, enjoying the day, when someone suggested we have a fish fry. We grabbed ab irons, spears, masks, snorkels and fins from our cars or from Rick's personal stash, and hit the water. An hour later we were cooking a variety of fresh seafood, more than we could eat.

Of course we couldn't hold a candle to some of the real old-time watermen, Older Guys like Bev Morgan who did it all, surfing, lifeguarding, skin-diving and even doing deep-sea diving and fabricating their own deep-diving equipment. We could only admire them.

1960: By train to Mazatlán

There's a line in the movie *Dances with Wolves*, when someone asks the Kevin Costner character why he wants to be sent to the frontier. His motive is simple: "I want to see it before it's gone." I don't know if we understood, in some vague way, that the Mexico we knew – like long-distance train travel itself – was going to disappear as surely as the old frontier had. But for whatever reason, there was a sense of romance and a special allure, almost as if we knew we were experiencing a time and place that was going to be lost forever.

In 1960 the train trip to Mazatlán was like a thousand-mile magic carpet ride to another world. In our case, the magic carpet was pretty ratty and threadbare, but for us that only added to the charm.

We boarded the train in Mexicali in the early evening, found our second-class – or maybe third-class – car, and lurched out of the station after dark. Off to adventure! Our travel companions were native women, native men, a couple of Mexican soldiers in uniform, a number of guys who appeared to be returning home after working as laborers or farm workers in the U.S., and a used car salesman from Hermosillo who introduced himself early on and peppered us with questions about life on the beach. There were also a couple of chickens; no pigs.

Mexico's northern desert is cold at night, especially in the dead of winter. Inside the train, it was roughly the same temperature due to an ample supply of outdoor air pouring in through leaky windows and the doors at both ends of the car. Plus a couple of hardy souls had left their windows partially open, perhaps to enjoy the brisk night air. The Mexicans had wisely bundled up in thick jackets (men) and heavy shawls (women). We had dressed for the semi-topics and we were miserable. Wearing three T-shirts and a thin windbreaker helped a bit, but not much. The wooden slat benches added to our misery.

The train clacked and swayed through the night, stopping now and then in the middle of nowhere for no apparent reason. When dawn came, we were moving through high desert, mostly rocks and cactus with scrubby bushes in between. Much like Baja California, but less rugged, and minus the ocean. Now the reason for the random stops became apparent: each time the train halted, a handful of Indians would get off and head out on foot across the desert, headed for a destination only they knew. At times, a similar handful would appear out of the wilderness and board the train. Then we were off again.

It was all very picturesque. Meanwhile, there was no drinking water and no running water in the bathrooms, the toilets were a stopped-up, stinking mess, and the conductor clearly hated gringos and would have loved to find an excuse to throw us off the train. The first-class carriages had all the amenities, but they were off limits and tightly guarded by the hostile conductor, so we hunkered down and endured.

Whenever we stopped at a town or village, the train was surrounded by Indian ladies selling food, soft drinks and beer, which we eagerly consumed. At one stop, when they spotted gringos, the word went out and our window was besieged by a small group that quickly swelled to a couple of dozen people, men and women, who gave up all pretense of selling us anything and simply held up their open hands toward our window, clamoring for money.

When a group of them peeled off away from our window and headed for the door of our car, someone saved the day by tossing a handful of coins as far from the train as possible. This created a mad scramble which ended the boarding attempt and distracted the locals until the train got underway a minute later. The whole affair made us feel privileged and targeted and callous, all at the same time. But what were we supposed to do? We were just kids trying to get to Mazatlán. The Mexican economy wasn't our fault.

We had been on the train all night, and by sundown we had added an entire day. And we weren't there yet. At least tonight was warmer; we were getting farther south. In the middle of the night we were awakened from a fitful sleep by a great lurching and banging and shouting in Spanish as the train ground to a halt. Mazatlán at last! It was somewhere between two and three in the morning.

Take a taxi to a cheap hotel, the first one available. We're too tired to be picky. Besides, anything will be an improvement over the train.

There's no electric light in our second-floor room, just dim light from the street somewhere. Exhausted, we toss our clothes on the floor and fall into bed, so tired that it's a luxury to sleep on lumpy straw-filled mattresses with sheets that feel like burlap bags, straw-stuffed pillows sewed to the bed (to prevent theft?), amid strange dreamlike impressions of snoring noises. We're too burned out to care about anything.

Morning: we discover that the center of the room is actually a large opening to the floor below, surrounded by a low wall. Some of our clothes lie scattered at the foot of the wall; others are randomly draped over it, just as we threw them. We go to the wall and look over it. Below is a large room – the really cheap part of the hotel – filled with narrow beds (more like cots, really), occupied by sleeping, snoring men. The fragrance of last night's beer and tequila wafts upward. A couple of items of our clothing have made it down to this level. One on the floor, one draped across the face of a sleeper. How to retrieve them? We decide it's best to let sleeping locals lie.

We get dressed, grab our bags, and proceed to a modest hotel across from the beach near Cannons, where one of the guys had stayed the year before. Three stories of Spartan motel-type units with small kitchens, overlooking the long curve of golden sand north of downtown and conveniently located between Cannons and the sheltered spot where the fishing *pangas* launched and returned filled with fish. We connect with the rest of the crew, a small group of guys from Windansea who had driven down by car, bringing our boards. Now we have wheels and we're good to go.

In the 1960s, the mainland of Mexico was a refreshing change from the border areas of Baja. There was still a sense of innocence, if you will. People were curious, inquisitive. There were actually entire towns and small cities where no one tried to sell you anything. A welcome absence of hustlers and scammers.

Mazatlán had yet to become a tourist town; it was still a combination of port town and fishing village. There was the old town center, built by the French during the short and tragic reign of Maximilian, with solid, European-looking stone buildings. Small *plazoletas* filled with trees and flowers, young children and old women. Bakeries, fruit vendors, *tiendas de abarrotes*. Openly curious children; curious adults feigning nonchalant indifference.

North of town, the long curving beach was backed by a low, swampy area dense with palm trees and undergrowth. Here and there among the foliage loomed the abandoned concrete hulks of empty buildings, empty doorways and windows staring vacantly at the sea. Most, we were told, were victims of the hurricane of 1957, which had made a direct hit on Mazatlán.

We surfed the point north of town and then hung out in the shade of the *palapa* at Lupe's cantina on the beach (now a gaudy fake Moorish disco or something of the sort) for a beer and a taco and to gaze at the offshore islands and listen to the locals talk about nothing and give us tips on places to go. We went to the endless sand beaches that bordered the swamps and lagoons north of Lupe's and rode isolated beach breaks.

If there were good waves, that was great. If not, it truly didn't matter. Being there and drinking it all in was enough. It was pure magic.

We dove for fish and lobster among the reefs near Olas Altas. We speared fish at Cannons reef when the surf was flat, being careful to avoid the thousands of long-spined dark purple sea urchins that filled every hollow and coated the bottom in the narrow spaces between the reefs.

We walked around the town and talked to people, practicing our Spanish. We went to the inlet where the fisherman went out before dawn and bought fish when they came put-putting back in the morning with their *pangas* filled with fresh catch and the pelicans flopped and danced awkwardly on the sand with their long beaks open, waiting for the men to throw them offal as they cleaned their fish. We climbed the endless steps to the lighthouse and drank in the sight of the city and the islands and the sea spread out five hundred feet below us. We ventured through the thorn forest into the interior, where enormous iguanas eyed us indifferently as they rested on the thick branches of trees.

We wandered through the big central market with its infinity of shops and marveled at the produce (huge papayas, mangos, coconuts, jícama, other tropical fruit), at the displays of *huaraches* (each village had its own distinctive weave) and hats and hand-embroidered *huipiles* and a thousand other items. We ate at the small restaurants on the second floor balcony and absorbed the sights and sounds and smells of the cavernous market below and the city outside.

We lolled in the plaza by the cathedral on Christmas morning, intrigued by the vultures perched on the crosses atop the cathedral towers. We even went into the mass, a delightfully disorganized affair where people got up and sat down and moved around and came in and went out at random. We grilled fish and lobster and made French toast and played guitars and drank Pacífico on the balcony in the evenings and watched the sun set somewhere in the deep Pacific Ocean beyond the offshore islands. We strolled along the *malecón* to the Copa de Leche to drink strong coffee and eat *pan dulce* and watch the sea shifting restlessly at Olas Altas.

The memories are endless: cooking stuff in the crude way that college kids have, riding perfect little lefts at Cannons, getting caught inside at Cannons and trying to become flat like a halibut to avoid being impaled on the hundreds of sea urchins, so thick on the reef that it looked like spiny purple carpet. Waking at dawn to the cries of street vendors and the gentle put-put-put of the *pangas* setting out to fish. Bat rays jumping all around us one day while we're out at Lupe's and we start wondering what was chasing them and we all paddled in without a word and then the fins in the water showed us we did the right thing.

Those days were sweet then; they're even sweeter now, and sometimes I'd give anything to get them back.

54

1961: Land of the Rising Sun

I really had the travel bug in the 1960s, and one of the destinations on my list was, amazingly, Japan. In those days Japan was synonymous with cheap junk and war brides and weird food. Today, everyone eats sashimi and sushi, but in the early '60s, the few people who had ever heard of it though you were nuts to even consider eating it.

So why Japan?

Wayne Land and several of the crew that had gone to the Islands in the late '50s to surf Mākaha and the North Shore had returned with something that is commonplace today, but as rare and exotic as anything could have been at the time: karate. And not only karate, but an appetite for an entire set of Japanese cultural artifacts as found in Hawai'i, from saimin and *zōri* to samurai movies.

When Wayne came back, he opened a karate school, and a bunch of us eagerly signed up. We really got into it, going to eat at dingy Japanese restaurants and even going out somewhere by San Diego State to watch grainy old black-and-white samurai films at a Buddhist temple. *The Hidden Fortress, Throne of Blood, 47 Rōnin, Seven Samurai, Yōjinbō* – we ate it up.

All this exposure created a desire to go to Japan for more karate, more culture, more experience in what was then exotic. San Diego State was about to start offering Japanese, and they told me I could get credit for language courses taken in Japan. I could even use my scholarship money to pay for it! I immediately went out and bought a teach-yourself-Japanese book to get ready.

I had it all figured out: use my scholarship money for airfare and survival – flying to Japan was expensive but once there it was insanely cheap – teach English for extra cash, and study Japanese language and martial arts. And that's what I did.

This meant a break from surfing, but not from the ocean. Japan, as an island country, has thousands of miles of coastline and when I could I took the train to the ocean. There were no surfboards in the country at the time, but I could swim and dive and bodysurf.

Japan was a trip. Everything was scaled to smaller size, so that I had to duck to enter a railway car or the doorway in a house, and on buses the seats were too close together for my legs to fit. If I stood up, my head was touching the roof of the bus and every bump – in those days there were lots of them – smacked the top of my head on the roof. I used to try to stand with my head in the opening of the roof air vent to give myself a bit more room to bounce.

The vast majority of Japanese had never seen a foreigner, which led to some interesting encounters. To adults, I was more or less like a poorly-trained talking bear; to kids I was a frightening monster. In restaurants I was chastised for using my left hand to eat (I'm left-handed), and once an old guy actually got up, walked over to my table, yanked the chopsticks out of my left hand and jammed them into my right. In Gifu, home of the famed cormorant fishermen, I swam across the river to check out the cormorants, which were kept in bamboo cages in the shade during the day. The locals didn't believe that a *gaijin* could swim. When I went to Sado Island for diving, the thing I remember – far more than the beautiful clear water and craggy shore – is having to get off a local bus because someone's baby took one look at me and couldn't stop screaming in terror.

I do remember bodysurfing some beautiful peeling lefts off a point break in Hokkaidō. When I came in, the locals praised my bravery.

"Oh, no," I protested modestly in my pidgin Japanese. "The waves are not so big."

They told me that wasn't the point. The area was so infested with sharks that no one ever dared to swim there.

Thanks for the warning.

On the way over to Japan, and again on the way back, I stopped off in Hawai'i to visit some guys from the Windansea crew in Mākaha, which was slowly being replaced by the North Shore as "the" big-wave destination in the Islands, but still had a reputation and a following. I didn't hit it big –

luckily! – but I got to ride some sweet overhead waves and experience the effects of the famous Mākaha backwash, which was like skiing into huge, moving moguls coming at you and tossing the entire mountain into the air with you on it.

By the following year I was back at State and back at the beach.

1962: Coast trip to Manzanillo

That winter, two years after the Mazatlán train trip, part of the same crew drove a VW van as far as Manzanillo, with the same mix of diving, surfing and general exploration.

Going by road added a whole new layer of adventure to the trip. In those days most of the highways in Mexico were two-lane roads and many of them were unpaved. Driving included avoiding dead animals, live animals, fatalistic people on bicycles (usually farm laborers riding to work before dawn, with no lights or reflectors, or riding back from work after dark, again with no lights or reflectors), slow trucks with no tail lights, stopped trucks with no tail lights, washed-out bridges, holes in the pavement, occasional debris. If a vehicle broke down, the driver might or might not make any effort to get it off the road and out of the way. Most roads had no shoulders; multi-lane roads were mostly non-existent. In short, a Mexico road trip was not for the unwary or the faint of heart.

Most of the time we traveled – okay, blundered around – on instinct. See something that might be interesting? Go check it out. Going farther down in Mexico? Keep the ocean on your right when possible and you can't go wrong. Going home? Reverse the process.

Like the early Spanish explorers, who managed to miss things like San Francisco Bay on their first go-around, we missed a lot of primo breaks, either because they weren't breaking at the time or because we just didn't find them. Access was limited and we hadn't the time or the resources to drive down every single sandy trail or dirt track leading toward the ocean. To find likely surfing spots we relied on tattered, grimy old AAA maps –

beer-stained and flecked with dried salsa and guacamole – and looked for obvious clues: points, river mouths, capes. For skin diving, we sought out clusters of rocky islets. Sometimes we got lucky, sometimes we didn't.

The trip down was, if possible, even more exotic than the train had been. Stoic *campesinos* riding bicycles at dawn, headed for the fields; cows and the occasional horse lying in the road to absorb some heat from the pavement. Once we saw a bull who had evidently lost a fight with a rival, swaying awkwardly as he walked aimlessly with blood flowing from a nasty wound in his side.

We hit Mazatlán for a couple of days of small surf, then continued south – we had five hundred miles of winding two-lane road yet to go. In Tepic there was a major *charreada* – a Mexican rodeo – being held at the bullring. We snuck in by walking along the tops of the narrow adobe brick walls dividing the pens where the bulls were kept before the event. It wasn't about saving money – the entry fee was cheap – it was just to see if we could pull it off. It was risky, but balancing precariously above the wild-eyed, hostile, snorting animals, we made it. I'm sure we were spotted, but perhaps in deference to our display of macho risk-taking no one threw us out.

Back on the road. A succession of hills and valleys, dense with foliage and studded with the glistening green fronds of banana palms. Local color: just as with *huaraches*, each village has a distinctive style of hat, seen in the variation in the tassels hanging down from the back.

Somewhere in Colima or Nayarit we noticed *campesinos* with especially interesting hats, so we decided to go into the next village to buy a hat. In a secluded valley, we see the earthy red of tile roofs. We turn off the highway, and find ourselves descending into a small village that looks like a movie set, or an idealized version of Mexico if Gauguin had painted Mexico. Whitewashed walls, tile roofs, dirt streets leading to a small cobblestone square; a dry fountain, a church, and finally our destination: a hat store.

We park the van, pile out, stroll inside. Already our arrival has caused a minor sensation. Nobody from the outside world ever bothers to stop off here, and gringos are merely a rumor, a mythical creature from Out There Somewhere. As we troop into the store, the owner tries to stay cool.

"Señores, ¿qué se les ofrece?" What can I offer you?

We tell him we want hats, the local kind.

By now the street outside the shop is packed with locals, all trying to get a look. I hear voices calling to friends and neighbors. *"Pedro, go get José! He's gotta see this!"*

We try on a couple of hats; they don't fit. It's not the size so much as the shape – our heads are too elongated. Some people are pressed against the glass of the shop window by the crowd. It looks as if the glass might break. A few brave souls slip in through the door for a closer look. The owner is still trying to act normal, as if this were just another day, but it's getting more difficult. As more people get brave enough to come inside, the shop gets so crowded we can barely move. Enough! We apologize to the shop owner, thank him for his time, push our way through the throng, get outside to the van and make our escape.

It's weird to be exotic.

The VW van had its own exoticism. From a distance, it evidently resembled a real bus, for peasants would sometimes step out into the road to flag it down. They couldn't seem to grasp that the van was something small and close, not big and far away. The anticipation on their faces morphed into confusion as we kept approaching but the van didn't expand to the size of a highway bus.

One old guy refused to believe what his eyes were telling him; waving vigorously, almost angrily, he stepped out into the roadway just as we roared past. I had to swerve violently to keep from hitting him, and the van fishtailed wildly until I could get it back under control. I braked to a shaky stop down the road and sat there trembling as the locals gathered in a little cluster around the old guy, glaring in our direction as if angry at our deception. Still pumped full of adrenaline, I drove on.

Finally we approach Manzanillo. The first impression is an aura of isolation and mystery. The approach to town is through a swampy jungle, and the only entry into town is across a railway bridge, the narrow highway bridge being unusable – actually, mostly missing – for some reason.

I drive across on the ties, inching ahead slowly and cautiously, our wheels outside the rails. The van rises onto each wooden tie, then bumps down into the gap between the ties. There are no guardrails to keep us from toppling off into the sluggish river below, and each time we bump down there's the unpleasant feeling that a wheel could somehow slip off the ties and send us plunging over the side. The crossing seems to take forever, and when we're finally across my fingers are sweaty from gripping the steering wheel and I realize that I've been halfway holding my breath.

Once across, we're driving through a dense jungle. Along the narrow road, Indians in huts raised on stilts above the sodden jungle floor gaze at us impassively as we drive past.

Somehow we found a small rental bungalow on the beach north of town, with an indigenous couple who lived in a nearby hut as caretakers. At night they would squat for hours by their open fire, gazing silently into the flames and occasionally exchanging a few words in their native language. When we asked about the lack of a highway bridge coming into town, they told us in pidgin Spanish that it was taken out by *un ciclón*, a hurricane. They said it had torn the roof off of the house we were renting. The death toll, we later learned, was said to be about a thousand people.

The bungalow, miles from any other structure, was literally on the beach. You stepped out the back door onto coarse, clean golden sand. The beach dropped off too steeply for surf, but the clear water had plenty of fish which provided some good meals. At night the sea made a soothing sound as it surged and receded on the steep sand beach.

The only uncomfortable thing was no toilet seats; they would have provided hiding places for spiders and centipedes. We did exterminate a couple of big centipedes on the living room floor, and once a very large and confrontational scorpion challenged us for possession of the bathroom. We won.

Exploring to the north, we came to a small island with a small, deep bay next to it. On the hill above the bay, cobbled streets lined with weeds wound up and around, devoid of any other signs of human intervention. The whole area was like a movie set for some apocalyptic vision of the future, as if an exotic, glittering civilization had once existed here and then been obliterated, leaving only the roadways. Today those roadways are a part of a high-density, upscale resort complex and the island is connected to the mainland by landfill, as part of a golf course. To be honest, I liked it better the way it was.

We went spear fishing in the small bay below the steep hills. One of the guys who had brought a speargun almost immediately shot a big pompano, which started towing him around so fast it nearly tore his mask and snorkel from his head until I was able to intervene by spearing the fish from the other side with my three-prong. We had landed the fish and were going back out for more when an enormous manta ray jumped out of the water and landed with a loud *smack*! and a huge splash, right where we had been diving. That put an end to our spearing for the day – if a ray that big landed on top you it would do some serious damage and could even be fatal – but what a meal we and the caretakers had that night!

We explored further north, to Barra de Navidad. Outside of town the wreckage of a hotel devastated by the hurricane sat empty and desolate, no glass in the windows, no doors in the frames. We got some nice little waves on the long sand spit, and traipsed the dirt streets of the primitive village, in those days nothing more than a cluster of thatched huts and a lone water tower inexplicably guarded (who, we wondered, would steal a water tower?) by a stone-faced indigenous soldier in a faded uniform, with an ancient single-shot bolt-action rifle. He ignored us.

On our last night in Manzanillo, to celebrate our trip and fortify ourselves for the long drive back, for the first and only time we treated ourselves to a meal in a "nice" restaurant at the main hotel in town. I splurged and ordered pepper steak with all the trimmings. Within hours I was feeling queasy, and by the time we left at dawn the next morning I was in full food poisoning mode. It was quite an irony: after all the questionable roadside meals and street-corner tacos I had consumed in Mexico, the one upscale meal I ever ate was the one that brought me down.

Barra de Navidad

All the way back to the US I lay on the back seat, only rousing myself long enough to get whoever was driving to stop so I could leap out and purge my GI tract. We drove non-stop, trading drivers (with me out of the rotation). For the last few hundred miles, all they talked about was going to a burger place and getting huge burgers and vanilla milkshakes. All I could think about was getting to a nice, dark place to curl up and die.

Back at San Diego State, I was a mess. My kidneys hurt, my intestinal tract was in turmoil, I had blood in my urine. I managed to drag myself to student health services, where they drew enough blood to feed an entire flock of hungry vampire bats. After multiple analyses, their diagnosis was that they didn't know what I had. Finally I recovered on my own.

It's amazing how well that works when you're young.

1963: The Great Malibu Surf Contest Bus Trip

The peak of that era, the zenith – or maybe, depending on one's point of view, the nadir – was the Great Malibu Surf Contest Bus Trip.

The year was 1963, and surfing was in the process of being transformed from an informal, small-scale artisanal activity to a commercialized mass-production monster. By the 1960s, it was obvious that there was money to be made from just about every aspect of surfing. The key was packaging and PR.

There had been a Windansea Surf Club dating from the 1940s, composed of Older Guys. Chuck Hasley, a charismatic athlete and former coach, surfer and entrepreneur, decided to monetize the Windansea concept. His first step was to trademark the Windansea Surf Club name. The next step was to form a surfing team. Not a team limited to Windansea surfers – although some of those were included – but rather a mega-team featuring the best surfers and biggest names he could recruit from anywhere up and down the coast. He probably would have included Aussies and Hawaiians and South Africans if they had been available for Southern California contests and PR.

The team was eclectic, but the Malibu trip itself was pure '60s Windansea.

The crew that surfed Windansea in the late 1950s and early '60s had a penchant for experiences beyond the pale of normal existence: lost weekends in Tijuana and Ensenada, searching for the *ola verde* deep in mainland Mexico, riding big waves in Hawai'i, bunker parties, all manner of surrealistic activities to fill the time between swells. They were on a constant search for adventure, and the Great Malibu Surf Contest Bus Trip of 1963 might have been the adventure to end them all.

Like all truly great events, it wasn't planned that way, any more than Columbus running into the Americas was planned. Sometimes you aim at one thing and end up with something much greater.

The situation was simple: there was a surf contest and Hasley, affectionately nicknamed the Coach, had entered the nominal Windansea team. The Coach could have just put the group on a bus like any other team manager in any other sport. He could have picked us up at the Windansea parking lot, or at a park or any other convenient spot. He could have scheduled the departure for a civilized hour. The trip up would have been high-spirited, fun, featuring rowdy horseplay and practical jokes. Sort of like, say, a minor-league baseball team's trip to an out of town game. But it would have remained earthbound, mired in the realm of the commonplace, the ordinary. And whatever the Coach was, he was neither commonplace nor ordinary. This trip had to be done with flair, panache and a surrealistic touch. So we departed from a bar in the middle of the night.

Before we get into the trip itself, it's important to get straight about the bus. When we think of "bus trip" the most common image is of a vehicle something like a Greyhound bus or maybe the type of bus used by tour bus companies, or by rock groups on tour. Large, comfortable, great suspension, tinted windows, with an onboard toilet, good sound system, tinted windows, reclining seats, A/C, and other amenities.

That was not this bus.

This bus was from Paul's Bus Company, driven by Paul himself. (There's no way to research it at this late date, but one suspects that the bus in question was the only vehicle in Paul's fleet, and that Paul was the company's only driver.) It was a converted school bus, painted school bus yellow, with thick rubber mats on the floor, straight-back unpadded metal frame seats covered with tough, seemingly bulletproof plastic, and small vertical sliding windows on metal tracks that opened only a few inches. It also had no sound system, no A/C, and – or at least that's the way it seemed after an hour or so of travel – no springs or shock absorbers.

Perfect for high school vandals, medium-security prisoners, and the likes of us.

The other thing to realize is that once we got started, Paul was basically a hostage. To this day, I'm amazed that he didn't back out. Either he really needed the money, or his ability to assess risk was grossly underdeveloped. Or maybe he was an old-school guy, a man of his word, a-deal's-a-deal kind of guy. We'll never know.

Put yourself in his place: you are going to fill your bus – perhaps your only real asset – with a large group of rowdy young drunks, at two in the morning, and drive all night to Malibu. Once you are on the road with this band of ruffians, there is no quitting and no turning back. You would be facing a mutiny if you tried. In the pre-cell phone era, there is no way to call for help. Even if you managed to stop the bus, bail out and run for it, the vehicle would probably be reduced to scrap in a matter of minutes.

Any normal, sane person would have realized this from the start, and either made up an excuse – surreptitious sabotage would have done the trick – or simply use a pay phone or the bar phone to contact the authorities and escape with official backup. Paul did none of the above. And so the die was cast.

The trip itself was like the cliché about the '60s – if you remember all of it, you weren't there. What I do recall:

We left from Maynard's bar in Pacific Beach at closing time, 2 a.m. Maynard's was a run-down watering hole that featured bullfight movies, butting contests – Butch Van Artsdalen was a consistent winner – and riotous behavior. The perfect jumping-off point for a trip to the unknown.

The bus, as noted above, was a yellow school bus, the kind with a big hood out front, as ugly as a failed cross-breeding experiment involving a cement mixer and a trolley car, sitting high on industrial-strength springs above its sturdy thick tires. On the side, in big black letters, was written:

PAUL'S BUS COMPANY

We trooped up the steps. Once inside, you were caught in a swirling current of drunken, excited humanity that picked you up and deposited you like flotsam from a flood. I found myself jammed into a window seat on the left, about half way back. The spot beside me was occupied by a non-surfer from the Windansea parking lot. (I am leaving most of the participants nameless, out of misplaced respect for their reputations.)

Maynard's

I was able to twist around enough to see that in the back the Coach had installed a live rock band, their instruments plugged into the power system of the bus. As people continued to board, the band broke into a deafening tune that more than made up in raw enthusiasm what it lacked in musicianship.

The bus filled up like a tide pool on an incoming tide, in a series of surges. No one in the bar wanted to be left behind. People sat in all the seats, in the aisles, on top of other people. My seatmate and I were partially covered by some guy we'd never seen before until he managed to slither through the crowd like a moray eel through a kelp forest and insinuate himself beneath a girl across the aisle. Her eyes widened and her mouth opened in surprise, then she smiled and wiggled herself comfortable on his lap and took a hit from the joint he had produced from his shirt pocket.

The bus became a gigantic yellow sardine tin bulging with squirming sardines, packed not in oil but in a rich, heady blend of beer, wine, sweat, smoke (both tobacco and weed), hormones and youthful insanity. For the duration of the drive up the coast, all social norms, as well as the very rules of time and space and physics, were suspended.

Acoustics were otherworldly. The noise level was roughly equivalent to an unmuffled jet engine, so that even words screamed directly into your ear were inaudible, yet other sounds, bouncing amongst the decibels like balls in a pinball machine, fell into your ear with crystalline clarity. A sigh, a grunt, the pop of a beer can being opened, a word or two would come drifting into awareness like emissions from the ether. Then the curtain of noise would descent again.

Underway! The sound of the bus going through the gears was felt through the floorboards rather than heard. The band blasted. Everyone shrieked and cheered. Beer cans popped. I felt a damp spray of foam on the side of my neck and turned my head.

"Hey, man, sorry," said the lips of a guy behind me. No sound, but words very clearly formed, like a person at a training school for lip-readers. "Here, man, you take it." He handed me the open can.

Our *bateau ivre* heads up the coast, following 101 North. By now we are in full Bacchanalian overdrive. More beer, more pills, more smoke. More noise jostling bodies jouncing bus total bedlam. Everything begins to seem a bit unreal. Someone in the seat across the aisle urinates into a beer can, then spills it as he tries to reach over and drop it out the window.

Suddenly a collective scream goes up, rising over the din like a barrage balloon above a battlefield. It sounds like a packed stadium cheering the winning touchdown, but it's emanating from us, from the bus. I look out the left-hand window. Two cops, California Highway Patrol, cruising along side, staring up at us. Dwarfed by the bus, their car looks like a pilot fish deciding whether or not to attach itself to a large, ugly shark. Amidst the din an orchard of arms protrudes from the bus, unsteady branches bearing a variety of fruit: joints, pills, open cans of beer. A beer can slips from a waving hand, falls to the roadway in an explosion of foam as we roll on by. The cops look on deadpan, then accelerate and pull away, disappearing around the bow of the bus.

Where are we? I guess that it's somewhere near Encinitas, or maybe Oceanside. Oceanside was only thirty miles from our starting point, but by now it might as well be Outer Mongolia. The bus careens off the highway and into a large parking lot. Is it a restaurant? A gas station? Something else? I'm not sure. There seems to be some sort of food and water and bathrooms.

Everyone piles out to drink water, use the toilet, whatever. We are a swarm of locusts, flitting and staggering and buzzing in all directions. Some purposefully, some aimless, all clueless. Why did we stop? To get gas? For Paul to call for reinforcements?

Then I see the same Highway Patrol cruiser, the two cops standing by it, doors open, the big 12-gauge pump shotgun gleaming in the rack on the dashboard, within easy reach. Next to them I see Paul, and the Coach. I can read the Coach's end of the conversation as I watch him, face earnest and expressive, hands moving in a series of placating gestures, head nodding in agreement with everything the cops say, then turning it around and giving it back to them in a different color, like a magician doing verbal magic tricks.

"No, officer, nothing like that." Vigorous shaking of the head. "Probably a Coca-Cola..."

Head is now nodding. Face filled with sympathy for the agents of law and order.

"Well, yes, I can see how you might get that impression."

Broad smile, flash of even white teeth.

"Oh, no, they wouldn't, they couldn't! These are athletes! They're in training."

Gesture toward his minions, now beginning to traipse back to the bus.

"But these kids are my surf team, we're headed for a contest up in Malibu. Of course they're excited."

Nod, then shake.

"No, don't worry. They're so tired that once they get back on the bus they'll sleep like babies. Everything is under control. You have my word."

The officers look skeptical but they get back into the cruiser and drive off. What's the alternative – arrest an entire busload (actually, two busloads in one bus) of drunks? The local jail isn't big enough.

Back on the bus. Somehow I end up on the right side, more toward the front. More driving, more drinking, more smoke, more noise. Things get blurry. Did we stop again? I don't know. The trip has become a fantasy, a dream, an independent reality orbiting erratically around the one I used to inhabit. There is nothing else in the universe, just the hard seat and the bedlam – a non-stop shrieking roar like a packed stadium screaming to celebrate their favorite gladiator, or an insane asylum filled with manics on uppers – and the rhythmic jouncing of stiff suspension and extreme sensory overload exacerbated by fatigue.

Just before dawn, when a faint light in the east is deciding whether or not to go all the way, the bus lurches and swerves violently. I look out the window to see a '56 Chevy careen off the road and into the ditch. Someone has tried to give Paul a beer and somehow ended up spilling it on his head. He has swerved, forcing the unsuspecting Chevy off the road. The bus, oblivious, roars on.

Finally we arrive.

The bus wheels into the gravel parking area of the restaurant across the street from the beach. Somehow I have managed to worm my way to a position next to the door, so that when it opens I am the first one out. But my legs don't work. I tumble down the stairs and land on my face in the gravel. In quick succession, two more people, apparently afflicted with the same temporary mobility issue, fall on top of me.

Then it's up and crawling and finally staggering, off to the bathroom and then to eat eggs and bacon and toast and drink O.J. and coffee. Lots and lots of coffee. I put in enough sugar to create and maintain an entire nation of diabetics.

We help the band stop traffic on Pacific Coast Highway long enough to run an extension cord from the restaurant across the highway to the beach, securing it to the roadway with some sort of tape. Which of course survives all of ten minutes.

We troop to the beach. The surf is maybe knee high, with some of the bigger sets reaching almost all the way to the hip. If you crouch. For me, this is the coup de grace. If there had been some significant waves, the cool water and forced vigorous exercise would have allowed me to wake up and feel somewhere near normal for a least a few hours. But this...I curl up in a fetal position on the beach with my T-shirt over my head, like a turtle in his shell, and try to pass out, but I'm too tired.

Someone calls my name:

"Hey, Dave, aren't you gonna surf?"

It sounds like someone I know, but I'm too tired to open my eyes or speak, so I give a little finger waggle of indifference. Whoever it is goes away.

The sun crawls upward, drags itself across the top of the sky, starts to slither over the hump toward its inevitable decline. I'm in a trance of exhaustion, hangover, and general physical and mental meltdown. The contest ends – I guess, I'm too far gone to notice or care.

Someone insists that I get up for the group photo.

"No, no, you go ahead; I'll just lie here and keep dying."

"Look, asshole, you're in the way. You're gonna have to move."

So I struggle to my feet and promptly sit back down, not far from my original spot. The photo is the standard composition: line up in ranks on the beach, first rows sitting, those behind us kneeling, finally a row or two standing. There were a lot of us – far more people than there had been waves, actually – and to get everyone in the picture the photographer herded us closer and closer together.

To see the camera (and thus for the camera to "see" you and include your face in the shot), you had to get your head between the heads of the two guys in front of you. Like everyone else I initially tried to do this, but some jerk behind me kept bitching about how I was blocking him. "So move your head," was my response, but he kept nagging and whining.

Finally I just said "screw it." The sooner he shut up, the sooner the photographer would shoot the picture, the group would melt away and I could go back to my fetal position on the sand. What difference did it make anyway? I never was going to get a copy of the photo (in fact, I never did), and if I had, so what? I wasn't going to put it in a scrapbook (I've never had one) or put it on the wall. Besides, I was too tired to maintain a heads up, erect posture.

So I just left my head mostly obscured by one of the guys in front of me, the photo was taken, and I'm the blond hair with no face, one or two rows from the front. And I, the guy who never really got included among the ranks of the cool non-conformists, ended up, well, not conforming.

When it's over I shamble back to my little dent in the sand and curl up again. I haven't slept for over thirty hours. Before our departure from Maynard's I unwisely imbibed a considerable quantity of beer which has left me hung over and dehydrated. I have spent the night in a series of cramped, contorted sitting positions, bombarded by high-decibel sound and second-hand smoke from tobacco and weed. I have had no food or liquid since we rolled into Malibu at dawn. I have spent the day frying under the relentless rays of the Southern California sun. My mouth seems to be lined with used oil rags from a gas station; inside my head someone has inflated a large dirty beach ball, covered with sand and beer and melted surf wax. All I want is to either die right here, right now, or go home.

I'm roused from my torpor by voices. Loud voices. One of them belongs to the Coach. The word "bus" is mentioned several times. Does this mean that we're finally headed back?

No, it does not.

Paul has hidden the bus. We had left it looking and smelling like a tribe of desert herdsmen and their camels had used it for a ritual slaughter and fertility festival. It was so filthy – Paul's description was graphic, but I'll spare you the details – that he had to wash out the interior with a high-pressure hose. Then there is the issue of all the insanity on the trip up. He is not about to submit himself or his bus to a repeat performance.

Hasley charms, cajoles, even threatens. Paul is adamant. The bus will not appear unless he personally inspects everyone as they get back on. And the fee for the trip has doubled.

Finally a deal is struck. We trudge to the bus, line up to be processed. At the door we chip in extra money, then turn our pockets inside out while Paul checks us for contraband: pills, weed, beverage containers and anything else that might reopen the gates to the living hell he has experienced on the way up. I'm cleared, good to go.

I stagger aboard, find a seat, put my hands on the seat back in front of me and rest my head on my arms. A steamy humidity arises from the rubber floor mat, still wet from Paul's hosing. I awaken to the rhythmic jiggling of the bus on the seams between the concrete slabs of the highway. For the first time, I realize that the bus is only half full. We must have been three or four times over normal capacity on the trip up; where did they all go? I decide I don't care. I go back to a fitful half-doze.

Paul's bus had been a magical vessel carrying us across an enchanted sea. Now, on the endless journey home, it seems more like the ferry to the underworld. I don't care if we end up in Hell, as long as I can lie down and sleep.

Back home, I'm so burned out that the next two days are pretty much a blur. Another Windansea adventure has come to an end, and it would be another ten years before I saw what Malibu was all about.

A cynic might regard the Great Malibu Surf Contest Bus Trip as a nadir of drunken idiocy by a group of degenerates. But it has another side. For me, at least, it was a true Dionysian experience, an interruption of contact with normal reality. I wasn't unconscious or delirious, or hallucinating or really drunk. I've been in those states, and I know the difference. But I was unable to account for large chunks of time, even though I was awake and experiencing the whole thing.

The only time I've had a comparable sensation was in Japan, when I was invited to participate in carrying an *omikoshi* to a *jinja*, or Shinto shrine, in an annual festival. The *omikoshi* is like a sedan chair for a god, an ornate lacquered wood compartment borne on two massive parallel timbers, curved and carved and polished. The entire affair weighs hundreds of pounds.

The rules for bearers are simple and sadistic: the supporting timber must be borne on the shoulder only, not using the hands to take up any of the weight. Furthermore, the hands must be resting on top of the timber, which adds weight to the load and puts the shoulder area in the most uncomfortable position possible. The net result is a constant force of dozens of pounds of pressure bearing down on the bony area of the shoulder and collarbone. In a very short time, this creates intense pain. To make matters worse, the chanting bearers dance rhythmically up and down in unison, creating more pressure and more pain with each bounce. This goes on for hours. To quit is a disgrace, a sin, a crime against the social order. I'm sure that in ancient times quitters were forced to commit hara-kiri. Perhaps in traditional corners of Japan they still are. I wouldn't be surprised.

By late afternoon, after hours of bearing and chanting and dancing, my shoulder was a flaming ball of pain, and I had no idea how much longer the self-inflicted torment was to last. To distract myself, I began to chant louder and louder, focusing on the chant, putting my entire mind into the production of sound.

The next thing I knew it was dark and we had arrived at the shrine and it was over. For at least two hours I had been outside of space and time, drifting alone in a universe of sound and motion without sight or feeling. And yet not once had I stumbled or missed a turn or failed to stop and start with the other bearers.

At the ceremonial supper for the bearers, the local Japanese who had dragooned me into the event congratulated me.

"You did well. You did not embarrass me today."

When we changed from our *happi* coats to regular clothing, I saw that everyone had enormous black bruises that covered the entire top of the shoulder area. And so did I.

The Great Malibu Surf Contest Bus Trip was all this, without the chanting and the bruises. But it wasn't for sissies and personally, I think the hangover was worse than any bruise.

1964: Moving on

The Malibu bus trip was the pièce de résistance, the grand finale, the biggest and best burst of collective insanity ever generated by the ongoing Windansea circus.

For me, it also marked the end of an era: a few months later I graduated from San Diego State (major in foreign languages) and left the area to seek new adventures elsewhere. I was opening another new chapter in my life.

Like so many other surfers I tried to do the socially accepted, mainstream thing and get a real job. After all, I was a child of the '40s and '50s: go to school, keep your hair short, get a job, buy a house, have 2.2 kids, live in the 'burbs. You weren't supposed to "find yourself"; no one told you to follow your dreams. My personal life in the '50s and early '60s – the beach, surfing, Mexico, *la vida loca* at Windansea and Aspen –

had definitely steered me off the straight and narrow path, but I had enough indoctrination left in me to guide me back.

My first attempt was in the international department of a major bank in San Francisco. Put those foreign languages to work! It sounded pretty exciting: get paid to learn banking and end up in a sexy location in France or Spain or Italy. (A buddy of mine from the beach, who stuck it out, got all that and ended up with a net worth of millions of dollars and a high-priced condo with a huge deck overlooking his favorite break in San Diego, so the potential was definitely there.)

But to each his own: it took a matter of weeks for me to be miserable, and I realized that this type of life was not and would never be for me. I felt like a hapless porpoise who had wandered into a holding tank at Marineland. I didn't fit in with the other porpoises who were eagerly learning their assigned tricks and gulping down their reward of dead fish. This was not my pod; these were not my people. I belonged in the open sea.

I hated spending all day in a windowless building. I hated the idea of fifty (that's FIFTY) weeks of drudgery before I would be eligible for my pathetic two-week vacation. I was bored by the work and hemmed in by the dense urban life – tall buildings, traffic, concrete everywhere. The sea was physically near but it might as well have been miles away. I was cut off most of the week and felt burnt out on weekends. There was lots of fog and wind. And the nearest beach was Ocean Beach – my old nemesis.

The worst thing was that I saw no point to all the paper-shuffling and money-moving. It wasn't interesting, it wasn't fun, it had no depth or purpose. Perhaps I was an idealist, or unrealistic, but I was looking for intangibles – some sort of meaning, or at least a feeling of forward motion, of progress, of accomplishment. Some reward other than a fistful of cash every month.

The future looked like an endless dark and dreary tunnel, maybe getting a bit wider and more bearable after a few years – in five years I would be eligible for a glorious three-week vacation – but still incredibly confining. Deadening.

An insight that I'd had in Mazatlán a few years earlier came to the rescue.

When we were in Mazatlán the first time, I noticed a couple of little blond gringo kids running around with local kids, jabbering in perfect Spanish and having a great time. I met their father, a Spanish teacher from California who spent all of his vacations in Mexico with his children. It seemed like a perfect life: he got a lot of time off, he was traveling in Mexico and perfecting his professional skills (he even got some sort of tax write-off) and his kids were growing up bilingual.

Now, unable to cope with rigid nine-to-five in a stultifying work environment, I saw the answer: I was going to be a Spanish teacher and get the same package that this guy had created for himself. For now, since I had no teaching credential, step one was to get a graduate degree, at least a master's.

So now "responsibility" and "main stream" meant more schooling and a career in higher education. Actually, as I soon found out, the total workload including class time, preparation and research, was at least as heavy and often much more taxing than at the bank. But I would have summers off – warm water and southern hemi swells! – and extended vacations during the school year – clear, dry winter weather and big, clean north swells from the Gulf of Alaska! – for local surfing and travel to Mexico.

1964, Spain: checking out the Med

The '60s were a golden era for higher education in the US. The nation still believed that education was an investment in the future, and that an educated population was the key to prosperity and success. The economy was on a roll unmatched in human history, money flowed freely to those in the right place at the right time, and I was right there with my hand out.

You had to earn it, of course – I knew that from my undergraduate scholarship. But it was there, I was ready, willing and able, and I still had a hunger to experience the world, so I got a scholarship to study in Spain.

Spain was mythical. Crossroads of the Mediterranean, occupied or colonized by Celts, Greeks, Romans, Phoenicians, Visigoths, Vandals, Arabs and tourists, it had absorbed something from all of them. It was Mexico with flamenco and paella, tapas and *tascas* and the residue of the Spanish Civil War. Lorca, Cervantes, Lope de Vega, la Calle Echegaray and the Teatro Nacional. The Prado. Saint Teresa's finger, complete with ring, preserved in a glass vial in Ávila. Gypsies in caves in the hills of Sacramonte. Flamenco. Bullfights at Ventas (¡el Viti! ¡el Cordobés!), with an ancient, cadaverous Franco sometimes in attendance and flashing a fascist salute, the crowd composed of real aficionados, not the mix of bored Mexicans and drunken tourists who filled el Toreo de Tijuana on hot Sunday afternoons. The bulls fifty percent larger than the ones in Tijuana, the entire event a matter of serious pageantry, deep significance and national tradition, not the type of tired, touristic performance one saw south of the US border. I drank it all in, day after night after day.

I wasn't there to surf – I had no access to a surfboard anyway – but I did what I could to get to the sea. And, ironically, being away from the possibility of surfing allowed me to interact with water and the sea in different ways and have experiences that I wouldn't have had otherwise.

On vacations I roamed up and down the Mediterranean coast. I marveled at the crystal clarity of the water and the rugged rock formations spilling into the sea on Mallorca and the Costa Brava and Alicante. On the Costa Brava I came across the most beautiful crystalline blue-green water and reefs and sand channels I've ever seen, a spot so enchanting that I did a hot, sweaty, dusty two-hour round-trip walk two days in a row, just to look at it.

In a small fishing village called Benidorm, I took a boat out to an island and tried my hand at cliff diving. After diving down to the bottom beneath a cliff to check the depth, I climbed the cliff and dove from a ledge ten or fifteen feet above the surface. On every succeeding dive I climbed a few feet higher, adjusting to the increased distance and time required to fall. Finally, on one dive, I failed to put my hands completely together before impact, and the water hitting the top of my head felt like the blow from a sledgehammer. I decided that I had gone as high as I was going to go.

At Tossa de Mar I had one of the most interesting experience I've ever had in the water. From the village, you could climb up a steep stone path that led over a rocky ridge, then back down to a beautiful cove filled with clean, coarse sand. In front of you, the sea, warm and inviting. To your left, the vertical face of a stony crag rising from the water.

I put on my fins and mask, put the snorkel into my mouth and drift away from the beach, face down. Within moments I'm in deeper water; I can see the bottom thirty feet below me. A few fish drift by and disappear into the distance. The temperature of the sea is perfect: I feel neither warmth nor coolness. The water is so clear that it is totally invisible, like air.

Suddenly the clarity and absence of physical sensation create the illusion that I'm falling through space. The feeling is exhilarating – like I imagine sky diving would be – but I can't hang onto it and it fades away until once again I'm floating in a crystal-clear sea.

I try to recapture the illusion without success. Maybe once is all you get. And maybe it has to happen by accident.

1965: Proving Murphy's Law

When I got back from Spain in the late summer of 1965, my first move was to head for the waves at Windansea. It was a classic late-summer La Jolla day: clear and warm under a calm blue sky – not as hot as the Mediterranean sky I had recently come from – slight breeze, ocean temperature in the high sixties. And a big south swell. Perfect Windansea conditions.

I don't remember if I didn't have a board, or just didn't feel like riding one that day. At any rate, I had a surfmat so that is what I used.

The classic surfmat, to refresh the memory of those who haven't ridden one lately, is the short, stubby kind they used to sell at gas stations near the beach in the summer: thick, rubberized canvas colored red, white and blue and formed into three fat, parallel tubes about four and a half feet long and five inches thick, with an air valve (just like the one on a car tire) at one corner of the back, and a rope handle attached to metal grommets at the two corners of the front.

Remember the rope handle.

Old-style surf mat

Getting out to the lineup with an old-style surfmat wasn't easy. They had to be inflated until they were tight and solid so that you could ride them. They were too buoyant to duck dive, and too blunt to roll through waves like you would on a longboard. You had to try to get out during a lull, and if you were caught by a wave the only recourse was to hurl the mat skyward just before the white water got to you, then dive under and hope that somehow the mat had cleared the top of the wave and would still be there when you came up. Otherwise, it was a long swim or body surf to the beach. At least swim fins made that part easy.

I wait for a lull and head out for the break, using a rip current to get more speed. As was still occasionally true in those days – especially on a weekday – there's almost no one else out. Pretty much any wave I want is mine. And here comes a set.

The first wave is a monster. I drop in and rocket part way down the face angling left, digging one edge into the wave to keep my line. For a moment, the mat holds. Then, as the wave goes vertical, the mat breaks loose. I skitter down the wave sideways for a few feet, trying in vain to get some sort of purchase on the wave face, then go airborne as I free-fall the rest of the way. The impact of my body hitting the trough is followed by several tons of water smashing down on top of me. As I lose my grip on the mat, I feel one of my fins being ripped off my foot by the force of the water. At the same time, I feel something tightening around my neck.

I have once again proved Murphy's Law: If something can go wrong, it will.

The explosive turbulence has jammed my head and one arm through the rope handle. Now the action of the water is spinning the mat around and around under water, causing the rope to twist tighter and tighter around my neck. I clutch at the rope with my free hand, but it's so tight that not even one finger will slide under it. The good news is that the arm and shoulder that are being wrapped up with my neck allow enough room for blood to continue flowing to my brain. At least I won't pass out.

Meanwhile, the front edge of the wave is dribbling the mat toward shore like a basketball, and I'm being dragged along underwater, unable to break free and dive beneath the turbulence. I do a quick mental calculation: even on a big day, from break to shore is under a minute. If I relax I can go with the flow underwater, all the way to the beach. After what seems like an eternity, we hit the shorebreak and the rope breaks.

When I stagger out of the water, gasping for breath, I have a rope burn on my neck that looks as if I had been hanged.

Who would have thought that could happen?

1965: Joe Grad School

I had my master's degree, and that put me on the path to my chosen career as a teacher. But there were other factors to consider besides my career path or my dream job.

In the mid-1960s I, like millions of other red-blooded young American males, was worried about the draft. By 1964 there were already over 23,000 of us in Vietnam, the following year the number jumped to over 184,000, and there was a steady trickle of casualties that was soon to become a flood. My draft board had been kind enough to let me know that my number might be coming up and that I might want to consider getting into some line of work or academic program that would allow me to remain a civilian.

Acting on their suggestion, I had been accepted to graduate school at Stanford, but I had no idea how I was going to pay for it. That was solved when I arrived at campus in the fall of 1965 and met my department chairman for the first time.

"How would you like to study Portuguese?" was his first question. Clearly this was an opportunity, so I told him it was something that I had always dreamed of doing. When I walked out of his office, I had a full ride: a free Ph.D., all tuition and expenses paid, even housing!

The program was called NDFL, National Defense Foreign Language, and the purpose was to recruit and train people who could supposedly keep places like Brazil from turning into the next Cuba or the next Vietnam. All I had to do was keep my grades up, and agree to spend a minimum of two years – either during or after completion of the program – working overseas "in a capacity deemed to be of value to the national interests of the United States of America" (or words to that effect). In other words, I would not be going to Vietnam. Unless there was an urgent need for Portuguese speakers in Saigon, which seemed unlikely.

My time at Stanford was uneventful. I managed to get out to Santa Cruz to surf a few times, and even got down to Monterey and Carmel. Nothing extraordinary in terms of surf, but I got some good rides and had a couple of interesting experiences – like being chased out of the water by a seal at Santa Cruz; and getting barreled at Carmel because my legs were so cold I was locked in a crouch on takeoff. After my earlier fiasco at Ocean Beach, I never even thought of trying to surf in San Francisco. During the summer I went down to La Jolla to hit the south swells and enjoy ocean temperatures that seemed positively tropical after the frigid waters of central California.

After a couple of years of this, the call came: I was wanted in Brazil! So in 1967, when 485,600 of my contemporaries were in Vietnam and nearly 20,000 had come home in body bags, I was on my way to Rio de Janeiro to fulfill my obligation to my government by working in the US Embassy.

1967: May I help you stow that spear?

In those days airline travel was simple. International fares were calculated by distance zones (1, 2, 3, 4) and your ticket was valid for travel to the zone of your final destination – in my case, Brazil, zone 4. You could stop off anywhere en route, as many times as you liked. The only rule was that you could not go through the same airport twice. My plan was to make full use of this system, so I allowed myself a couple of weeks to get from California to Rio.

Since the U.S. Government was shipping my personal effects, including my van, to Rio at no charge, I put my board in the van and sent it off. I did bring a mask, snorkel and fins on the plane. And in those wonderful, trusting, pre-terrorist days, I also brought my Hawaiian three-prong spear, carrying it on the plane with me and stowing it under the seats. The idea was that if I found waves I could bodysurf them; if not I could go diving.

In those days, incredible as it seems today, there was no airline security. You walked out to the plane and got on. Nobody screened your carry-on items, and you could carry on just about anything, as long as it would fit on board.

So on my way to Brazil, nobody paid any attention to my spear, except to help me stow it below the window rows of seats. I guess no one had ever hijacked a plane using a Hawaiian three-prong as a weapon.

Not that anyone would have cared.

At the time, hijackings were so commonplace as to be normal. Between 1968 and 1972 there were more than 130 aircraft hijackings in the US. More than once there were multiple hijackings on the same day. It was just part of flying.

The most publicized ones involved Cuba. And, amazing as it seems today, hijacking to Cuba didn't sound all that bad. In fact, it added a little spice to the journey. As one aviation site explains, "...hijacking wasn't considered a serious threat by airlines or passengers. It was more of an inconvenience than anything else. The passengers assumed that if the plane was hijacked, they would simply be flown down to Havana, where the hijacker would be taken off of the plane. Maybe they'd have to spend the night in Havana. Maybe they could catch a show and buy some cigars and rum and have a good story to tell back in the United States... Whenever the idea of physically screening of all passengers was suggested, the airline lobby would shoot it down... After all, a hijacking only cost an airline twenty or thirty thousand dollars, whereas X-ray screenings and security personnel would cost millions." (*Aerotime.aero*)

So, like a warrior of the sea, on each leg of my journey to Brazil I boarded the aircraft with my trusty spear in hand.

My first stop was Jamaica.

1967: From the Caribbean to Copacabana

As soon as I had gotten to my hotel room and unpacked, I put on a pair of shorts, grabbed my diving gear and went out into the ocean. The weather was tropical, the sea warm and calm – it was like another Hawai'i! The water was crystal clear and filled with fish.

As I started snorkeling my way among the reefs, I felt a tickling, tingling sensation in my legs. At first I thought I had run into some kind of jellyfish, but when I stopped and looked, I saw that I was under attack by a couple of tiny but aggressive reef fish! They were only about an inch long and their little mouths were too small to get a grip on me or do any damage, but apparently I had intruded into their territory and they were defending it courageously.

I speared a couple of small fish, just a couple of pounds or so each, but they looked excellent for filleting or pan frying. Being new to the concept of staying in a real hotel (my limited previous hotel experience was cheap dives on road trips in Mexico), I blithely wandered in through the back door of the hotel kitchen with my fish – still dripping blood and sea water – and asked if it was possible to get them cooked.

Instant hit! The staff were amazed that a Yankee hotel guest would go into the ocean and come back up with his own food. They not only cooked the fish, but a couple of guys from the kitchen wanted to see how I did it. They were used to fishing with rod and reel or with drop lines, but they had never speared anything. The next day the three of us went to the sea with my gear but they were apprehensive about putting their faces in the water while wearing the dive mask – the look of things underwater was so different that they were actually frightened – and they absolutely refused to put their face in the water and breathe through the snorkel.

My next stop was Curaçao where I did the same hotel restaurant routine, this time with a large conch and then a lobster. This time the hotel guys were so impressed that they took me on a tour of the island and showed me all their favorite fishing spots. I would have stayed longer to check everything out, but by now time was getting short: I was almost due in Rio.

1967: Rio, cidade maravilhosa

Rio de Janeiro, the *Marvelous City*, was everything a Southern California surfer dude could want. Beaches, samba, string bikinis, the whole *carioca* lifestyle; it combined the best of Southern California and Tijuana. Apparently the locals agreed: in theory the capital of Brazil had been moved from Rio to the newly-created city of Brasilia years earlier, but since nobody wanted to leave the fun-loving, hedonistic, slightly decadent *cidade maravilhosa* for the raw, boring landlocked legal capital, all the embassies and ministries simply stayed put. (They finally made the move, but it took fifteen years.)

What made my situation even better was the location of our office: five blocks from my apartment on the beach in Copacabana. Normally we would have worked out of the US Embassy, but it was too small and several programs were run out of rented buildings. Ours was an old, three-story house perched on a hill next to a cobblestone street and backed by wild banana palms. I could get up early, hit the waves, stop by my apartment for a quick shower, and walk to work.

What was Brazil like in those days? Not always quite like the Demi Moore/Michael Caine film *Blame it on Rio* but sometimes better.

Carnival was awesome. The official celebration – a nonstop orgy of drinking, partying, dancing in the streets and whatever else you could imagine doing – was only four days, but Rio being Rio the *cariocas* took an entire week including both weekends. Nine full days and nights of madness. On the beaches, people would ignite ether-filled balloons at night, causing spectacular explosions and frantic trips to the nearest hospital emergency room. At wild carnival parties people fell or were thrown from windows. In the neighborhoods, including Copacabana, small flat-bed trucks with samba bands on them would cruise slowly

85

around, music blasting and anywhere from dozens to hundreds of people dancing along behind them. One of my Brazilian co-workers was doing samba on the back of a truck when he fell off. He ended up with a broken leg – not from the fall, but from a hundred fired-up *sambistas* dancing over him as he lay in the street. Each morning the daily papers documented the carnage with lists of incidents and victims.

In the best medieval tradition, the streets – and especially the night – belonged to the working class, while the upper crust, terrified by the very real mayhem taking place all around the city, fled to the gated precinct of the Rio Yacht Club or their summer homes in Petrópolis. For those who stayed, it was party all night, sleep when you could during the day, and then do it all over again. My personal formula for greeting each day was to hit the waves in front of my apartment for a brisk dawn bodysurf; then breakfast (espresso, toast, fruit, cheese, guava jam) and pass out until early afternoon. It was like Southern California beach culture on uppers, set to a pulsing samba beat.

And of course there was the sea, and surf. I wish I could tell you dramatic tales of surfing huge waves in Brazil, or riding a tidal bore up some dark and dangerous river filled with piranhas and menacing tribes launching curare-tipped darts with blowguns. But I can't. I saw some insanely large and nasty-looking waves off Copacabana during big swells, but I didn't attempt to ride them and I never saw anyone else try it, either. My favorite spot was a bit out of town, at Recreio dos Bandeirantes or nearby Praia da Macumba.

I did surf a lot, but nothing epic and I never hit any of today's famous spots like Florianópolis. In fact, if you asked me where I surfed besides Copacabana and Arpoador, I would have to mostly say I don't know, at least not specifically. General areas, of course: Saquarema, Barra da Tijuca, Recreio, Cabo Frio. But as to the myriad specific break names, I'm clueless. I sampled various breaks.

As in Mexico, my standard tactic was to find a place that looked promising and then go out and surf it. If I could, I'd try to get a look at it at maximum low tide to get a feeling for the reefs and any unpleasant topographical surprises that might be hidden by the water.

1967, Brazil: Fishing village. There was good beach break outside the bar.

Another great way to preview a new break was to go snorkeling or skin diving on it when there was no surf. You can really get a feeling for the bottom that way. In addition, some of the snorkeling and diving in places like Buzios and Saquarema and Cabo Frio was incredibly beautiful: crystalline blue-green water, reefs, dazzling white sands. In many places the diving was excellent, and you could even spear some decent fish just off the beach at Copacabana. However, you ran the risk of antagonizing local fishermen who still launched boats with nets from there, so I held back. There were plenty of other places to dive.

My main surf memories are mellow days riding the beach break at Copacabana, and lazy sundrenched sessions at Recreio, outside of town.

Big, fat lines forming user-friendly overhead waves. Afterwards, sipping chilled coconut water straight from the shell through a straw, at a thatch-roof open air stand behind the beach.

Surfing in Rio in the late '60s was like surfing in San Diego in the '50s: almost no people. The whole time I surfed Copacabana, I don't believe I ever saw a single other surfer. At local surfer magnet Arpoador, a dozen people was a crowded day. It's not a very spacious break, but still. Outside of town, it was the same. Drive out to catch some waves at Recreio, and more times than not you would have it all to yourself. I guess no matter what era you live in, there are always unsurfed places somewhere in the world. But it sure was nice to have them right in your own back yard.

There were drawbacks, of course, to living and surfing in and around Rio. The city pumped untreated sewage out to sea via a pipe that released it a couple of miles off shore. The outfall was located so that the prevailing currents would carry the sewage away from shore, but of course prevailing currents don't always prevail, and on more than one occasion I surfed through used toilet paper and other reminders of urban life. Even the colorful aspects of local culture could damage the beach: out by Recreio practitioners of some sub-cult of *macumba* had littered a stretch of sand with broken glass left as part of their ceremonies.

Daily life could be risky. The dictatorship was harsh and unpopular. The Death Squad was kidnapping and killing people: petty criminals, opponents of the dictatorship and anyone they didn't like. (Once in a while they offed the wrong person by mistake.) At times there were tanks in the streets. A few blocks from my apartment, an entire movie theater full of people was arrested and hauled off in commandeered city buses after someone booed a propaganda newsreel featuring the current military leader. The following year I found myself trapped in the US Embassy, choking on tear gas, while rioters smashed the windows and fought pitched battles with hordes of police in the surrounding streets. Another time I was surrounded by left-wing students atop a parking garage who threatened to throw me off the roof. (I got out of that by threatening to grab the first one to touch me and take him off with me.)

Even in laid-back Copacabana, far from the disturbances downtown, I narrowly missed being kidnapped by an unidentified group. Those days it could have been anybody, from radicals to a right-wing squad to ordinary thugs.

I was a long way from the Windansea parking lot and coast trips and lost weekends in Tijuana.

But most of the time in Copacabana – and even more so in super-cool Ipanema and Leblon – the disturbances and mayhem downtown and in other parts of the country seemed light-years away. I was young and confident and I was used to a certain degree of risk and violence. Negative incidents quickly faded from memory, and I paid more attention to a life of surfing, hanging out, sipping a *chope* (draft beer) in a beachside bar and watching the shortboarders rip waves at Arpoador – a great novelty to me, since I had never seen a shortboard before leaving California. I resolved to get one when I got back to the US.

After two years, I had fulfilled my required service. My boss offered me the chance to extend my tour for another two years, but after giving it much thought I decided against it. Rio had been great, but it was still a huge, gritty city and I was ready to get back to California and my plan of being a surfing teacher.

1970s: Academic surfer dude

After my last class in grad school the money faucet turned off and I lost my free housing. Since job options – and surf – were more plentiful in San Diego, I put my stuff in my van (my rule in those days was simple: if it won't fit in or on the van, don't bring it) and headed south, moving back to La Jolla.

The beach and surf scene in Southern California was relatively unchanged, and I could pick up more or less where I left off. The main difference was shortboards – I had seen them and even ridden one in Rio and I made the switch as soon as I could.

Once again I was free to tap into my inner surfer and embrace a full-on surfer dude lifestyle. All I had to do was get a job and finish writing my dissertation. But not a day job. I would work evenings and have my days free to interact with the ocean and the waves.

I considered going back to the Aspen formula of waiter and bartender, but what works for you at eighteen doesn't necessarily work when you're pushing thirty. I had gotten an M.A., which qualified me to teach at any community college in California. Community colleges offered lots of evening courses to accommodate working people, so I could teach evening classes and have my days free for the ocean and my dissertation. Best of all, community colleges were always eager to hire someone willing to work evenings, since most people preferred to teach during the day and have their evenings free for home and family. I would make less money than a bartender, but I could get to bed at a decent hour, I wouldn't have to put up with drunks, and I wouldn't end the night stinking of second-hand cigarette smoke. And in the morning I could be fresh and ready to hit the waves at dawn.

As a community college instructor, I could live modestly and indulge my passion for the sea. My needs were basic and few.

I had a stripped-down existence. Except for basic clothing, all I needed was my van, a surfboard, diving stuff, skis (until that ended due to knee problems) and a bicycle. And a typewriter. I had no TV, no radio, no stereo. I had no laptop or PC because they didn't exist. I taught my classes, read books, worked on my dissertation, surfed and dove and lived a clean, simple life.

I lived in a small cluster of modest cottages half a block from the beach, with a real sense of community. There were spur-of-the-moment potluck dinners and little parties for various occasions. I was the only surfer but no one held that against me. My nearest neighbor – our cottages were side by side – was a drug dealer who gave frequent dope parties with lines of coke on the coffee tables and neatly-rolled joints in snifters. I wasn't a user but I did like the sweet aroma of good weed wafting in on Saturday night.

It was truly an idyllic life. A surfboard, a bike, a mask, fins and a spear. A VW van. A job that kept my days free. The sound of waves exploding on the reefs when the surf came up, shaking the house, so close and so powerful that you could feel the vibration in your skin. Lazy afternoons in the sun, soaking up warmth and energy with the peaceful sounds of waves lapping on the sand. At night I could hear the tireless booming and sighing of the sea. What else did a guy need?

I was within a few hundred yards of five insane breaks. North swell, south swell, west swell, smallish to big – and practically deserted. Big but forgiving waves at La Jolla Cove. More hollow and less forgiving waves at Boomer and the Casa reef. South Boomer, fickle but fun. The powerful bowl at Horseshoe. Beyond these, a couple of bigger-swell breaks known mostly to locals. My old home break, Windansea. And more.

Reef after reef, break after break. And on days with no surf, they were all great for snorkeling and skin diving.

My job was better than I had imagined – far more than just a paycheck. My night school classes were mostly working adults or university grad students who were occupied during the day and needed Spanish for some specific purpose – dealing with Spanish-speaking employees or co-workers, going on archeological digs in Latin America, doing research on some Spanish-language topic. I loved watching them make progress in the language, learning to communicate, breaking down the barriers to understanding. I saw how they went to Mexico or beyond and came back with a new perspective and new awareness of who those people were. This was what teaching was supposed to be! I was giving them something of value, something they wanted and needed and appreciated; we were all in it together.

I taught my classes. I had friends and girlfriends. I went on all-day bike rides – north, east, south to Mexico – alone or with a buddy or two. I surfed and bodysurfed, dove and speared fish and grabbed lobster and popped abalone. I studied Japanese, repeating sentence patterns as I rode my bike. I knew the sheltered spots to sit in the sun at the beach on cold or windy days. My life was in balance; I was contented.

1970s: The joy of bodysurfing

I loved surfing with a passion, but you don't always need a board to ride waves, and living a stone's throw from Boomer – one of the top bodysurfing spots in Southern California – led to a lot of bodysurfing.

Bodysurfing has its own unique charm. First of all, you're riding the wave itself, not a board skimming on the water. There is an incomparable, sometimes almost otherworldly experience you get from being in the water with the waves, in them and, in a sense, of them. Not just riding them, but being enveloped by their energy and power.

Even swimming out on a big day is an experience to embrace and remember. Underwater at Boomer with a big set breaking and creating roiling balls of turbulence, each wave generating a liquid whirlwind cloud coming at you like an express train above the huge, round boulders on the bottom. Winter water as clear and cold as a mountain stream; seeing the roiling mass of churning foam reaching down from the surface – sometimes touching the sea floor – as it races toward you. As it hits, you extend yourself full length face down, arms stretched forward. Then, as the main force passes, you tilt yourself upward and with a few strong kicks of your fins you let the rushing flow of white water lift you to the surface. All the beauty and power of a hold-down without the helplessness.

Then there are submarine takeoffs: just as the wave jacks up you duck under facing the shore and – using the surge of the wave and a couple of strong kicks for push – extend yourself in a flying Superman pose and let the wave drive you out through the face. One instant you're in the world beneath the surface, the next moment you break free into air and sunlight and the sight of a steep wave face waiting for you to ride it.

Bad timing, or bad wave selection, can lead to comical moments. I do a submarine takeoff at Boomer on a solid eight-foot day. When I pop out through the face, there is nothing beneath me but air. I'm near the top of the breaking wave, and the bottom has dropped completely out. I flail frantically, trying to somehow get into a better position. Guys on the bluff nearly died laughing: they said the only thing in the wave was the tip of my right fin, and I looked like I was trying to grab an invisible rope to safety. I hit the water face first, so hard that when I came up I felt pressure below my eyes and when I rubbed them water squirted out. I had two black eyes that lasted almost a week.

1970s: Murphy's Law revisited

Bodysurfing also provided me with a new application of Murphy's Law, this time with a wetsuit.

The first real wetsuit I ever owned was a zip-up top with long sleeves and a beaver-tail closure – a rubber flap hanging down from the back of the wetsuit, with two snap fasteners on it. You put your arms through the sleeves, zipped up the front zipper, pulled the beaver tail between your legs, and snap-fastened it to two snaps on the lower front part of the top.

The first time I wore this getup, I was excited. This wasn't some glue-it-yourself model like the one I had gotten in the '50s – this was the real thing! For the first time in winter, I was going to be warm in the water! Or at least warmer.

The suit got its trial session at Boomer in La Jolla. It was a pretty good-sized day, which made the idea more attractive. Warmer body, longer session, more waves. What could go wrong?

What, indeed. I made it out without incident, floated around for awhile, marveling at how toasty and buoyant I felt, and caught the first wave of the next set. Roll right, extend the right arm, and start planing across the face. I missed the direct feeling of water on skin, but I loved the added buoyancy. The neoprene also seemed to slide faster through the water, like gliding over Crisco. I was happy! When the wave jacked up and closed out I tucked and rolled, already thinking about how many more waves I was going to ride.

The wave I was on had some size, and it broke hard. The next thing I knew, the beavertail had come unsnapped and the washing-machine action of the wave had pulled the wetsuit up over my head. I was now trapped underwater with my arms tied up over my head in a rubber straight jacket and a tight-fitting neoprene bag full of water wrapped around my head. The pull tab on the zipper was rolled up somewhere inside the bag, out of reach. I had about thirty seconds to get out of this thing or I was in big trouble.

I managed to kick my way to the surface, but there was still no way to breathe or swim or see. I could feel the next wave crashing and rumbling toward me. Somehow I ripped the suit off my head and got a gulp of air before that wave hit, and between that one and the next I got my arms free. I kept the beavertail for surfing, but I never wore it bodysurfing again. And never on a big day.

1970s: Making up for lost time

Some people might say that I was trying to compensate for what had been a geeky, late-blooming childhood and adolescence – making up for lost time, trying to belatedly experience what everyone else (or so it seemed to me) had enjoyed since their teens: athletic ability, the joy of pure physicality, spontaneous adventure. And there is clearly a lot of truth to that. But in life we don't always choose the timing of events and opportunities. There's an old saying: do what you can with what you've got. There should be a corollary: do what you can when you're ready to do it. Or when you're able to.

From time to time, as I indulged in my chosen lifestyle and watched others move on, I would ask myself why. After all, I was no surfing legend; I hadn't even ridden Waimea. And I certainly was no hard-core, full-on waterman. My idea of an accomplishment was to spot an ab while snorkeling, swim back to the beach to borrow an ab iron, and know the reefs well enough to find my way back to the same spot so I could pop the ab and bring it back to shore. Meanwhile, serious local diving clubs would require new members to find their way back to a spot a quarter mile offshore, and to free-dive down in twenty to thirty feet of water and bring up two abs on one dive.

So I would ask myself the question, and each time, the answer was more or less the same, at least when it came to surfing.

I once read a description of near-death experiences that spoke of "a distortion of time, accompanied by high-level mental processing." That pretty much describes one aspect of surfing, and you don't have to have a near-death experience to get it.

Take, for example, an intense, critical takeoff on a powerful wave on a crowded day. You seem to have ample time to consider details, ponder options, come to a conclusion and take action, all in milliseconds. There is no rush, no anxiety, no confusion and no hesitation. You fit perfectly into the situation, and your decisions are both instantaneous and flawless. You're in tune with the moment, in tune with your surroundings, in tune with the wave. Few activities allow you to enter this enchanted realm of pure harmony.

When you're in this zone, even a journeyman can transcend his normal limitations.

You take off on an overhead bomb; it breaks on you just as you get to your feet. You ride down and forward in a welter of foam, flying blind, not even thinking about balance or what's happening, just riding the board. When you come blasting out through the foam and onto the shoulder, you have plenty of time and presence of mind to savor what you have just done – something far beyond your normal capabilities.

You've attained a few moments of transcendence, and a sensation and a memory that will stay with you for years, perhaps forever. There are far worse things to build your life around.

1970s: *Good vibes*

And then there are the beautiful soundless harmonies produced by sea and sky and swell, independent of any wave.

One summer in the mid '70s a big south swell arrived. It was a long-period swell that built fast: nothing much in the morning, four to six feet by early afternoon, a solid ten to twelve before dark. The surf had been above overhead in the late afternoon, when I went out. Now it was dusk and the sets were double overhead and more. The water was warm, the summer sky was clear and calm and filling up with stars, the rides were outstanding.

There's something special about sitting way outside on a big day. Not just the waves. Farther from shore, there is a completely different perspective. Up and down the coast, you can see other breaks and landmarks that would not be visible if you were in the normal lineup closer to the beach. Objects to line up on have a different relative position, so you have to pick new ones. It's almost like surfing a different break in a different ocean. And at dusk it's even more special.

I had been surfing for hours and still couldn't get enough. I was in my prime, early thirties, riding my 7'6" semi-swallowtail, my "two to ten" board. Everything was effortless: paddling out, getting into position, catching waves, making late drops. The sets were long, at least four to six waves each. The length of ride and consistency of surf thinned out the crowd – which in those days was still pretty minimal anyway – so there were plenty of waves to pick from. I always let the first couple of waves in a set go by for other guys to catch, meanwhile setting up for the bomb I wanted.

A few quick strokes, pop up, feel the exhilaration of standing ten feet or more above the trough below. Fade left, cut back right, get into the pocket and fly. Alternatively, stall in the peak, do a slight right turn, then turn back and rocket straight down the face and out into the flat, then put the board up on the rail and feel the G's as it digs in and carves a sharp turn and heads back up the face. This, to me, was a supreme moment: low over the water, moving at high speed, facing off with a monster face topped by a fringing crest. Just before the pocket, on the steepest part of the wave, ease off and turn left going up, to end up tucked in just below the lip and going right. The high from a wave like that lasted all through the rest of the ride and the paddle back out.

During a lull before my final ride of the day, I drank in the scene – the darkening sea, the intermittent white of other breaks to the north and south, the way the sky shaded from deep indigo above to pale glowing cyan at the horizon, with faint tinges of rosy gold showing where the sun had just set. As I looked up at the stars in the waning light, I have never felt more serene and at peace with the sea. That feeling has stayed with me far more vividly than any of the waves I rode that day.

September, 1976: South to adventure

In the early '70s I had made several surf safaris to mainland Mexico: a couple to Mazatlán and Teacapán; once all the way to Puerto Escondido and Puerto Angel with stops along the way. I got a ton of waves, although nothing epic, and some great skin diving. And plenty of the sort of bizarre episodes that I came to expect on trips like this: a dead body by the side of the road (Sonora), an attack by rabid bats (Sinaloa), two unnerving encounters with drug dealers (Culiacán and Pinotepa Nacional), being chased out of the water by a bull shark (Puerto Escondido), forced to fork over money at gunpoint (Guerrero), a car breakdown (Esquinapa) and a sleepless night in the mountains south of Culiacán nervously clutching a cocked speargun as various groups of persons unknown walked around my van in the dark conversing in low tones.

It had all been fun but I was ready for something different, so when my surf buddy Pete suggested a Baja trip I engaged in some skillful class-swapping with a teaching colleague and managed to free up a couple of weeks.   At the tail end of summer, we set out to the south in a VW van, headed for the tip of Baja.

Our timing was perfect.

After decades of existence as an often-impassable dirt track, Mexico Highway 1 had finally been paved all the way from the US border to the tip of Baja California. The commercialization and overdevelopment that had overtaken so many places in California and Hawai'i was still in the future; the natives were still friendly. And there were countless miles of unsurfed breaks waiting to be ridden.

The Baja California peninsula is a gnarled, bony finger of land pointing crookedly toward the Tropic of Cancer. A thousand miles by road, somewhat less as the seagull flies. Thanks to plate tectonics, it's destined to end up somewhere off the Bering Strait.

In the meantime it's the ultimate land of contrast, freezing mountain peaks from which you can see both the Pacific and the Sea of Cortés and a lot of baking desert in between. Mountains surrounded by desert surrounded by ocean. A land aged and withered, cracked and parched and besieged on three sides by salty, undrinkable wetness. There's never enough water, except when it rains and there's too much – fierce flash floods scour the rocky hills and drown the flats in sheets of muddy water and debris, like dirty glaciers morphed and speeded up by a factor of thousands. Racing to get back to the sea and lose themselves in the bottomless deep.

Baja was halfway between heaven and hell, with a little bit of both. What better place for an adventure?

As an indifferent Mexican cop, reflective shades and drooping moustache and bulging belly conforming perfectly to the image in a thousand caricatures, passed us through the border with an indifferent wave of the hand, we were ecstatic.

"All right, man, this is it. On the road to adventure. We're gonna get some waves, I just know it."

As we crossed the border and entered Tijuana, a torrent of memories and associations came flooding in. No matter how many times I came here, there they were.

Trips as a kid, marveling at the candies made of cactus or coconut and the stoic Indian ladies making tortillas by hand in a small "factory" – complete with a rickety, clanking conveyer belt – just off the main drag, and the countless people living in cardboard boxes in the river bed we crossed over on the old, two-lane concrete bridge that connected the border with the town.

Later in life, wild nights in the seedy bars and clubs near Avenida Revolución. The time we got caught in a spasm of popular outrage after an election which the local PANistas were convinced was stolen by the PRI, and the Hotel Nelson was set afire and troops took over the streets.

The very smell in the air – roasted *elotes* and tamales and burned corn husks mingled with the distant echo of a mariachi group warming up for the evening, the cries of vendors – promised exoticism and adventure. We were pumped.

The Long Bar – site of countless wasted nights and wild times – beckons but we are on a mission. We get through downtown and head for the road that leads south.

While still in Tijuana we stopped at a roadside vendor and bought ceviche for the road. Then it was up the hill by the smoldering city dump, out to the coast, and south.

The splendor of the coast road from Tijuana to Ensenada is matched only by some stretches of Big Sur and along the Central California coast. Steep cliffs, rocky promontories ringed with foam, the sea surging cobalt blue and blinding white over the reefs.

If the sun is out. Right now it was not.

There is nothing as deadening as the white glaring overcast of Baja California when cool, moist maritime air meets the warmer air heated by the land. Not at ground level, but a few hundred feet above.

Low fog has mystery, charm, atmosphere. We used to get this in La Jolla: a San Francisco-style fog, a Dashiell Hammett fog. Fog like a living presence, muffling all sounds, wisping between buildings, dripping from the eucalyptus leaves like soft spring rain. At night, sometimes, you had to drive by rolling down the window to follow the center line of the road, and you could get lost in the middle of an intersection where the line ended and left you stranded like a wayfarer on the trackless sea.

High fog – overcast – has no such charm. It is a harsh gray-white sheet of oxidized tin stretched taut and implacable above everything. Over the Baja California coastal desert, it's even more oppressive.

The air is stiff and overcooked. The opaque layer refracts the light and breaks up the wavelengths into something that should be confined to a microwave oven. Your head feels stifled and pressurized, not as from holding your breath, but from breathing too shallowly for too long, against an excess of gravity. We weren't usually much for in-car conversation – we had known each other so long that there was nothing new we could say – but the oppressive lid of the sky pushed down so hard it made us positively taciturn.

We were hoping to surf our way down the peninsula, but so far we had seen nothing worth waxing up for. We reached Ensenada, stopped for food and gas, mounted up again and set our course south on the thousand miles of two-lane road that would take us to our destination.

As the miles drifted away behind the van like a vanishing wake of foam behind a boat, the dull white overcast turned to hanging fog and then rose, turned to torn clumps of cumulus, and dissipated with the ocean breeze. High overhead a pair of vultures took advantage of the weather to ride a thermal, soaring upward in lazy circles until they were mere specks against the blue.

South of Colonet, the emptiness of the coastal desert took over in earnest. The sameness became an almost palpable presence dragging at the wheels. After an hour or so, it seemed that the van was immobile and the road was unspooling beneath it, an endless treadmill emanating from somewhere just beyond the horizon, the landscape parting around us as it floated past in perfectly synchronized choreography.

Lost in our separate reveries, neither of us spoke. Judging from Pete's almost complete immobility – broken only by minimal movements of the steering wheel – and the aroma of the smoke curling from his pipe, his reverie appeared to be something approaching a stupor. From time to time he would sigh deeply, overcome by some random emotion wandering through his synapses. At one point we passed a dead cow lying just off the road. "Man!" was his only comment, and he never let up on the gas. The van, unimpressed, clattered and wheezed through the desert like an asthmatic armadillo. As we went farther south the sparse traffic disappeared altogether.

The road was finally paved but there were few people to use it. The new road would eventually bring them but until then it was just us, for mile after countless mile. The VW van clattered along like an industrial sewing machine, mindlessly stitching the ribbon of asphalt to the sandy, rocky desert littered with cactus. The blue sky had given out miles behind us, as if tired of the trip. Here the overcast was softer, the light less intrusive. The miles clattered on. Highway 1 took us south, flirted with the ocean between Rosarito and Guerrero Negro, headed back across the peninsula.

At some point it got dark. Somewhere before Santa Rosalía we pulled off on a dirt side road leading to nowhere and slept in the van for the night. At dawn we were up and on the road again. It carried us further south, along the breathtaking primitive beauty of the Gulf: sudden oases filled with the green of palm trees, islands baking sere and black in the crystalline blue water. Back again west into the interior – Ciudad Insurgentes, Ciudad Constitución, Santa Rita. Once again we paralleled the coast. Even at this distance we could sense the presence of the sea.

To the edge of the Earth

As we approached the point where Highway 1 would swing left to take us back across the peninsula toward La Paz, we felt an external tug that made us hesitate like pieces of iron feeling the pull of a magnet. After so many hours of silence, the idea was expressed in minimalist terms.

"Be a shame to not even surf the Pacific side up here."

"Yeah."

Reflexively, whoever was driving slowed down. The van, ever alert to changes of velocity and RPM, altered its sound to something resembling a weed whacker in a gravel pit.

Serendipity struck. Rising from a small pile of jagged stones like a monument to an obscure local deity, a gnarled and withered branch held up a primitive sign, crudely painted on a cracked and splintered board.

The lettering was so weathered that it was impossible to decipher. It might have said "*playa*" or "*pescado*." For all we knew it said "golf course" or "yacht club" or "road to hell." But whatever it said, it was a sign indicating that the double ruts leading off toward the west went somewhere that someone had thought worthy of note. We turned off.

Going in, the road was an incomplete idea, a road in name only. After a few hundred yards of firm sandstone and rock the track became looser and less definite. A bit further, and it began to follow an arroyo, or dry wash. Where the sandy banks were steep, the rutted track clung precariously to the rim. Where the banks had collapsed, we found ourselves following the ruts down to the bottom of the arroyo, where the sand was softer and there were fewer rocks for the tires to grip. The van skittered and wriggled up and down the sandy banks and dusty ruts as nimbly as a lizard. Already we could smell the sea.

We arrived at a scruffy-looking sand beach, strewn with driftwood and a jumble of worn, rounded rocks and boulders, none of them very large, deposited on the shore by what must have been centuries of periodic flash floods through the arroyo. We would have to pull up stakes and leave in a hurry if it started to rain. Otherwise the arroyo would fill with raging water and we would be stranded indefinitely with just the food and water we had brought.

The sky hovered motionless above the landscape, with only an occasional stirring of air to reveal its presence. This was as close as one could get to nowhere without falling off the edge of the Earth.

The rocks and sand deposited by the arroyo had formed a classic alluvial delta, small but well-formed, that created a point protruding out from the beach. To the left, as we faced the ocean, was a flat expanse of beach and sea. To the right, the shore curved inward to form a broad cove, not quite a bay. We had warm air, warm water and the perfect point break setup for a south swell. Now all we needed was a south swell.

A hundred yards or so to our right was a small site, partially sheltered by a ramshackle set of scrawny poles topped by crooked cross-members and desiccated brush and fronds, that must have been a seasonal fish camp. Near the poles was a rough ring of blackened rocks evidently used as a fire and cooking pit. The entire area was littered with fish bones and the mica-like glitter of fish scales.

We parked the van next to the poles, spent a few minutes cleaning up the most obnoxious litter, and set up camp. Remarkably, there was no odor and no flies or other insects – the desert air had mummified the fish remains that hadn't been carried off by gulls and scavengers.

Surfer's Log, Day One: Flat

As a surf site the place had potential, but that afternoon it looked anything but promising. The sea was rough and hung with drab clouds stretching to the horizon like dirty laundry. A murky-looking chop slapped half-heartedly at the shore. The air was sultry and oppressive. Even the few gulls that coasted by looked dispirited and pessimistic. But after the long drive we were ready for a break, and we were here.

We spent the rest of the day relaxing and puttering and improving the campsite and napping in the heat. If nothing improved by morning, we agreed, we were gone. Surely the Tip would be better than this.

The day drew to a close. The forward motion of travel had kept both of us at least partially emotionally inflated, but now that we were here with nothing to do, I could feel the pressure leaking out. I felt like a balloon slowly losing air, the surface starting to go slack and flabby and cave in on itself. The sullen smacking of the ripples on the gritty shore was like a soundtrack designed to emphasize the dismal ambience that surrounded us and infiltrated our souls. From time to time a seabird would glide by, too tired to flap its wings. A gaggle of bored sand-flies perched indifferently on clots of dried seaweed and the occasional fish bone. Occasionally one of them would crawl lazily to a new perch. Maybe he was looking for a scrap of something to ingest, or maybe he just wanted a change of scenery.

I built a small fire in preparation for nightfall and possibly a warm meal. We sat in the waning light with our backs to the van, watching the chop on the ocean. It was like watching litter blow around in a vacant lot.

Pete rolled a joint, lit it, took an enormous drag. When he handed it to me his motion was sort of pent-up and squeaky, as if his hand were holding its breath and offering me a hit through a constricted throat.

Normally I didn't smoke weed, but this was a special situation. I had obligated myself to put in some serious extra teaching hours to free up the time for this trip and for what? I'd had more interesting evenings watching the clothes in the washing machine at the Laundromat. I needed something to change my outlook.

"What do you think?"

One of us said it; it might have been me. The implication, if there was an implication, might have been that we might want to do some short range planning.

The idea, if it was an idea, sank back into a bottomless pool of lethargy. Our small campfire crackled merrily. Fires are like that – it's always all about them.

We sat and smoked and watched the scruffy-looking wavelets lick little scraps of flotsam off the beach. A seagull drifted by at low altitude, eyeing the fish camp as he passed. Maybe he was remembering happier times there, the *palapa* ringed with fins and heads and fresh entrails as the fishermen cleaned their catch. He soared up, banked sharply and glided back to land a dozen yards away and stood there staring at us as if expecting us to conjure up a fish for him.

The sky was still a dirty gray dome, with a gap at the western edge between the dome and the horizon. Above the overcast the sun was a large luminous circle, like a spotlight seen from the inside of a dust-covered window. The circle slid down the dome, hung from the edge for a few seconds, then let go and tumbled into the sea. It was like watching an invisible hen laying a flaming egg.

"Pretty good smoke," I said to Pete. Give credit where credit is due.

Pete just grunted and nodded. Who knew what he was experiencing? He never talked about his inner life. It's a guy thing.

The sun was trying to stay afloat, but it was only postponing the inevitable. Finally it fell off the edge of the sea like a drunk going over a waterfall. There was a brief eruption of multicolored light memorializing the event, then the band of color above the horizon began to turn to indigo. No green flash. I raised my hand toward the afterglow in salute. *Sic transit gloria mundi.*

We sat. The wavelets lapped in the dark. The fire crackled. Now that the sun was no longer around, stars began to come out cautiously in the narrow band of sky above the horizon, like sand crabs emerging from their holes. Another glowing circle, this one whiter and more tentative, appeared above the dome of overcast. Pete lit another joint and I took a small hit just to be polite.

When it was dark and the fire had burned to embers we crawled into the back of the van, where I fell asleep immediately and slept hard and silently and without dreams.

Surfer's Log, Day Two: Into the dunes

Day two dawned. Well, not dawned, actually. The cloud layer got brighter in uneven splotches, like a dirty bed sheet dipped in weak bleach, until our surroundings came into partial focus. It's always darkest just before the dawn, but what happens when dawn looks like the bottom of a used skid-row mattress? Today the sand looked dirty, the water murky and roiled, the chop as ugly and raw as poorly filleted fish.

Inside the van, a groping hand emerged from the welter of sleeping bags and towels that served as a bed. Like a sightless and misshapen slug, it groped blindly about until it made contact with the bottle of tequila left over from the night before. Another hand appeared, eager to share in the spoils. Using amazing teamwork, the hands found the cap, unscrewed it, and dragged the open bottle into their lair beneath the blankets. A muffled gurgle, the sound of raspy swallowing, a satisfied sigh.

Pete emerged from his cocoon, blinking and wiping his mouth, putting the cap back on the bottle. The start of another day in paradise.

As an adventure, our trip so far was a bust. We had been living on hope and anticipation; now we were running on fumes and momentum. The good news was that from this far down there was nowhere to go but up. The interior of the van reflected our mood: a confused welter of clothes, towels, food, water bottles, tequila bottles, trashy paperbacks, flashlight, boom-box, tapes (pre-CD era!), toilet paper, eating utensils, matches, wax, trunks, extra fins, fin key, first aid kit, miscellaneous junk. At least everything we needed was there.

Surfboard-wise, I was set: on my 7'6" semi-swallowtail single fin shaped by Rusty when he still worked at Canyon, I could ride anything within my comfort zone and beyond. It was my "two to ten" board, fun in knee-high waves and capable of dealing with double overhead and more. Reef break, point break or beach break, it didn't matter – it handled everything. On smaller days the board was quick and responsive, and on any wave it made it easy to set up for getting barreled. It was the perfect board for our trip into the unknown.

So I had the right board – now we needed waves. Big or small, either way. Just something to ride before we left the Pacific side of the peninsula.

We piled crumpled paper on last night's ashes, gathered driftwood, lit a match, started a fire for coffee and eggs.

By the time we finished breakfast, improvement was in the air. The marine layer retreated toward the horizon, pushed by a new air mass that sailed in from the east, dragging long thin trails of stratus clouds. The chop turned to a smooth, almost glassy surface, then took on a slight texture dancing with small sparkling ripples. Still no surf, but the sunshine had us in a good mood and the change of weather might mean that our luck was about to change and waves were on the way. We puttered around all morning, gathered firewood for later, straightened up the van, skipped flat stones on the water. After lunch we dozed, lulled by the rhythmic lapping of the waves, the gentle sigh of the breeze in the palapa, the occasional distant cry of a gull.

By mid-afternoon relaxation was slowly curdling into boredom. Pete walked to the shore, looked out toward the horizon, stretched, and turned south, walking toward the point formed by centuries of periodic detritus from the arroyo. On impulse I started walking north along the beach, away from where we had come in.

Not far from our encampment, the desert spilled down onto the beach in a series of low hillocks of sand – small, but technically dunes – devoid of rocks and supporting only a slight stubble of scraggly wild grasses. I left the beach and headed among them, the sea on my left, moving north. The sky was brilliant blue, laced by long fragile brush-strokes of white. The sun, still warm at the end of September, made the ocean shimmer. There was little sensation of heat, just a pleasant warm dryness, free of insects.

Barefoot and wearing only surf shorts, I walked on, the sand of the dunes coarse and clean and warm on my bare soles. With each step it whispered of times long past, of lost worlds and forgotten native tribes. No need to bring food or water; I'd had a good lunch and we were used to spending all day at the beach, surfing and lying in the sand or walking along the shore without anything to eat or drink.

The walk took me gradually upward, as the underlying ground had risen imperceptibly but steadily. A half hour or so later the dunes and I ended up atop a sandstone cliff, perhaps a hundred feet above the narrow beach and the glistening sea. I stopped and sat in the sand to admire the view. The sun was low to the horizon now; in a while – minutes or hours didn't really matter – I'd be able to watch the sunset. With this weather, I might even get a glimpse of the green flash.

Except for an occasional seagull gliding by below me, there was no life for miles. No fishing boats, no aircraft, nothing. Pete was miles in the other direction; I might as well be the last person on earth. It was a good feeling, relaxing and peaceful. And my bare feet had left no clear tracks in the sand; it was as if I had floated in and wafted down to this spot.

It was easy to imagine that no one had ever been here, and that no one ever would. There was no reason for it, nothing to come here for. Only the stark soft purity of the place itself. It was elemental, Creation in the middle of the process. Sand, sea, sky. After I left, my faint tracks would remain for as long as it took the wind to erase them, and then there would be no record of anything at all. Somehow this though seemed comforting. Bring nothing, leave nothing, take nothing away.

I sat, the gulls glided, the ripples twinkled, the sun finally set.

Surfer's Log: Night of the snakes

At sunset the indigo of the sea touched the red at the lower end of the sky, as if the spectrum of color reached all the way around the globe to reconnect at the horizon. A flattened but hugely inflated moon lifted off from the southeast like a hot air balloon and glowed its way upward at the speed of time. A pair of fat planets loitered serenely above the scene like patrons at an outdoor art installation. Stars and constellations glittered and wheeled in the heavens. A meteor sliced across the sky. I rose to my feet and started back, my shadow like a photographic negative on the silvery sand of the dunes, a dream rising from my own footsteps.

After the Technicolor of the sunset the subtropical night was sudden. The moon recast the dunes in liquid silver still warm from the heat of the day. It felt good beneath my bare feet. Everything was beautiful and mysterious and filled with magic. The sand was clean and brilliant, the surface a glittering luminescence like a movie screen. The air seemed charged with its own faint chiaroscuro glow. Each dune was like a wave, pushed up by the wind and frozen in place, then coated with liquid ebony shadow that flowed down the sides and pooled in the troughs and hollows between the dunes. Some pools of darkness evaporated slowly as the moonlight moved languidly over the dunes; others seemed to seep beneath the nearest dune and reemerge on the other side, dark stains welling up through the sand.

I had lost all track of time and distance. There was no reason to care about either one. Keep the ocean on my right, keep walking until the dunes merged with the shore. I drifted on, moving through a soft haze of moonlight and solitude. The dunes rose and fell in gentle swells around me, undulating in lunar brilliance. Up one, down the back side, up the next.

Then I saw the stick.

Odd, I thought, *I don't remember seeing any sticks on the way out.* There were no trees in the dunes, not even bushes, just small clumps of desert grass. I changed course to move toward the stick. It might come in handy as a walking stick, or just something to fool around with as I walked back. As I drew closer, the stick morphed into a coil. The transformation was amazingly quick. A dry rattling noise, like seeds being shaken in a desiccated gourd, drifted across the sand. I stopped in my tracks. A rattler. A big one, maybe five feet long.

Instantly, the poetry of the night congealed and shriveled.

One definition of panic is encountering a rattlesnake at night, miles from anywhere, when you are wearing nothing but surf shorts and surrounded by sand. No rocks to throw, nothing to use as a weapon, no defense, no protection.

My mouth suddenly dry, senses ramped up to high alert, mind racing, I was running through possible moves like a chess player with only one piece left on the board. The snake, its outlines blurred by the night and the shadows, seemed to expand as I watched it, wishing it would go away. My heartbeat was thunderous in my ears. Above it, in the absolute stillness of the desert, amplified by my paranoia, the dry rattle sounded as loud and piercing as a defective car alarm.

If I ran, would the snake chase me? How fast could they slither? I had seen films of huge snakes somewhere darting across the sand at incredible speed. Black mambas? Sidewinders? I didn't think this one was that fast, but who knew? How about throwing sand at it as a distraction? Or would that just make it angry? In the harsh glare of the moon, the snake's eyes were hard and dark, with a slight surface glitter like chips of obsidian. If I just stayed where I was, would it go away? As I pondered, its coiled body seemed to swell and grow. If I waited long enough, it would be the size of an anaconda.

The patience of snakes was legendary, and this one seemed to be in no hurry. It didn't seem inclined to stand down, so I decided there was nothing else but to go around it.

Deliberately − try to remain calm; they can smell fear! − I circled warily around the snake, alert to any sudden moves, my body compressed and ready to explode in flight like a sprinter waiting for the starter's gun. The snake remained coiled, tail aloft, periodically brandishing his rattle. I cleared the next dune, and the next, but the tranquil innocence of the night had been shattered. In my suddenly febrile mind the dunes were filled with rattlesnakes − tens, dozens, hundreds − lurking and slithering, hunting mice or kangaroo rats or lizards or whatever they were after. And they got nasty when disturbed.

The moonlit mounds and crests and ridges of sand seemed to shine with their own silver-white light as they floated in seas of inky impenetrable blackness. But now it was beauty with an undercurrent of menace. In my imagination each shadow-flooded hollow now teemed with venomous reptiles. I eyed the terrain in front of me warily, like a migrating wildebeest faced with fording an endless succession of crocodile-infested rivers. There was no way around, only across and through. If I tried to stay on the moonlit sides of the dunes and search for hollows with better illumination, I risked wandering away from the sea and getting lost. There was nothing to do but retrace my steps to camp.

I could feel my heart pulsating in my chest, hear the muffled thunder of blood cascading through my veins. Below the cliff the sea shifted and murmured in its sleep. The dunes lay still, bathed in light and shadow, waiting for whatever came next. Along the edges and through the hollows the shadows slithered in reptilian undulations.

I could feel myself losing it. By now each shadow was a nest of vipers, gaping mouths dripping venom. My mind filled with vivid images of fangs sinking into unprotected calves, pumping lethal venom into quivering arteries. I felt the hopeless dread of a hapless explorer wandering alone in a hostile wilderness teeming with death.

The ground was lower here, and on the seaward edge the dunes skirted a low bluff, a steep slope of rocky sandstone, fissured by countless narrow gullies formed by rainstorms past. Stalked by the predatory reptiles of my imagination, I snapped. I bolted down the slope, risking a sprained or broken ankle with every panicked step, leaping over narrow crevasses, imagining hissing rattlers hiding in each one, hoping that I would be past them before they had time to react.

I hit the beach at a dead run – almost falling on my face due to the sudden change to flat ground – and kept going until I got to the water. Did rattlers hunt on the beach at night? It seemed reasonable to assume they did. To be on the safe side I walked in ankle-deep water all the way back to camp.

When I finally got back the sky was profound and clear, a distant sea hung with gentle reefs of cirrus cloud. In the channels between the clouds fleets of stars twinkled at anchor while the moon floated like an enormous illuminated buoy, sending a river of light cascading across the water.

Pete sat staring into the flickering blaze of the campfire. He mumbled a greeting while I guzzled water from one of the bottles, stuffed my face with half-rotten bananas and a left-over *torta*, the guacamole turned brown with age and heat. I could still feel the tension in my body, and my feet had been turned to dill pickles by my extended salt-water stroll.

As usual, our conversation was minimalist.

"See anything?" I said.

My voice was still a little shaky with adrenaline.

"Naw. Walked a couple of miles down past the arroyo. Nobody there. Did you?"

I told him about the rattlesnake. My brush with agonizing death appeared to leave him unmoved.

"Could be a good sign, you know?" He was obviously deep in smoke, in touch with his mystic inner core. "The Aztecs didn't have all the hang-ups that the padres had, they knew how versatile snakes can be. Quetzalcoatl? He wasn't a bird, amigo, he was a feathered serpent."

He nodded sagely and held out a joint with a slender plume of fragrant smoke wafting from its glowing tip. To neutralize the adrenaline still coursing through my system, I took a deep hit and put a tape in the boom box – Handel's *Water Music*. Normally the sound of wind and wave is enough for me, but now there was something soothing, almost necessary, in the sounds of a creation that had survived its author for centuries. Under a smiling moon the gentle harmonies swirled and rippled out across the sea and toward the stars.

Surfer's Log, Day Three: Jackpot!

During the night, a warm wind began blowing the stars past holes in the clouds, which were growing thicker and more substantial than before. Drifting in and out of sleep, I was aware of the change. Wind would kill it. Even if there were waves, they would be blown out, choppy and crumbling. This was the last straw – we'd leave in the morning. I hoped Pete remembered our agreement: at the first drops of rain, we would have to leave. Otherwise we'd be trapped indefinitely. Meanwhile, sleep.

I'm sleeping in the back of the van as it clatters south. I become vaguely aware of motion, the sounds of wind and engine and highway. We're on the road again. Pete must have awakened to the sound of rain and driven back out. I want to keep sleeping – nothing worth waking up for now – but the engine noise won't let me. Through the curtain of sleep, the noise of the engine is louder than it should be. He must be driving flat out; the usual wheezing clatter has become a steady roar, the sound of speed. Something's wrong.

Now I'm struggling to wake up, tell him to ease up, but I can't. More roaring. The wind from our speed whips unabated through the open windows, making concussive flapping sounds. The engine noise increases. Suddenly a cylinder explodes. Somehow the van keeps moving, shuddering in the wind. The roaring engine noise continues. I've got to wake up. Another explosion, more roaring, and another. What's happening? Thunder! Confusion turns to panic. We've waited too long! Once the rain starts coming down the arroyo will fill to the brim in minutes and we'll be trapped. Another crashing explosion, followed by prolonged rumbling.

I sit bolt upright in the van, still half asleep, confused and sweating, tangled in bedding. We're still parked under the ragged palapa, which is being lashed by a stiff breeze. The gusts are buffeting the van. Outside a faint gray tells me that it's almost dawn. There's a strange roaring in the air. The normal chill of early morning is gone, replaced by a humid warmth. An explosion. The fronds on the palapa rustle excitedly, murmuring among themselves. The next explosion is accompanied by a dull white burst from offshore. I jump out of the side door of the van barefoot, oblivious to the danger of thorns or bits of broken glass we may have missed when we cleaned up the site.

The sky is completely overcast, the wind straight offshore, blowing off the desert and rushing out to sea. From somewhere beyond the horizon, cresting three hundred yards offshore, enormous waves sweep toward the beach in endless ranks, plumes of spray fringing on the crests, the sea at their backs and the wind howling up the faces. Each one rises up to its full height, held up and hollowed out by the wind, then hurls itself forward in a thunderous crashing explosion of foam.

For a moment I'm paralyzed, mesmerized by the scene. It's a perfect counterpart to the day before, another of the days of Creation. Enormous waves, each one magnificent and without flaw, arriving like destiny at this deserted spot with no one to bear witness to the event. Except us.

I break loose from the scene and tear off my shorts and T-shirt, put on board shorts, look for wax. The whole time I'm calling, almost chanting in ecstasy, babbling with joy. "It's here, it's happening! Surf! Waves!"

My frenzied activity, more than my voice, awakens Pete. No tequila starter needed – he's up and out of the van and ready to go even before I am.

We wait for a lull, leap in, and paddle straight toward the horizon, sprinting out and around the edge. The waves are coming off the point a couple of hundred yards to the south. They're huge – easily double overhead and higher in the sets. We make it out and reach the lineup, directly off the mouth of the arroyo. The force of the wind pushing us out and enormous volume of water coming off the point and moving north makes us paddle constantly to stay in one place.

A set comes, I set up for it. I miss the first one – the wind holds it up so long and makes it fringe so hard that I back off, thinking it's going to break. Blown back over the top, I take a few strokes out and set up for the next one. Paddle harder this time, feeling the energy of the wave surging through me and I'm in, dropping down and to the left. The wave jacks up above me, held up by the wind. The face is beyond vertical, in front of me it stretches forever, a half-pipe tipped up on edge to form an overhang, the upper lip suspended in space, reaching toward the shore. Behind me I hear water crashing, Niagara, engulfing me in a rush of air, a blast of spray as the tube collapses behind me. Rocket across the face – no chance of cutting back or doing any turns – glide up and out before the outer shorebreak, paddle out and do it again.

As I paddle back out, I see Pete streaking across an enormous face. He's not a small guy, but he looks tiny compared to the wall he's on. We each catch another wave, and another. The conditions are so perfect that we can do no wrong. Once we're in a wave, the wind seems to guide us to the perfect spot. It's like riding on rails with a jet engine strapped on our back.

Even the wait between sets is magical. We have gotten into a rotation: Pete catches a wave while I'm paddling out – or waiting for a lull if I have ridden too far to get out over the back of my wave – then it's my turn. Due to the size of the surf, Pete isn't visible once he has dropped into a wave, so between waves I have the experience of sitting hundreds of yards offshore from an alien desert with no signs of life anywhere. The shore looks tiny, with everything rendered in miniature: the van and the ragged palapa, the dry wash where we drove in, bushes, rocks, cactus. The immediate shore is obscured by the waves, by blowing spindrift, by churning white water. Any mountains that might have been visible are hidden by the clouds.

The desolation and solitude are absolute and almost overwhelming. Add the currents, the wind and the surf, and the effect is incredibly intense. Our universe has been compressed into a space ruled by wild, raw energy.

The waves are arriving from somewhere deep off the coast of Mexico and they have the cleaned-up, hyper-regular configuration of swells that have hit from an angle and wrapped around the land to come ashore. They are awesome. Double overhead plus, and uniform – no sections, no discreet peaks or shifting takeoff spots; just set after set of massive surging walls that come driving in from the southwest, pushing north from deep water off the cobble point; held up by the offshore wind until they form massive tilted concave faces that defy gravity as long as they can and then collapse with a thunderous crashing rumble.

Wave after wave after wave.

Finally we've had enough. My shoulders are hurting, the rest of me is exhausted. One last ride in, get through the shorebreak, trot back up the beach to the van, high on excitement, giddy with joy, laughing like idiots. Minutes later we're drinking camp coffee, eating some kind of more or less nourishing breakfast cobbled together from our eclectic larder.

I have paddled so much that my shoulders are throbbing, so strongly that I almost expect to see motion beneath the skin. The area is warm to the touch and it feels like I've irritated the tendons or something. But I'm so happy and full of endorphins that I don't pay much attention.

We spend the rest of the day recovering. Will tomorrow be this good? It doesn't seem likely. The gray overcast is thickening and the horizon is taking on texture. As the day progresses, the wind changes from a steady offshore to something more fickle, shifting this way and that as if trying to avoid a commitment. A few seagulls huddle warily on the beach, their reptilian yellow eyes narrowed to slits. Usually before a storm they will soar in rising spirals as if practicing for higher wind. Maybe they sense that the approaching storm is too fearsome to practice for.

By afternoon the surf is ragged, still big but with an ugly churning component that tears the waves into unruly jagged slabs. We wouldn't stay for these conditions, but we cling to the hope that somehow they may improve.

1976, Hurricane Liza: Deluge

The first drops of rain, fat and tentative, begin to explode against the van like tiny artillery shells, driven by the increasing wind. If we wait too long we'll be stuck here, and when the rain stops there will be no source of untainted water except what we've brought with us. We quickly break camp, make a halfhearted attempt to organize the chaos inside the van, and leave.

By the time we reach the arroyo the rain is pelting down almost horizontally and the first insidious trickles of water are beginning to form in the sandy stream bed. On the way out, the trickles turn to playful rivulets, then streams. For the first time, we're worried about not making it out. The footing is irregular, crumbly and clinging, and the van, slick with water and grimy with sand and salt spray, crawls and wriggles awkwardly as it picks its way up the arroyo, away from the sea. Behind us the waves sweep through the bay, tearing the shore apart in a mad welter of noise and movement and kicked-up spray.

It's tight, but we make it out. Back on the highway, we head for La Paz. Within minutes the rain is torrential. The storm is emptying itself onto the earth below. Moisture-laden air spirals upward, driven by the heat contained in the late summer ocean. As it rises, it cools; the moisture condenses, forms drops, plummets back to earth by the ton.

When we reach La Paz late in the afternoon, the world is eerie. The rain is falling in sheets, turning the road into a shallow expanse of water filled with currents and eddies. A strange glowing light fills the sky above the pouring rain. The city is without electric power. In windows, kerosene lanterns glow and flicker, trying to hold off the advancing gloom. The side streets are awash. Gusts of wind play soccer in a rain-swept park, using an empty paint can for a ball. Cars move like cautious cattle, hesitating at every pool and current as water swirls around them.

We pull into a gas station. The power is out here, too, but the pumps are being operated by hand. The rain falls in sheets that twist and flutter violently in all directions. We wait in line, fill up, pay in cash.

We hold a strategy meeting. Stay here, we risk getting stuck here. The Pacific coast is over, at least for now. The odds seem better at the tip. We eat and set out again.

The going is slow; the rain makes it hard to see; my hands are tired on the wheel. The steady pounding of the rain is deafening, like a fire hose on a tin roof. We leave the lowlands, rise, descend again toward the Gulf near Los Barriles. From there it's one more mountain range, then a final descent to San José del Cabo and the sea.

The road climbs into the Sierra de la Laguna. The scrub and dry vegetation give way to an exotic forest of pines, oak and the occasional palm tree. Once again we have transitioned into another world. The van almost drives itself, crawling up the mountain like a gigantic metallic trilobite, rain-slick and rattling and murmuring to itself, driven by a primitive instinct to seek higher ground. Once we get high enough into the mountains, feeling the fatigue now from this morning's epic session, we pull off at a gravel turnout and try to rest again. We're safely above any flooding that might keep us stuck in the lowlands. We'll rest awhile, then cruise on to the Cape.

When we awaken, it's still dark. Four a.m. The wind has abated, leaving only the steady monotonous drumming of the rain. Might as well get started; we'll be in San José del Cabo for breakfast.

Pete had lit another doobie and was enveloped in wreaths of fragrant smoke, plus whatever his imagination could generate. Onward and upward we drove, following the twisting road into the dark and forested Sierra, with only the pouring rain and the muffled sounds of engine, tires and windshield wipers for company. No music, no radio, no talking. There wasn't really anything to say at this point, so we didn't say it. We were immersed in recent memories and the pure experience of the moment. Anything else would have been a disruption.

1976, Hurricane Liza: Trapped

As we passed the summit of the grade and traversed the side of the low mountain range in the dim gray just before dawn, we came upon a scene of carnage. The road at that point had been built atop a culvert at a narrow point in the canyon of the Río San José. This made sense from the point of view of construction – easier, cheaper and quicker to build than a bridge – but it was not so good during a major flood event like the one that this storm was producing. In the narrow part of the canyon the water moved much faster and put more pressure on the road. Forced into a confined space, its energy was concentrated.

During the night the floodwater had swept out of the mountains and down the ravine, carrying all before it. Battered by a barrage of water, rocks and debris, the road had held firm for a time, then crumbled, overwhelmed and swept away. The first car to arrive thereafter (traffic would have been light because of the hurricane) had seen the deluge and stopped short. Then – with no thought of leaving the parking lights on or putting any sort of marker or warning in the road behind – the occupants had simply hunkered down inside the car to wait until morning. A second car, coming along later in the dark, had smashed into the rear of the unlighted car.

Both vehicles were full of people, two families' worth, and each carful had a couple of serious injuries. One man's face had a broken nose surrounded by deep cuts, apparently from going through the windshield, another had an enormous swelling bruise that was cut to its core like a rotten plum, probably from a steering wheel or dashboard. There were also a couple of serious whiplashes and an assortment of cuts and contusions.

We sprang into action. Superheroes to the rescue! The only shelter in sight was a pair of dilapidated buildings set back from the road, adobe shells with walls melting where the protective whitewashed coating had broken away, roofs mostly collapsed with time and age and their own weight. We found a dry area in one of the ruined buildings, a corner that still had a roof. We cleaned out dirt and leaves, built a fire from debris. From our camping supplies we got pots, pans, cereal, utensils.

In a few minutes we had shepherded the accident victims into the shelter, provided an old blanket for the women to sit on, fixed hot oatmeal for the children. Our first aid kit was basic, but adequate: peroxide or Bactine to clean the wounds, band-aids for smaller cuts, improvised butterflies for the deeper ones. The broken nose and the more serious injuries we left for whatever help might arrive later.

Once our humanitarian chores were attended to, we went back to the van. In front of us the two wrecked vehicles sat in a little rubble field of broken headlights and taillights, their interiors gradually soaking up the rain through their broken windshields. Beyond them, the flash flood roared, an endless monologue punctuated from time to time by what the locals call a *golpe de agua*, a sudden rush of water created when a natural dam of dead vegetation and rocks upstream is broken by the pressure of water building up behind it. The result is a low rumbling growl like the sound of distant thunder from upstream, followed by a foaming wall of water – usually only a couple of feet or so high, but with tsunami power – that brings the level of the entire flood up with it as it passes.

We held another conference. Since we couldn't continue, we decided that the best course of action was to return to La Paz. We could send somebody – the Cruz Roja, the Tourism Assistance Patrol, somebody – to help the crash victims. Then we could either enjoy the limited attractions of La Paz for a couple of days, or head back to the Pacific coast. We were down, but not out! We had options! Armed with optimism and a sense of purpose, we checked on our patients, told them our plan, and set out for La Paz.

Behind us the flood raged on, sweeping away cactus and scrub trees, scouring the sandy valley floor, carving and grinding the stony bluffs that had suddenly become the banks of a surging temporary river.

The rain was still falling steadily, alternating between hard and harder, drumming on the roof of the van. Somewhere above the vast lid of clouds the sun was struggling to clear the horizon, but on the road the thick sky and pouring water soaked up all the sunlight, so that it wasn't much brighter than it had been before dawn. Lights and wipers set to full max, the bus whirred and clattered gamely as we went through the gears. The mere fact of being on the road again improved our spirits. We were going somewhere! Maybe there would be waves at Los Barriles. Maybe the wind would turn offshore and we'd replicate our Pacific coast experience. Maybe pigs would learn to fly.

Barely a mile from the washout we were driving through a narrow canyon, steep on both sides. To the left of the road, a low rocky cliff tumbled abruptly down to a narrow gorge, now a raging torrent. To the right, the slope rose sharply among scrubby, nondescript trees and undergrowth. If it had been a movie set, this is where bandits would lie in wait to ambush the unwary travelers. But this was no movie, this was real life. So instead, the road disappeared.

A wall of muck and stones twenty yards across and ten feet high came hurtling out of the rain from the hillside to our right and surged across the road in front of us, an enormous inanimate slug slurping wetly over the ground, devouring everything in its path. With deceptive speed, leaving a trail of mud and mangled plant matter six feet deep, it heaved itself across the road and into the gorge. If we had come this way half a minute earlier, we would have been swept away and buried alive.

We stopped just short of the pile of sludge, which was still flowing weakly, its edges oozing moisture. We stared at it dully, like cows herded through a chute and into a pen with no way out. It was like being blocked by a lava flow, one with the temperature of cold oatmeal and the consistency of wet cement. No way over, around, under or through. Still stunned and digesting the idea of total encirclement, we had little to say. Besides, we were exhausted. Our conversation was minimalist but expressive, as primitive as the situation.

"Sonovabitch!"

"When it rains, it really fucking pours."

"Coulda got us."

"Now what?"

With no way out and no way forward, we got the van turned around and returned to the scene of the accident. What choice did we have?

When we got back, nothing much had changed. The wrecked cars were still there, surrounded by chips of paint and bits of chrome and broken glass. Through the rain the faint smell of smoke and a wisp curling from the ruined adobe buildings indicated that the families were still keeping relatively warm and dry inside. We gave them the news about the road, then returned to the van.

Like water soaking into mud, the realization began to sink in. We were not going anywhere at all. No waves, no more trip, just rain, rain, rain.

"At least we can't get rear-ended."

"Yeah, not with the road closed."

"How long do you think we'll be here?"

It was the question we had put off asking. Two days, a week, longer? At least we weren't injured, we had food and we had the van to sleep in. Things could have been worse.

Then we noticed that the road where we were parked was getting narrower. The shallow ditches at each side had filled with rain and had formed rivulets that flowed briskly toward the main flood crossing the road in front of the two wrecked cars. The raindrops pecked at the fringes of the roadway like birds pecking at a cracker, dislodging larger and larger crumbs. From time to time a narrow crack would appear in the surface near the edge of the road. The crack would widen, hesitantly at first and then more rapidly, until at last it opened up and a chunk of asphalt dropped into the ditch, where it was devoured whole by one of the roadside rivulets, which were growing at an alarming rate. Our little slice of the planet was growing smaller by the minute. All we could do was sit and watch it shrink.

The rain on the roof of the van put up a continuous dull roar, amplified by the sound of the torrent pouring across the washed-out road. Gradually, emerging from behind the sound of water like a dream seeping into consciousness, I heard another sound. Like little bells.

We had been up most of the night and our environment was dissolving into chaos. Now I was hearing things.

Then, from behind the layered curtains of rain, a goat appeared. Then another, and a dozen more, followed by an elderly man, gnarled and wiry, covered to the knees with a poncho, face of tanned leather beneath a tattered straw hat. The classic Mexican kind, with water dripping from the little tassel hanging down the back. On his feet, *huaraches*, the worn leather straps soaked through, the tire-tread soles thickly clotted with mud. He stopped to greet us with the welcoming air of a man who didn't get many visitors and was glad when they showed up – even two gringos in an old van.

"Mucha lluvia. Mejor suban p'allá con el carro. Donde mi choza. Aquí no se puede." Come up to my hut. From beneath the poncho one gnarled arm gestured vaguely through the rain.

A pair of roughly parallel goat tracks studded with jagged bits of stone – eroded gullies that might once have been the semblance of a road – led straight up the rocky hillside. Above, barely visible through the curtains of rain, was a clump of scrubby trees and the dim outlines of a rustic shack. The old man was already gone, his back a receding patch of dark surrounded by bobbing goats like a weather-beaten boat surrounded by buoys.

We tried to follow him but the normally sure-footed VW van couldn't make it up. The tires slipped, the engine roared in protest, the frame scraped and threatened to bottom out on the hump between the gullies. We stripped to our shorts, leaped out and began collecting rock after broken rock, tossing them into the ruts until there was enough clearance and firmer footing. Slipping, skidding and rattling complainingly, the van made it to the top on the third try.

Within minutes we were dried, dressed, and sitting in the snug interior of the one-room hut. Dirt floor, one door, a single small window, everything neat and shipshape. A couple of wooden stools, a crude wooden table. Bedroll on a low platform against one wall. Food, utensils, tools and clothing hung from the gnarled branches that made up the rafters. Above, a thatched roof, as old and withered as the goatherd, but so tight and well-made that not a drop of rain leaked in.

The old man lit a kerosene lantern that bravely pushed a golden yellow light a few feet into the room. With it the dim beginnings of an idea stirred somewhere in a corner of my brain. Pete broke out a bottle of tequila and offered it to our host.

"Tequila, sí? Bueno."

Pidgin Spanish was all he had, but it was enough. They each took a drink from the bottle, then another. The rain, which had been falling with considerable force, dropped back to a steady, sullen background noise, like the hissing static of a midnight television set. Outside, water dripped from the edge of the roof with monotonous repetition.

So there we were, stranded in the middle of the Sierra de la Laguna, cut off from La Paz by a massive mudslide and cut off from our destination by a raging torrent of muddy, debris-filled water.

As we sat in the goatherd's hut, I could feel the need for action rising inside me. Maybe it was the aftereffects of our epic day of surf: man against nature, the pure, simple physical pleasure of dealing with the elements in primeval conditions. Whatever the cause, I was feeling stifled, confined, hemmed in.

I started thinking about rain and flash floods and how all rivers end up in the sea. I darted back out to the van and came in with the beat-up, dirty Triple-A map of Baja. Opening it up, I found our approximate location. On the map, a squiggly line ran maybe twenty-five miles to a spot near San José del Cabo. Gradually a simple but daring plan took form in my head.

Pete was still chatting in pidgin Spanish with the goatherd and trading swigs of tequila from the now half-empty bottle. Probably if he had been totally sober he wouldn't have gone for what I was about to propose.

"Hey, Pete, listen – where's all this rainwater going?"

He looked at me with tolerant bemusement.

"To the ocean, where else?"

"Right. And where are we trying to get to?"

A moment of stunned silence, then an incredulous outburst: "That is the dumbest, most irresponsible idea I've ever heard!"

Fifteen minutes later, it was a done deal. We would leave the van with the old man, in return for the remaining tequila, some supplies, and the promise of more supplies and another bottle when we returned.

We might have been crazy, but we weren't stupid. We had both seen *Deliverance*, the movie where Burt Reynolds and a group of urban yuppies attempt a canoe trip down a rural river, get attacked by pervert subhuman rednecks, are stranded and shattered by rapids and waterfalls, and generally have a rotten time. We'd asked and asked again, and the old man had assured us that the valley floor was essentially flat, a normally dry wash that meandered down a gentle slope all the way to San José del Cabo. He'd covered most of it himself, in dry weather – which was almost always – with his goats. He knew the terrain as well as anyone.

We suited up. Shorts, tennis shoes (no socks) for rocks and thorns, T-shirt – even through the clouds you could get serious sunburn this far south. A change of clothes (T-shirt, underwear, shorts), money, credit cards and ID carefully wrapped and taped in plastic bags and stuffed into our day packs. Half a dozen oranges each, for liquid and nourishment in case we had to end up trekking twenty miles or so through the desert to the coast. Extra wax. And that was it.

We said *adiós* to the old goat-herder and picked our way through the rain, past the VW van and half walking, half sliding down the slippery, rocky slope to the arroyo. The rain, which was still falling steadily, had let up a bit. The roar of the muddy brown torrent raging over the remains of the road and down the embankment below it seemed louder than it had before.

At the water's edge I did a quick scan of our surroundings. The canyon where the road and culvert had washed out was steep and narrow and the flood below the washed-out road was torrential, gushing through the gap and pouring over the edge in a tight waterfall. The opposite bank had been cut away into a vertical cliff by the rush of water. On our side the bank was precipitous, slick with rain and mud and loose rock; downstream it might well be worse. Once we got into the water, there would be no turning back. I felt like a character in *River of No Return*.

1976, Hurricane Liza: *River of No Return*

As we reached the margin of the swirling flood, a sudden surge swept like a mini-tsunami over the remaining pavement and dumped down into the roiling water below the road with a sound almost like that of a breaking wave. This meant that somewhere upstream a mass of rubble, collected and piled up by the pouring rain until it acted as a small dam, had broken from the pressure above it, releasing a sudden rush of water into the torrent.

A photo taken of us at that moment would have shown two eager young gringo surfers, rain-soaked and outlandishly dressed in tennies, shorts and T-shirts, with day packs on their backs and surfboards under their arms, scanning the maelstrom for the best place and direction to launch. What the heck – one spot was as good as another. We jumped in.

As soon as I hit the water I could feel that this was going to be different from anything I had ever done. We were used to decent-sized surf – not North Shore O'ahu, but still we had plenty of experience with hard-breaking, double-overhead-plus waves. We had gotten pitched, gone over the falls, been through long hold-downs, rag-dolled in washing machine turbulence, body-slammed in various ways. But this was different. The power was there, but most of it was hidden. Not explosive like surf, but relentless. No lulls, no channels, no shoulders. This was pure non-stop, gravity-fed, no-holds-barred energy. And that was just the first challenge.

In the silt-filled current, wax was useless. Our boards were instantly coated with a film of ultra-fine mud, like brown cold cream. There was absolutely no traction. You had to sprawl face down on the board, keep your feet and knees wide apart for balance, and use one hand to hold onto the rail, leaving only one hand to paddle with. And you had to paddle; not for propulsion – the flash flood took care of that – but for any semblance of directional control.

For the other thing we learned immediately was that no matter what your fin setup, fins were useless in the swirling, racing current. Our boards yawed wildly, the noses swinging left and right in random surges. At times we found ourselves traveling sideways, even backwards. Occasionally, in really serious eddies, we did 360s, some slow, some fast. We were going the same speed as the water, carried like leaves on a swirling flood, and fins gave absolutely no control. In reality, paddling with one hand didn't provide much, either, but it was slightly better than nothing. Or maybe we just imagined it was better.

Other than that, we got off to a good start. At least the flood water, like the rain, was warm. We were, after all, in the weather created by a tropical hurricane.

At first – by luck more than by design – we stayed pretty much parallel to each other, a few yards apart. The arroyo at this point was maybe twenty yards wide and the water was several feet deep –although given the murky, silty quality of the water, there was no way to know exactly how deep. We were rocketing along, getting used to our new environment, yawing wildly in the current and struggling to keep from slipping off our boards, but generally making out okay and without any notion of trouble.

We slipped, we spun, we drifted. Within a couple of minutes we had been separated from each other by the vagaries of currents and the individual idiosyncrasies of our boards. All my energies were quickly funneled into two priorities: staying on the board, and attempting to face downstream often enough to see what we were getting into.

As I spun helplessly on the water, trying to hang on to the slippery board, I realized that I hadn't thought of one key thing. I had no leash, and if I went off the board for whatever reason, it would be difficult to impossible to get it back. The board and I would be spun and whirled and dragged in different directions. And one of us – either the board or me – would move downstream faster.

Pete not only had a leash, one of his girlfriends had made him a macramé ankle strap for it. The ankle strap was like one of those woven finger traps we used to buy in Tijuana when we were kids – you stick one finger in each end of a woven tube, and when you try to pull them out the direction of the weave makes the tube get tighter, trapping your finger. The harder you pull, the tighter it gets. There was no way Pete's leash could be pulled off his ankle by a wave, or by the river. If he slipped off, all he had to do was grab the leash and reel his board back in. I started wishing that I had a leash.

That brought up another problem. I wouldn't be able to swim far in the roiling current with a waterlogged day pack on my back. If I fell of my board I would probably have to ditch the day pack, and then I would be stranded in the desert with no oranges, no spare clothes, no ID and no money.

Maybe Pete had been right: this was a really, really dumb idea. But we were in it now, there didn't seem to be any way to turn back – or, at this point, even to reach the shore and hike out – so I tightened my grip on the rail and hung on.

Eventually the canyon widened and things got easier for a while. We were still riding the swirls and eddies more or less passively, but the turbulence had diminished. There was still the occasional *golpe de agua*, but the width of the current dispersed the energy. What had been mini-tsunamis topped with dirty foaming crests became swells, a quick rising that passed without much aftereffect. We began to relax. This was working! The current still toyed with our trajectory in unexpected ways, shooting one of us in front, or to the side, without warning or apparent cause.

Then Pete disappeared.

I was still trying to figure out some way to keep the nose of my board pointed more or less downstream, when out of the corner of my eye I saw a quick movement. At the same time I heard a strangled, gurgling cry, and by the time my board rotated toward the direction Pete had been, he was gone.

Holy crap! What the...? Had he slipped off his mud-slicked board? But if so, where was the board?

I heard another stifled, gurgling cry just as my board spun around again to point upstream, and I got a glimpse of Pete – just his head, actually, which came to the surface of the water for an instant and then went down again as if he had been pulled by a gigantic hand. Then I saw his board, half-submerged, caught against some underwater object and jerking roughly in the current.

As Pete's head popped up again, my board rotated downstream, but I understood what had happened. His leash had gotten hooked on something, probably a tree, and pulled him off his board. Unless he could get to his ankle and get free of the leash, he was done for. Savagely buffeted by the powerful current, he would manage to get a shallow breath from time to time until he was too exhausted to fight or his oxygen deficit built up to the point of unconsciousness. Either way, he would drown.

I tried to get control of my direction, somehow get to shore, figure out a way to get back up to him before it was too late. No luck. The channel here was full of bends, with fairly flat shores of sediment on the insides of the bends and sheer cliffs on the outsides where the current of hundreds of flash floods over the years had torn away the desert. At each bend the current dragged me around the outside of the bend. There was no way for me to get to a flat shore to haul out. I couldn't even control the direction of my board, let alone change course. I was completely at the mercy of the current, and racing downstream and farther away from Pete every second.

The current swept me around the next bend and out of sight of the spot where Pete was fighting for his life. I had been carried a couple of hundred yards when another crisis loomed. I was swept toward an especially sharp bend topped by a very tall cliff – three stories of round river rocks precariously held together by a crumbling mortar of crushed rock, sand and the roots of desert plants. The cliff was vertical as a plumb line, broken off sharp as a razor at the top, and crowned with an enormous, Menorah-like *cardón*, the archetypal desert giant cactus, its central spire and curving arms towering at least thirty feet higher than the cliff.

This impressive sight had one very troubling feature: starting a few feet above the waterline, and extending to the top of the cliff, was the dark line of a fissure. Saturated with rain and weakened by the carving of the flood, a gigantic section of the cliff was starting to detach.

Ignoring the futility of paddling in a maelstrom and forgetting the need to hang onto the board, I began paddling like a madman with both hands. There was no hope of changing course, but maybe I could get past the cliff before tons of sand and rock, topped by more tons of evilly-barbed cactus, collapsed onto me and pinned me to the river bottom.

As I struggled, gasping open-mouthed, paddling for my life, the *cardón* quivered, swayed, and began to topple over into the flood.

A warning shower of small round stones rained down on the muddy water like meteorites, each one creating a small, viscous crater that came into being, paused for a moment, and dissolved into thick, concentric ripples. They scattered around me like grapeshot. Intent on paddling, distracted by the shower of stones, I couldn't look up or back to see whether or not the next impact would be the last.

Suddenly there was an enormous blast, followed by a wave of water several feet tall that surged into my board from behind, almost knocking me into the water. Confused and dazed by the concussion, for a moment I thought that lightning had struck, or that a big *golpe de agua* had overtaken me like a rogue wave. Then I realized what had happened: I had shot the gap just before the cliff and the *cardón* came down thunderously behind me, cratering the water like an exploding asteroid.

The wave from the collapse had pushed me toward a small island, covered with some sort of scrubby willow plants cowering forlornly in the mud, in the center of the flood. I managed to get myself to it and haul out, pumped with adrenaline and fright. I was alive, but by now Pete was surely dead.

My mind was in turmoil; a dozen emotions were swirling inside me. I'm now alone in the mountains of Baja, isolated, more or less trapped on a raging river. My best friend has just drowned. The nearest town is unimaginably far away in terms of time. Just trying to get back to the van could take hours, and then what? There's no one to turn to for help, and it's too late for anyone to help anyway. What should I do? Continue on? Try to get to shore and work my way back up to the place where I last saw him? What could I do then?

As I sat there shivering, suddenly cold, trying to adjust to my new reality, a miracle: around the bend past the now foreshortened cliff came

Pete, on his board, heading with the newly-redirected current toward the island. Another minute and he was on shore. Shaking with emotion, mumbling to himself.

"Jesuschrist. Sonovabitch. I almost died back there."

I stammered a sort-of apology. There was no way I could have turned back, I had a problem of my own...

"No, no, it's not your fault. Nothing anyone could do...Fuckin' leash got hooked on a branch or something and pulled me off the board. The ankle thing had a hold of my leg. So I'm down there on my back trying to get some slack into the damn thing so I can get my ankle out. Finally – can you believe this – the leash broke but one of those eddies spun me right back into my board."

Some people are just born lucky.

Suddenly, Pete tore the sodden day pack from his shoulders as if it were on fire. I stood there openmouthed and blankly amazed as he dug through the pack like a deranged badger, tossing things aside on the wet, sandy soil and grunting in desperation.

"Damn. Gotta be here somewhere. I know it put it in here. Where the fuck..."

Had he lost his money? His I.D.? His sanity? Maybe he needed food?

"Hey, ah, you want an orange? I've got plenty."

Finally the digging and rummaging stopped. His hand found something in the depths of the day pack, disengaged it like a paleontologist loosening a fossil from its surroundings. With a snort of triumph he brought it forth into the light of day.

"Found the fucker!"

A snorkel, the old-style kind with no fancy balls or flutter valves or filters, just a simple rubber tube in the shape of a letter J. *What the...?* Was this supposed to be some sort of defense against drowning? Was he planning on making the rest of the trip semi-submerged, like a frogman or an iguana?

Surrounded by the debris of his previous search, he dove again into the depths of the now mostly empty pack. A bit more peering and groping about, and he came up with the rest of the treasure. A bit of aluminum foil and a small baggie protecting a brownish lump of some elemental-looking substance and some matches. Now it was my turn to explode, but as calmly and eloquently as possible.

"Hey, ah, amigo, in case you hadn't thought? We're a few miles into a twenty-five mile journey through hell. We have both, each in our own unique way, come within seconds or inches – pick your measuring tool – of being killed in the middle of nowhere. And the best thing you can think of is to get fried on hash?"

"Helps me think."

He loaded the improvised pipe, lit it, and took an enormous hit. Immediately the tension left his face. His eyes took on a comfortable, benevolent glow. His voice was calm, mellow, avuncular. He held out the smoldering snorkel. A thin coating of saliva shimmered on the upper rim. He addressed me like a New-Age pastor gently pressing faith and salvation onto his flock.

"Have some. Good for you."

"I'll pass."

The flood flowed and rushed and swirled around our small island, the current made more turbulent as it adjusted itself to the sudden obstacle created by the rockfall in the main channel. Upstream I could see the massive spiked body and thick, clublike arms of the *cardón* resting on its own little island, the pile of stones and sand and lesser cacti from the collapse of the cliff. The trunk of the *cardón* sagged brokenly, its thick arms lolled and swayed drunkenly in the current. The entire mass shifted and settled heavily as the flood ate away at the heap of rubble supporting it.

"Suit yourself, man."

A couple more puffs, great long sucking inhalations followed at length by enormous sighs of satisfaction and relief.

"Ooohkay! Let's hit it."

He tucked the gear back in the day pack, we picked up our boards, and put ourselves again into the river.

Just before we launched ourselves back into the current, I cast a final glance back at the *cardón* that had come so close to taking me out. It sprawled in the water like a punch-drunk prizefighter, wallowing back and forth, buffeted by the current which by now had carried off most of the supporting rocks and plants. The water lapped and splashed noisily against it.

As we floated and swirled our way toward the Gulf, our spirits improved. Or rather, mine did; Pete's had already been adjusted upward by his hit of hash. The rain had let up somewhat, and the flood seemed to have stabilized. There hadn't been a *golpe de agua* for some time – either because all the rubble and driftwood barriers upstream had all been broken, or because the rainfall in the mountains had decreased.

Around us, the muddy water seemed almost festive, rippling and burbling cheerfully, playing with the twigs and branches of desert trees uprooted or simply engulfed by the flood. We mostly sat upright, straddling our boards in the current as if waiting for a wave.

For the first time since entering the flood, we engaged in cautiously optimistic banter.

"This is some ride, huh?"

"Beats driving."

It was hard to say much or carry on an extended dialog. The currents made it hard to stay together, and a space of five or ten feet could quickly become ten or twenty yards. We didn't feel like yelling back and forth; even if we had the surroundings were somehow against it. It would have seemed unnatural, a violation of nature, a disruption of the fengshui of the moment. Besides, what was there to say? So we simply sat and swirled and steeped in the experience, surrounded by a vast desert rimmed by distant hills, held together by water and rain and endless leaden sky.

Somewhere above us a faint, persistent sound hovered on the edge of awareness. Then I heard it – a faint, repetitive thwacking, like the rotors of a helicopter. It wouldn't be a search party; no one knew we were gone. And anyway, we weren't missing, just more or less cut off from the outside world. The sound, regular and insistent, seemed closer.

Thumpthumpthumpthump

There was nothing above us but the heavy blanket of clouds. Who would be flying in this weather? I didn't think they had the facilities to medevac the car accident victims from their isolated refuge where we had left them. And how could anyone have made contact with the authorities?

As the sound grew louder it seemed to be coming from within the canyon. It sounded wrong, too heavy and too wet – even with the rain – to be a helicopter. As we drifting along a straight stretch, we looked back. There it was.

I got that sick feeling you get just as you lose your balance on top of a cliff, or at the moment you perceive a car running the red light when you're in the crosswalk. Around the bend upstream came a nightmare, all sound and fury and churning kinetic energy: the huge *cardón* that had been toppled from the cliff, the bottom of its trunk and parts of its enormous thick arms broken off in the fall. Like an enormous jagged boulder tumbling down a hill, the *cardón* was rolling erratically towards us through the flood, driven by the force of the water. The stumps of its multiple arms, each studded with thousands of needle-sharp spines glistening with water, churned and flopped in an irregular rotation like the blades of a broken paddle wheel. They flailed the water, tossing spray into the air, as the *cardón* bore down on us.

Stunned paralysis was followed by panicked action. Desperate to avoid being overtaken, shredded into pulp and ground into the muck beneath the flood, we paddled like men possessed. But whatever energy we put forth was converted into random motion guided only by the caprice of the eddies. Mainly we just spun faster while drifting in whatever direction the current chose.

Thumpthumpthumpthump

The *cardón* was unstoppable and with its size and momentum it was closing the gap; while we were being whirled by the eddies the *cardón* plowed right through them without slowing down. The slapping and chuffing of its massive arms grew louder, a sinister counterpoint to the trip-hammer pounding of our hearts, the hoarse insistent panting of our breath and the ragged desperate splashing of our fruitless paddling as the thumping, whirling behemoth gradually overtook us.

Just when the thumping and thrashing reached a climax behind us, it stopped. A few scuffing noises, a scrape or two, then silence broken only the water and a gurgling rushing sound, audible over our own frantic splashing and gasping. Risking a look back, I saw that the *cardón* had run aground, its massive bulk caught on a sandbar.

For at least a mile we neither spoke nor paddled, just lay limply on our boards to recover.

At intervals there were rutted tracks leading to the edge of the water, what in normal times were desert roads and paths leading across what should have been a dry wash. In many of them we saw people – singly, in pairs, in groups – waiting patiently for the flood to subside so they could continue going wherever it was they were going to.

The current drew us close to a sandy track where a couple of *campesinos* squatted stolidly beneath a bower of low bushes bent lower by the storm. Belatedly eager to find out what we had gotten ourselves into, we made it to the shore and greeted them. They were an old couple, maybe late seventies, mostly or entirely Native American. Skin tanned by age and weather, tight across the bones and surprisingly smooth. Ropy and tough like the desert vegetation. They may have been squatting here for an hour, or a night and a day, dressed in huaraches and shirts and ponchos, pants on the man, a skirt on the woman. There was no sign of any baggage or equipment, no blankets, nothing but the clothes on their backs. They looked at us without surprise and without curiosity, as if the sight of a couple of half-naked gringos emerging from a flash flood, hair caked with mud and carrying strange boards like flattened porpoises, were the most natural thing in the world. They probably wouldn't have shown any emotion if we had been the second coming of Emiliano Zapata.

After a polite but cursory greeting (our social graces were being seriously eroded by the adventure) we cut to the chase: what was the terrain like downstream?

They were calmly emphatic in their agreement. No boulders, no cliffs, *no problema*, nothing but more of the same valley sloping continuously from here to the Gulf. *Pura arena no más.* Nothing but sand; not to worry.

"¿Cuántos kilómetros?" How far?

They had been together so long they operated in unison, as if connected by invisible wires. A pair of shrugs. "Está retirado." Some distance away.

We said our good-byes, picked up our boards, and returned to the river.

More water, more drifting, more of the same scenery. Water, mud, rocks, sand. Cactus, hills, bushes. People and cows along the bank, more of them now. A good sign. The canyon was widening into a valley. At times the current got so spread out and shallow that we had to walk, always downstream, ankle-deep in flowing water. At these times, the silt and sand beneath our feet was surprisingly firm. Then a narrower stretch would squeeze the banks together and make the water deeper and faster, and we were back in flotation mode.

At some point the adrenaline from our mishaps wore off. The flash flood, the steep desert banks, the gray sky, all became normal. We had habituated, the same way that sailors on an extended voyage habituate to their world of water and sky. The flash flood and our surroundings were our universe. We never thought of leaving the river to go overland; it was as if the outside world had never existed. Our original goal – to get to San José del Cabo – had faded from memory. Everything now was pure immediacy. So we focused on the task at hand, which was to make it through the next stretch, get to the next bend, see what lay ahead.

Life on the flood took on its own pace and shape. There was no sense of time, nor of progress, nor of urgency. The sky remained a muddy flannel blanket hung wet and low from horizon to horizon. The rain continued its sullen, monotonous falling, giving the murky water the dimpled texture of a large, dirty golf ball moving sluggishly beneath us. There was no sun, no directions, no landmarks. We had no past and no future, no goals other than staying on our boards and reaching the next bend in the torrent.

We settled into a variable but repetitive routine. Paddle to avoid a snag or rock, struggle to stay on the board, drift, paddle to avoid any anomaly in the surface that might indicate a dangerous object underneath, spin, paddle to stay facing forward and downstream, sit up, lie down, paddle some more. It was a tiring grind in an indifferent world of sand and cactus, stones and water and low-hovering sky.

In the middle stretches of our journey the water calmed down, and life settled into a more agreeable routine. Paddle, glide; lie prone, ride sitting up; ride the current, walk the shallows. In shallow stretches it felt good to walk. Here the sand was coarse and firm; the constant flow of water had percolated the silt and small particles downward. We chatted about nothing, or walked in silence, savoring the sensation of walking itself, the relaxation of not having to fight the current or worry about the next unexpected challenge, the solitude.

We were the living embodiment of the Zen of the moment, poster boys for the slogan "be here now." There was no thought of are-we-almost-there-yet or when-are-we-going-to-get-there. We were adjusting to the little universe we had chosen to commit to. When the torrent widened and slowed and became shallow, we were glad to be able to walk for a while. When it narrowed and deepened and gained velocity, we were happy to be riding the current again. The past, including the near misses with death by drowning, death by collapsing cliff and death by rogue cactus, was behind us. The future was unknowable. All we had was the present, and we were learning to embrace it no matter what form it took.

As we descended from the sierra, the land became flatter. No more mountain torrents or narrow gorges. The flood widened to several times its usual width and stayed that way for a while. The sand beneath our feet was firm and dense in the gently flowing water. We actually managed to put an optimistic spring in our step. The clouds were as impenetrable as ever but the rain was letting up. We must be more than half way there.

But we had no idea of our actual position, and the show was far from over.

Ahead of us stretched the water, a muddy ribbon pulled along by its own internal workings. On one bank, a hundred yards away, a steep rock outcropping composed of overlapping crags rose perhaps fifty feet above the shore, with a cluster of Mexicans on top. As we slogged closer we saw that beneath their perch was another flood, a large tributary flowing in at roughly a right angle. The water was moving briskly, descending through a channel narrower and steeper than ours.

As we approached the Mexicans atop the crag waved and hooted and whistled. Whistling in Mexico is ambiguous; it can indicate scorn and displeasure, but can also be a simple signal to attract attention. We chose the latter interpretation and waved.

At the junction of the two streams, the tributary was absorbed into our main flood. Where the two joined, the shallows ended and there was a dynamic sheen to the water, a subtle velvety rolling on the surface that revealed the presence of the entering current. Based on our surfing experience, we figured it would be easy to make this transition to deeper, swifter water. After all, we had done this a million times in big shorebreak: run at top speed, leap as far as possible in a flying broad jump, and come down prone and paddling. This would allow us to clear and glide beyond the lateral current and any turbulence and drag it might produce.

Pete went first. A ten-step run-up worthy of an Olympic broad jumper, a flying leap with board poised, a perfect landing followed by a series of quick, smooth, powerful strokes. He cleared the critical area by several feet, and quickly reached the featureless water beyond. Ten feet, twenty, thirty... Suddenly his board stopped as though he had run aground. Still paddling mightily, he was dragged backward by an invisible hand, faster and faster until he was almost back to the slight roiling caused by the confluence of the two streams. Another instant, and he was going down stern first. As he slipped beneath the surface there was no whirlpool, no visible turbulence. One moment he was there, the next he was gone.

I was too stunned to move or make a sound. High on their rock, the Mexicans more than made up for it, waving their arms and shouting their enthusiastic approval. I hardly heard them; I was focused on Pete and his situation. I started counting: one-thousand-one, one-thousand-two... Pete was in good shape and he knew how to deal with a long hold-down. But we were tired and he had been paddling hard. One-thousand-fifteen, one-thousand-sixteen... Had he had time to take a breath before he went down?

Something broke the surface thirty yards downstream, submerged for an instant, then came up permanently. It was Pete, sitting astride his board like a rodeo cowboy on a bull, spouting water like a whale. With his first breath he let out a war-whoop that cut through the frenzied shouting and applause showered on him by the Mexicans.

Now it was up to me. No worries – I could see what his problem had been: he hadn't gotten up enough speed before he launched. I took a few steps backward to give myself a longer run-in. Five steps, ten, twelve... airborne! I soared above the confluence, hit the water fast enough to leave a wake, paddled as if my life depended on it. The excited shrieks of the Mexicans and Pete's deeper bellows of encouragement seemed faint and distant. All my focus was on forward motion. Five yards, ten, fifteen... I was close enough to Pete to see the congratulatory look in his eyes. I had made it!

Suddenly I was being reeled in from behind, with increasing force. Over the years my fear of getting caught by waves had made me a strong paddler, especially in a sprint-type situation, but all my efforts were as useless as they had been in the whirlpools and eddies farther upstream.

The tail of the board seemed to shudder, and then tip down. Then, with surprising speed the board, with me clinging to the deck, was sucked down by the tail.

Just as I went under, I wrapped both legs around the board. I wrapped one arm as far around the board as I could, and with the other arm I reached up and over the nose, gripping with my whole hand. Death grip! No way was I going to lose the board!

In an instant we were submerged – and suddenly driven down so deep that my ears hurt. There was no sensation of churning or twisting, just an underwater elevator drop that sent my stomach up into my mouth. It seemed to me that we were still vertical, at least relative to the direction of motion. But there was really no way to tell. I tried to take a peek, but all I got was a glimpse of inky blackness and a coating of gritty silt on my eyeballs. *Okay, fine*, I reassured myself, *the board floats – it's got to come up sometime.* After all, I had experienced bad underwater situations before. So now, in the grip of the undertow beneath a Mexican flash flood, I was in a bad situation, but nothing unique. Keep calm. Ride it out.

Underwater, time slowed down. Surrounded by impenetrable gloom, I could only clench my eyes shut and hold my breath and wait. They say that when you're dying, your life flashes before your eyes. My life wasn't flashing, so I took it as prima facie evidence that I was going to get through this okay. Besides, Pete had popped to the surface. But that was him. What if I got jammed into an underwater cave, under an overhang, between two boulders? I pushed the thought as far away as I could get it.

The pressure wasn't increasing, but holding constant. Did I detect a bit more turbulence? I couldn't be sure. I recalled that keeper holes drain from the bottom. Down, around, and out. At least, that's what the water does. It may or may not allow you to come out with it.

It was completely dark down there, and there was a lot of turbulence and pressure, so I had no idea what direction I was facing or pointing at any given moment. I could have been upside down or sideways. I was concerned about the possibility of being slammed against something that might dislodge me from my board, so I kept a tight grip. I would have given anything to have clear water, so that I could see what was down there and what was going on, but that wasn't the way it was.

I became aware of increasing turbulence, not the kind of washing-machine industrial cycle you get beneath a big wave, but more of a sharp twisting and jerking motion. My thoughts became confused, probably as the result of less oxygen for my brain to work with. If this didn't end soon, Pete was going to have to continue without me.

A couple more shakes, a twist, and I was up. I flooded my lungs with air as the group on the crag gave me the same rousing response they had given Pete. I felt like a matador who has killed the bull, had it fall on him and somehow crawled out from beneath the beast, unscathed. A victory wave to our audience, and we continued downstream.

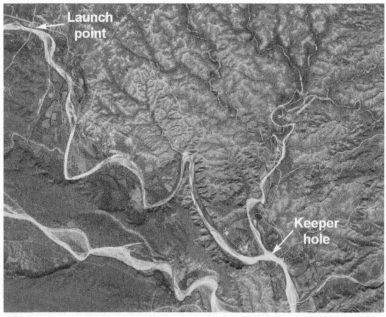

Our position estimates were wildly optimistic. Above: "halfway there."

Below: our actual situation. We had a long way to go.

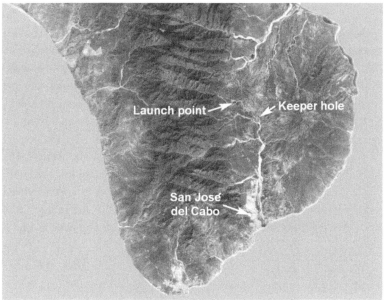

Images from Google Earth

For the next two or three hours, the trip was easy. As bend after bend revealed no new surprises, we relaxed. The current was much slower and weaker now, and from time to time we found ourselves paddling to move faster. Here and there, protruding from the current or washed against the bank, were reminders of what had happened upstream: an uprooted tree, the broken arm of a *cardón*, a dead animal, a bit of fence with a crude post attached.

The rain had almost stopped; the sky was higher but still a featureless gray sheet, illuminated from somewhere undefined, that obscured any hint of sun or time of day. The heat and humidity were stifling.

143

Swamp things

As we progressed, the shallows became shallower and more extensive, and we spent more and more time slogging through the sluggish murk on foot. We were getting seriously tired now, not the intense fatigue of high-output effort, but the bone-wilting deep burnout of total organic exhaustion. We had started sometime in the early morning; by now it must be approaching late afternoon. The lark had become an adventure, the adventure had turned into an ordeal, the ordeal was over, and now all we wanted was to quit. But quit what? It was too late to abandon the flood and walk out; it had abandoned us and now slogging through muck was our only option. Before, we had welcomed walking as a change from paddling prone; now we would have given anything for the chance to lie down. We encountered one last bit of reluctant current to paddle in, and it was over.

We found ourselves at the edge of a forest of palm trees, the water transformed into a trackless sea of mud. We had made it! We had reached the delta formed by silt and residue and debris deposited by this flood and hundreds more like it over thousands of years. And that meant that we were somewhere near San José del Cabo and the sea. And a place to lie down.

But as someone once said, it's not over until it's over.

The mud beneath the palms is softer and deeper than the silt of the flood. Primeval ooze rises to our ankles, then our knees, then higher. We struggle along, the tails of our boards dragging in the slop, our day packs seeming to increase in weight with every step.

In the palm forest the air is dead, the heat is intense. In places the silt is like quicksand: leg movement only serves to sink us deeper.

Beneath the mud is a welter of branches, thorns, cactus, barbed wire, palm frond spines, dead creatures, things unknown. You can feel them when your foot sinks down. Sometimes they support your weight, other times they give way – maybe with a slow rotten bending, perhaps with a sodden crack like a gasp of pain muffled by the mud.

Occasionally your foot encounters a sturdy object just inches below the surface; when you step on it you are temporarily elevated out of the morass, only to plunge back down when the next step comes down on nothing. From time to time whatever you put your foot on will twist or draw back in such a way that your sole slips off – backward, forward, to the side – causing the hidden obstacle to scrape the length of your shin or calf as your foot slides down past it. This is happening in a toxic, germ-filled environment. I try not to think about it.

Lifting each foot is an exercise in caution – the mud sucks at our shoes, and a sudden pull upward will forever separate shoe from foot. And we need the protection the shoes offer.

We quickly learn the proper technique: raise the foot with the heel down and the toes up. Bring up the heel first, and there goes the shoe and you'll never get it back. With all the unidentified sharp things buried beneath the delta mud, this would be disastrous. This style of walking makes our progress twice as exhausting, but it keeps our shoes on our feet. We resort to traveling more or less prone: pushing our boards across the slime, upside down and sideways, a few feet at a time, then pulling ourselves forward on our bellies toward the board.

We try to navigate by dead reckoning: keep moving south toward the sea and west toward the town. But directions are pure guesswork; in reality there is no way to know which way we're headed. The palm trees all look alike, the surface of the mud has been troweled smooth by the receding water, there is no sky or sun or shadows.

The absolute stillness and desolation are prehistoric in scope. No breeze, no rain, no birds, no insects, nothing moving. I half-expect to see a dinosaur – or maybe a monstrous pre-saurian slime creature – materialize among the palms. But there is nothing. Just the sound of our slurping and panting and muffled grunts and curses each time we lose some more skin or are stabbed by something penetrating the thin rubber soles of our tennies.

I feel a delirious rush of nostalgia for the power of the flood, the falling cliff, the pursuit by the giant *cardón*, the grip of the undertow where the two rivers had converged. At least that was struggle with a purpose. This is mindlessly draining and utterly lacking in dignity.

Beneath the canopy of palms and the invisible backlit sky, we slog on, slip, swear, slog some more. We have come across no footprints – or, more accurately, crawl marks – which means that at least we aren't moving in circles. At some point, a lifetime later, the trees gradually become thinner. A dozen yards ahead and to our right a clearing appears, and a low, steep bank, and beyond that, behind a clump of real trees, the hint of a tiled roof. The edge of the delta! Dry land! Victory!

When we finally emerge from the muck a few minutes later, we are coated with mud and slime. From beneath the covering of muck, small red flowers blossom shyly as blood oozes from the cuts and scrapes received in the delta.

As we stagger up the bank and into the streets of the town, passersby give us looks that run the gamut from horror to disgust. Two bedraggled, mud- and filth-clotted creatures from the swamp, day packs caked in slime sprouting like tumors from our shoulders, boards clutched under bloody, dripping arms. An old woman crosses herself, scoops up her grandchild, and scurries to safety around the nearest corner.

We reel down the cobbled side street, drunk with fatigue. A cheap backstreet building advertises a vacancy: *Se rentan cuartos*. Before we reach the door to ask for a room, a burly Mexican in a grimy tank-top undershirt moves menacingly to intercept us. Spouting threats and insults, he angrily chases us off the property, insulted that we would even think of staying there.

We change strategy: spying a garden hose, we humbly ask permission, then take turns hosing each other off in the street while a gaggle of grade-school kids gather around us to point and laugh. Dripping wet but reasonably clean and odor-free, we find a room. A rickety table with a jug of water, an old double bed with brass head- and footrails, too narrow for two full-sized people and too short to stretch out on unless we stick our feet between the rails. Between us we drain the water jug, then fall onto the bed.

"There's a good place to eat a couple of blocks from here. Let's rest until dinner time, then head down there for a couple of beers and a meal."

Agreed. It's after four in the afternoon; we have fought nature for at least eight hours. I lie down on my back near the edge of the bed, stick one foot through the footrail and leave the other one on the floor, and close my eyes.

When I wake up, I haven't moved. The room is drenched in sunlight. At first I'm confused; then I realize that it's late morning and I've been out for a good sixteen hours. Pete is still out cold. I get up stiffly and look out the window. An ordinary day. Sun shining, kids playing, neighborhood women chatting, the distant cry of a vendor rising from somewhere beyond the corner. It's as if the last twenty-four hours – the wrecked cars, the mudslide, our battle with the flash flood, our near brushes with death – had been nothing but a dream.

After the flood

The insides of our day packs had to be hosed out, but our plastic-wrapped clothes and money were still intact and dry. We washed up – this time with soap – dressed, and hit town for breakfast. We spent the next couple of days moping around, the ocean filled with filth and driftwood from the storm, waiting for the water to dry up so that we could go back for the van.

There were a couple of echoes of the event. One day we encountered one of the accident victims, his face still heavily bandaged, and got his expression of undying gratitude. He called a friend of his who worked for the local paper, and we found ourselves being photographed and interviewed for the next edition. He promised to send us a copy of the article, but of course he never did. Maybe it never appeared in print.

Between the car guy and the newspaper guy, we were the subject of a localized flurry of interest. No one seemed to care that we had played the role of Boy Scout paramedics by tending to the casualties from the accident at the washout. The only thing that mattered was the fact that we had shown *cojones*, been recklessly macho enough to risk the flood and make it through alive. Real men.

Our notoriety was fleeting. Like a lot of other things in Mexico, it was here today, gone tomorrow. Who has time to dwell on yesterday's news when there are so many other things to cope with?

When the waters had receded and the road had been reopened we hitched a ride on a truck, back to the mountains to reclaim the van. The sky was a hot blue, the air tropical and laden with moisture. The heat was humid and oppressive; everything was saturated with the earthy, clinging humidity of storm water being steamed from the soil.

When we reached the site of the washout, the damaged road had been reasonably well repaired. Without the rain, everything seemed more ordinary, prosaic, but there was still a hint of a time warp, as if the normal pace of days had skipped a beat and then continued as before. The ruined buildings were still the same, the space we had cleared already filling up with rubble blown in by the storm or falling in gentle erosion from the roof and walls. The cooking pot and utensils we had left were gone.

The goatherd was out somewhere with his goats, the open hut waiting patiently for his return. We left the promised goods and tequila on the hand-made table, along with a few dollars. It might be months before he was anywhere that he could spend the money; it would be a good souvenir until then. With nothing more to keep us there, we started up the van and left, inching and sliding our way down the crude roadway we had built until we were back on the main road.

Back in the Cape area, we surfed several spots between San José del Cabo and Cabo San Lucas – for us they were no-name breaks; if they'd had names we wouldn't have known them and wouldn't have cared. Our approach was simple: drive the coast, see a break that looked good. Stop, surf, move on. Only once did we see anyone else on a board in the water. We skipped that spot; the two guys surfing it were onto a good thing and there was no point in creating a crowd. There were plenty of other places to surf.

In comparison with our epic offshore day on the Pacific side, all the breaks seemed pretty much the same. I do remember carving S-turns up and down the faces of some nice overhead rights somewhere closer to Cabo than to San José. And in Cabo, on the short, steep beach by the hotel on the point, we got in some bodysurfing on very powerful waves outside an extremely nasty shorebreak. Monkey see, monkey do: a tourist saw us in the water and we had to save her when she decided to go for a swim.

The few remaining days were uneventful, and then it was time to go back. When we got to the point of the washout, we pulled off for a moment to take one last look. The flood area was unrecognizable. A couple of weeks of sun had dried everything to the same parched state as before the flood, with the exception of occasional slightly darker spots hinting at residual moisture beneath the surface. The valley was beginning to reclaim itself. The new boulders and dead branches littering the sandy valley floor were already bleaching out beneath the dry summer sky. Among them, a delicate carpet of sprouting grasses and desert plants had appeared in pale, hesitant patches of green. Nearby, small desert birds flitted from bush to bush as if reorienting themselves to the changed terrain. In the sky the omnipresent buzzard wheeled, looking for the remains of animals left over from the storm. There was nothing that spoke of the experience we'd had, nothing but a softly-contoured valley, cloaked in shrubs and fresh green and studded with cactus, rolling gently down toward the invisible sea. It was as if the flood had been part of a dream, or experienced in another life.

We both were keenly aware that nothing like this was ever going to happen to us again. Most people never got one chance like this in life and it would be foolish to hope that we might be granted another. The thought might have left me a little sad, but mostly I felt fortunate. If I may use the word, blessed. We had been to another world, entered mythic time, and returned. Not to tell the tale, but to carry the reality of it inside ourselves, forever.

We drove away without looking back.

Once we left La Paz, the drive back north was uneventful, meaningless, hypnotic. We never considered revisiting the site of our epic surf day; to do so would have been pointless. Whatever we might encounter there would only detract from what we had experienced just a few days before.

We drove north. Road, desert, plants, sun, sky, the clattering of the van, the pungent sweetness of sage tempered by the smoke from Pete's joints and pipe. Once, bored beyond mindlessness, I took a hit from the pipe and watched the road ripple and bend, changing width like an accordion in a polka concert, forming rolling waves, the van working its way up each face and gliding down into the following trough. Pete, ever alert to defects in my driving style, pulled me over and I was relieved of duty until further notice and cut off from foreign substances for the duration. Beyond that, nothing notable. The scenery was exactly as it had been coming south, except we were seeing the other side of everything going north.

The only sign of the recent deluge was a profusion of wildflowers blooming and grasses sprouting hopefully among the rocks and cactus. I suppose that there was some symbolism in this – renovation, renewal, rebirth and all that – but we were indifferent to it. We had been, for a time, in an alternate reality, a universe not parallel to the normal one, but contained within it. Now we were returning to the same ordinary lives that had caused us to set forth in the first place.

By the time we approached Ensenada we were burned out from driving and catatonic with boredom and fatigue. The van was unleashing periodic bursts of angry rattling and clattering like a grumpy raccoon rummaging through a row of trash cans. The sky was a featureless gray shroud, the land dry and dispirited. It was almost over, we were almost home.

During the trip, in the span of a hundred hours we had witnessed the Creation, communed with the sea, been swept to the gates of Hell and come through in one piece. We had each had many moments of magic while surfing, but never a series of experiences like this. And I think we both realized that this adventure marked the end of an era, a high-water mark in our lives that neither of us would ever reach again.

Back in San Diego, I settled into a beach-oriented routine.

1970s, Malibu: Share the barrel

The trifecta of my great Baja adventure – snakes, epic waves, riding a flash flood – was something that I would never top, but there were still memorable experiences to be had. One of those occurred at Malibu.

I had never really "gotten" Malibu, never understood the attraction and the mystique. I'll admit I had never seen Malibu at its best – in fact, I had hardly seen it at all. Growing up surfing in San Diego County, which arguably has the best collection of breaks in California – stretching from the Trestles to the Tijuana Sloughs and including such classic spots as Swamis, Blacks and Windansea – we had little reason to leave the county, let alone drive all the way through L.A. to get to Malibu. From what I had heard it was always crowded, and had been since the '50s. Full of ego and drop-in artists.

OK, yeah, nice point break, a long ride when it was on, but was it worth the crowd and the 'tude? Rincon was at least as good, with more variety – Indicators, River Mouth and the Cove all broke differently and on good days they would connect and you could make it from one through the next – and in the early days far less crowded and less self-conscious. And there were plenty of spots in Southern California – not to mention Hawai'i and Mexico – that offered at least as much overall fun.

But in the 1970s, when I decided to go up and visit a friend who had, for some obscure reason, moved to the Valley, I tossed my board – the same 7'6" Canyon that had gotten me through the flash flood – in the back of my van, figuring I might get a wave somewhere on the way back. Malibu? Why not give it a look?

It was actually a fun evening, a house party with some weird LA music people. The next day I took the canyon road out to the beach. I was up here and maybe I should go check it out. Just in case. Maybe I would get a chance to see what all the hoopla was about.

My personal experience of Malibu was limited to the ballyhooed contest of 1963, which was more a test of riding shin- and ankle-slappers. But on this day, when the beach came in sight I got that disbelieving adrenaline rush you'd get if you just realized you had won the lottery. Huge clean lines, curving majestically along the coast and stretching halfway to the horizon, each one generating a mathematically peeling barrel trailed with white foam. Few things in life are more exciting than stumbling across an epic swell, and even now I get a little short of breath thinking back on it.

The sea floor at Malibu has created three main "points" – actually submerged cobble-and-sand formations – each of which can be a good place to sit and wait for a wave. But on that day there were just two main takeoff spots: to the north near the outside point, and another to the south, closer to the pier.

However, occasionally a wave with just the right size and angle would snap shut on surfers taking off outside, allowing anyone lined up at the middle point to take off unimpeded. That was where I would set up. And no one was there – they were all concentrated at the other two locations. I positioned myself there, and waited.

When my wave came, it was a beauty.

I see that none of the pack at the outer break is going to make it this far, so this wave is mine. I turn and start to paddle. I feel the incredible rush of energy going off all over: outside at the third point, inside at the first point, and the unseen power of the set rolling in behind me. A few quick strokes and I feel the water change around me as the energy of the wave takes over. There's that incredible, sensuous thrill as the tail of the board feels the drive and lift of the wave and responds, God this moment is the best, the first feeling of what's coming, almost like the anticipation of sex.

And then I'm in and up; a quick turn on the face and it's even better than I thought it would be, an endless concave wall, getting more hollow, curling up and over my head. I hear the roaring noise behind me and feel the wind as spray blows past from the collapsing tunnel. I'm in the mouth of the tunnel now and nothing ahead of me but a circle of sky and the distant pier, framed in sky and crystal blue water.

Then ahead of me, a guy from the next takeoff spot dropped in, maybe twenty yards in front of me. I don't think he saw me, or maybe he didn't think I would make the wave, although from what I had heard about Malibu he probably would have dropped in regardless. Anyhow, he did.

By the time he made his turn and pulled up into the fast part of the wave, I was maybe two or three board lengths back. Not a whole lot I could do; the wave was way overhead, I'm flying, and he's doing the same.

He had no idea I was there, so I started yelling, my voice echoing over the rushing crashing sound of the wave collapsing on itself behind me, "Go! Go! Go!" I'd give it a rest and then shout it again, just to be sure he heard me. My main fear was that at some point he'd either turn straight off or bail, and either way there was a high risk that I would run over him and almost literally cut him in half.

We went on like this for what seemed like forever, me shouting intermittently, the wave zipping and roaring and crashing. A couple of times it looked like he was going to try to grab a quick look back to see what was going on behind him, but under the circumstances it just wasn't possible. Finally the wave let up a little and he sliced up the face and over the back, leaving me alone. The next moment the entire wave jacked up and slammed down in a section that must have been fifty feet long, with me inside of it.

When I got back out past the surf line and paddled toward my takeoff spot, I passed a huge, muscular guy who looked like he could have been an NFL linebacker.

"Was that you behind me?"

He didn't sound friendly. He didn't look like he ever sounded friendly.

"Well, yeah," I stammered, "you know, I wanted to be sure you didn't cut back or something..."

Suddenly his ominous scowl broke into a grin.

"Shit! Great ride, man. What's your name?"

I told him, and he turned and yelled to everyone within earshot, "This here's my buddy Dave. Next set comes, he gets his pick. Anyone takes off on him, I'll kick their ass!"

It was, to paraphrase Bogart's line in *Casablanca*, the beginning of a brief but beautiful friendship. I even got invited to a beach party that night. You never know what a drop-in will lead to.

Looking back, I realize that one of the best things about the entire experience was this: I had no expectations. I hadn't looked at any weather maps, and of course there was no internet and no surf reports to turn to. Beyond a vague intuition, I didn't expect that there would be surf. I didn't have any high hopes for Malibu in general. And therefore, coming in sight of Malibu and seeing those incredible waves rolling in was an unbelievable thrill, a real rush. I came into the situation with a truly open mind – you might call it a beginner's mind – and I think that helped me experience it to the fullest.

Late 1970s: Trial by speargun

That Malibu day was something extraordinary, something I'll always remember. It was soon followed by another extraordinary event, one that wasn't so nice.

The beach subculture didn't create damaged souls, but it did seem to attract them – and for some of them even the soothing balm of the sea and the waves wasn't enough to calm their inner demons, at least not for long.

One of these people was Jeff Junkins. Jeff had been a certified wild man even before his tours as a Special Forces sergeant in Vietnam. After his return we occasionally got together at his small rented house a few blocks from the beach, where over beers and the occasional joint he would regale me with tales from the boonies. He had been involved in some seriously heavy stuff, both on the receiving end and the delivery end. Some of it was so disturbing even to him that he would start to talk about it, then abruptly change the subject.

Since his return from Vietnam, Jeff had dabbled in various things, often absurdly dangerous. Every time I saw him, he seemed to have a new bandage or a different sore body part. Once, he showed up at the beach sporting a huge, ugly-looking scab that covered most of his right side – arm, body, and leg. He had tried to set a new world speed record on a skateboard, he told me. He had fallen at over sixty miles an hour. Knowing Jeff, he had probably gone down with style and a big smile on his face. Savoring the rush.

In one of our last conversations he was totally pumped about a new opportunity.

""I got great new gig!" he announced proudly. "It's like Special Ops on the border! Like 'Nam only better: three hots and a cot!"

He had applied to join the Border Force, a special unit created in 1976 to fight the problem of rampant crime along the US-Mexican border.

"It's gonna be a piece of cake! I dress up like an illegal alien and wander around in no-man's land, on the US side of the border. When the bandidos come to rob me, I whip out a gun and a badge, shout "*¡Policía – te arresto!*" and take 'em in!"

It sounded like an idea lifted from the Charles Bronson movie *Death Wish* (which had come out a couple of years earlier), but I was happy for him. He had always been an adrenaline junkie; his war stories always gave him an enthusiasm and spark I rarely saw in him at other times, so if this was what he needed to do, more power to him.

Jeff was dark, almost swarthy, with black hair, and he often sported a thick black moustache. He would have easily fit the profile of a lost would-be immigrant, but I never found out if he got into the Border Force or not, because for me Jeff became too risky.

Due to his war injuries Jeff used a variety of prescription drugs and electric devices to block the sometimes intense pain in his back and legs. He also had been feeling down due to breaking up with his girlfriend. Jeff was sure that someone had stolen her away from him, and he had shared with me his fantasies of finding out who her new boyfriend was – it never occurred to him that maybe there wasn't anyone else, that she just didn't want to go out with him anymore – and gutting him slowly with a dull knife.

Junkins and I were different on the surface but very much alike underneath. There was a simple basis for our otherwise unlikely friendship. He hung out with a totally different crew, people I didn't really know. So what did we have in common? Simply this: we were both trying to prove something, and although our motives and methods were different, they led us to act in certain similar ways.

I spend my formative years – and beyond – trying to be as capable and tough as the guys from the beach who used to kick my ass and make me look like an incompetent twerp in everything I did. Junkins spent his formative years – and beyond – overcompensating for an overly protective mother, trying to prove he was not a mama's boy. We both sought out situations and trajectories that would allow us to prove ourselves, to believe that we were at least equal to our peer group.

The big difference was that I had a powerful aversion to getting locked into anything. No matter what I did, I wanted to be able to quit if I felt like it. Junkins, on the other hand, loved situations where the only way out was through. No backtracking, no quitting. The result was that Junkins was far more extreme than I could ever be. He would do things like try to set the land speed record on a skateboard, where once into it, he had no choice but to try to make the end of the course. And his decision to join Special Forces put him in any number of potentially lethal, past-the-point-of-no-return situations. But underneath, in a weird sense we were kindred spirits.

This is probably why I wasn't shocked or even really surprised by our final encounter. Like so many other things, it happened at the beach.

One activity on surfless days was the beach patrol. You would start at the extreme south end of Windansea beach and walk north along the sand, stopping to chat up the occasional lone girl, or say hello to friends encountered along the way. Each beach had its own crew, some of which overlapped, and we all knew each other. On this day I had barely gotten started when I saw a local girl named Gina.

Gina was not my type – she was undeniably good-looking (she did a lot of modeling) and very kind, but for whatever reason I never imagined going out with her. She was just a casual pal. Today she was as nice as always and we were in the midst of a pleasant conversation about nothing when a shadow fell over me. When I looked up, I saw that the shadow was cast by none other than my good buddy Junkins.

There were three main reasons why I was not happy to see my pal Jeff: (1) he was holding a speargun, (2) it was cocked, (3) he had it aimed right at my chest.

I also noticed that Jeff was not carrying fins, nor a diving mask, nor a snorkel. This lack of equipment indicated that he was not intending to go skin diving or spear fishing. Rather – and taken together with the unusual fact of having a cocked speargun on the beach – it indicated that Jeff was going after different prey. I believe this is what is called "malice aforethought."

I still wasn't sure what the issue was. Was this his idea of humor? Windansea guys were known for extreme practical jokes, and Junkins had told me about some pretty sick pranks that guys had pulled on each other in Vietnam. Was he having some sort of flashback? Whatever it was, Jeff had seen all kinds of extreme action in Vietnam, and judging by the tales he told, shooting me with a speargun wouldn't even register on his top-fifty list.

I was in the very worst possible position for any feeble self-defense or evasion attempt I might have considered making. I was lying on my back, in a partially sitting position with my weight resting on my elbows and one outstretched leg crossed over the other. From this position there was zero chance of taking evasive action or blocking a spear, especially at close range. If Junkins pulled the trigger, I was toast.

His tales of violence in Vietnam and elsewhere flashed through my mind, along with gruesome images of me, skewered like a sea bass, flopping and floundering on the sand in a pool of my own blood and internal organs. I recalled a recent incident in which a scuba diver had mistakenly shot his buddy in the chest with a speargun, generating lurid articles in the local press, replete with graphic descriptions of the writhing victim being transported to the ER with the spear – rusty, dirty and covered with sea slime that mingled with the victim's blood – still sticking out of his body, the barbs having prevented its removal.

In some situations the best thing to say is nothing, and I instinctively grasped the fact that this was one of those times. I concentrated on lying still, appearing relaxed. Stay calm, maintain eye contact. I had no idea what Gina was thinking during all this – and I wasn't about to enrage Junkins further by looking in her direction – but like me she must have sensed that any spoken words would be not only futile, but dangerously counterproductive. She remained silent.

Jeff was quivering with rage.

"So it was *you*! It was *you*, you dirty fuck!"

My mind was racing to keep up with all this. *Me? Me what?* Had someone stolen his stash of drugs, prescription and otherwise? Why blame me?

Suddenly all the pieces fell into place.

Jeff. Gina. Their breakup. The supposed existence of some other guy. All my metabolic processes seemed to stop at once. Junkins thought that I was the mystery man who had stolen his woman, and he was here to inflict retribution.

Stay calm, maintain eye contact. I was alert for any sign that his finger was tightening on the trigger of the spear gun. Even though there was nothing I could do to avoid the spear, hope springs eternal.

The seconds ticked by. Or was it minutes? I have no idea. Like a kangaroo rat cornered by a rattler, I was frozen in the moment, living in the timeless here and now, but anticipating the deadly strike.

Jeff was shaking now, working his way to a potentially explosive rage. Teeth clenched, jaw muscles working, fists tightening on the weapon, arms quivering to the point where the spear gun was trembling like a branch in a high wind. He emitted a couple of guttural animal sounds, halfway between a snarl and a moan. Suddenly he whirled around and with a great primal shriek of rage and frustration he hurled the cocked speargun into the shorebreak, turned toward me one last time, then wheeled away and ran up the beach to the street, possibly to get better weapons.

I decided that my chat with Gina was best left unfinished. I headed on down the beach, feeling that a giant target had been painted on my back and stifling the urge to break into a dead run. When I returned home, I made sure to take a different route.

What made Jeff decide to spare me? I believe it was that he didn't want his theory to be true – didn't want me to be the man who had come between him and Gina. I was at the time his closest friend and confidant, and to decide that I had betrayed him would have been too much, almost a form of suicide. I think that was the only thing between me and a barbed spear right through the sternum.

1970s, Dunemere: It's only water

I escaped from Junkins unscathed, but I didn't get off as lightly at a break called Dunemere.

Like many areas, La Jolla has a few spots that only break – or only break properly – if the surf is significantly bigger than usual, double overhead or thereabouts. One of these is Dunemere. A year or so after the flash flood adventure and a few months after my Malibu experience, I happened to hit it on one of these epic Dunemere days.

The conditions were less than ideal: cloudy, with intermittent rain, and a sideshore wind that made the surface rough and bumpy. It was late afternoon, with weird lighting, and there were some nasty sideshore currents running. But the swell was clean and massive, great long-period lines from the north, emanating from a faraway storm in the Gulf of Alaska.

Once again, my surf buddy was Pete. We got to the beach – each with the same board he had used on the flash flood descent from the Sierra de La Laguna to San José del Cabo – and were instantly stoked. The tide was very low. There was no one out, but four or five surfers were standing in shallow water far out on the flat reef at Little Point, waiting for a lull. We quickly waxed up and hurried out to join them.

At the first lull, we all hit the water. Of the half-dozen or so surfers who launched at the same time, only four of us made it outside. The others, caught by the next set and dragged in a bad direction by the currents, never reappeared.

I've never had much luck chasing peaks or shoulder hopping, so my strategy has always been to watch a set break, set up outside that spot, and wait for a bomb. Quality over quantity. So I carefully observed the first set, went to a point a couple of dozen yards outside of where the biggest wave had broken, and set up. Everyone was pretty far outside, but I was farther out and a bit farther north than the others when the next set – perhaps the set of the day – began to show on the horizon.

Trying to act casual so as not to tip the others off, I took a dozen or so strokes out and northward, wanting to be absolutely sure of being in position. I let the first wave go by, and there it was: the second wave was absolutely perfect and a real monster.

I waited, waited – *Come on, stand up, don't break* – then turned and started paddling. As I did so, the wave behind me blocked out the weak afternoon sun, casting a dark and ominous shadow on me and the water in front of me. It was frankly quite a spooky effect, and for a moment I felt a surge of the old dread from my childhood, hidden deep memories of twilight and clutching waves and no way to get out.

To quiet this unwelcome feeling, I reassured myself with a comforting thought: "*It's only water*." Big mistake. Niagara Falls is only water. I calmed myself so much that without really meaning to, I eased up on my furious big-wave effort.

Pete said afterward that I suddenly slackened my paddling so much, as he put it, "You looked like you were paddling for a four-foot wave."

Several things happened in rapid succession. My speed relative to the wave dropped off. Just as I popped up, high in the wave, the lip pitched. I was tossed, catapulted forward. My board hit the water first, twisted, and rammed a rail into the front of my shoulder as I was hurled down on top of it. A moment later the lip slammed down on me with far more force than it should have. Carried by the lip and driven into me like a ton of cement was a huge floating mass of kelp, hundreds of pounds of it, which had been torn loose by the storm and drifted into the impact zone.

Now I was underwater, my right arm already throbbing and almost useless, held down by hundreds of pounds of tangled kelp, with my board (this day I was using a leash) caught somewhere in the mess. I had about thirty seconds to get out of this or I was in real trouble. Keep calm.

I pushed up on the kelp to push myself down and clear of it, then swam underwater to the edge of the tangle where I could come up for air. I could feel my leash pulling on my ankle but not enough to keep me trapped. The next wave was only a few seconds away, but I managed a couple of deep breaths before I had to dive again. My leash tugged violently as the huge, tangled mass, with my board embedded in it, was pummeled and dragged by the wave. The good news was that the large volume of inert material absorbed some of the energy of the wave and lessened the turbulence of the churning water after the wave broke.

One more wave, and somehow my board popped free of the mess. And the set was over. With my right arm all but useless, there was no question of trying to catch another wave. Obviously I was done surfing for the day.

Now all I had to do was get to shore.

I was going to have to do that on my own since everyone else was still far outside and there was no one on the beach. In fact, in the low clouds, dim light and intermittent rain it was hard to even see the beach, and if anyone had been there it would have been even harder for them to see me. And I was just as invisible to Pete and the other surfers.

I pulled myself up on the board and started paddling as hard as I could with one arm, heading for the shore. I had to weather one other set (which I simply dived under, hoping that my leash would not break) and then I was just outside the shorebreak.

This is where things got interesting.

On the back side of a shorebreak I slipped off my board and tried to get my footing to run up and out of the water, only to find that the side-shore current had carved a trench in the sandy bottom inside the reef, parallel to the beach. The shorebreak was jacking up and breaking on the shoreward lip of this trench. As a result, there was no way to touch bottom outside the shorebreak and no way to avoid it. And it was breaking hard in just inches of water.

As I floated next to my board, I realized that the current was dragging me southward toward an area appropriately known as Rock Pile. If I didn't get out of the water soon, I could end up being beaten to shreds on the rocks. So with the next set I abandoned any pretense of a controlled exit from the water. Still in the water next to my board, I undid my leash to avoid tripping and rode the surge right into the shorebreak. Stay flat, stay low. I took quite a pounding but the wave washed me up onto the sand, still in one piece and with my board.

By the time I got home my right arm from the shoulder to the elbow was black with internal bleeding from the impact with my board. It was weeks before I could use the arm normally again. As usual, it never occurred to me to seek medical treatment – what are they going to do, sew the muscle together? Just put some ice on it, take it easy, and gradually work back to full use of the arm. It's amazing how well that works when you're young.

Late 1970s: End of the line

Sometimes it takes a perfect storm of circumstances to force major change.

The breaks I had known and loved since high school were starting to get crowded and full of 'tude. This was unpleasant to be around. And, as I discovered when my elbow was shattered in a spearing incident, more than just unpleasant. Downright dangerous.

Some of the old time Windansea crew were quitting surfing due to all this, but my solution was to change the times and places where I surfed. After all, I still had my idea of the perfect life: teaching night school at community college, days free to surf, living in a picturesque – and cheap – cottage just steps from outstanding surfing, bodysurfing and skin diving.

I was in my mid thirties, at the top of my game and on top of the world. Through hard work and repetition, I had overcome my youthful clumsy incompetence. In the process, I had pretty much conquered my childhood fear of gnarly ocean conditions. (I decided that the Dunemere experience was an anomaly.) I was riding high.

If I had been able to continue, I might well have painted myself into a corner from which I might never have escaped. If I had owned a crystal ball, it would have revealed that within a decade rents would soar, the cottage I lived in would be torn down for a condo project, and housing prices would rise beyond my reach. Ignorance may be bliss, but it was leading me into a very unblissful situation. More importantly, I was living a seductive but very narrow existence, seemingly idyllic but actually stultifying.

In any case the final decision was out of my hands.

My back had been bad for as long as I could remember. In junior high, I remember sitting in the lineup waiting for a wave, a constant dull pain in my lower spine. I just assumed that everyone's back hurt when they were surfing. It was just another thing to get used to. But that's not the way it worked – and it wasn't just my back.

I had subjected by body – back, knees, shoulders, wrists, elbows – to severe strains and outright physical abuse (surfing, skiing, martial arts) for years, and it was catching up with me. To make matters worse, my joints seem to have been lined with an inferior brand of cartilage, the assembly done by a cut-rate contractor who made his profit by skimping on quality. Instead of surfing, I probably would have been better off if I had fallen in love with chess or bird-watching or beekeeping. But we can't always choose what we love.

The pain in my lower spine when paddling prone had become more intense and more frequent until I couldn't take it anymore. The tipping point was a small day at a beach break. By the time I got to the lineup my back was so bad that instead of sitting up I had to roll off the board and float limply in the water until I recovered enough to kick my way in, lying face up in the water.

My orthopedic surgeon – the fact that I had an orthopedic surgeon should have told me something – put it this way:

"Think tires. There are tires that are good for a hundred thousand miles, and there are tires that are good for thirty thousand miles. You got the thirty-thousand-mile version."

I think he overestimated: my guess would have been twenty thousand, tops. Either way, my lower back was done.

Since I couldn't paddle a surfboard anymore, I reverted to bodysurfing. Luckily I liked bodysurfing and I still lived just a short way from Boomer, the premier bodysurfing beach in San Diego.

My favorite takeoff was still submarine style. I loved every moment: the sensation of total involvement as the energy of the wave reaches you, the boulders on the sea floor suddenly rushing past as you are driven forward, the sensation of being thrust upward as the wave jacks up and hurls you out through the face. You're almost part of the wave. It's not board surfing, but it's a moment like no other – living for a brief period in the underwater world and then being reborn into the world of air and sky. This I could live with.

Until I couldn't. No matter how I swam out or took off or rode the wave, no matter how I ended the ride, my neck was now becoming my new major problem. After a couple of tuck and flip endings on a big day at Boomer, I was sitting on a beachside bench watching the waves and suddenly felt a stabbing pain as if someone had inserted an ice pick in my neck. Diagnosis: bone spurs, arthritis, degeneration of a disc or two. Basically, my lower back problems reproduced higher up my spine.

By now it was dawning on me that my problem wasn't just a matter of cheap tires. The whole machine was falling apart, the components frazzled and frayed from a combination of design flaws, poor construction, misuse and excessive wear and tear. This time it was really over. I had no more fallback positions.

I had already been forced to quit martial arts, skiing, tennis, golf, and even long bike rides. Now it looked like I might have to give up all forms of surfing.

Like many endings in life, it wasn't a quick, clean break. I rationalized. My spine would calm down and I would delude myself into thinking I was cured. Then it would flare up again. Finally I had to face the inevitable, and the love affair that I had with waves since I was ten years old was over.

But not really. What you have experienced becomes part of you, forever.

A few years ago, an off-beat movie was released in Japan. Titled in English as *Afterlife*, it had a simple premise: after dying, the spirit of the departed – looking and acting exactly as he or she had in life – proceeds to a supernatural pre-heavenly bureaucracy. There, assisted by counselors, the deceased must select one memory to have and experience for all eternity, to the exclusion of all others.

I always thought the best memory would be of riding a wave.

It's a beautiful day, and you've just dropped into a smooth, glassy wall, blue-green face fringing white a few feet above your head. You rocket down the face, gathering speed, then make your turn. Ahead of you, ecstasy: a perfect, endless wall with no one and nothing in your way, for you to ride forever.

One moment, pure joy. The next, life everlasting.

What a memory to carry into eternity!

Endless wall - John Ahlbrand photo

Waves aside, just being on the ocean, alone on a surfboard, had given me a lifetime of mental images, any of which could have been a candidate for permanence.

Fish shining like a shower of silver coins as they mill aimlessly round a reef. An enormous sea lion coming up with an octopus in its mouth, so close you can hear the chomping and crunching as it tries to subdue the catch and reduce it to something that can be swallowed. The bright wary red-eyed stare of a cormorant that surfaces next to your board, assesses your intentions, and dives down again.

Squadrons of pelicans, lumbering across the waves like torpedo bombers, with an agile seagull or two as fighter cover. The aerial acrobatics of terns and gulls fighting over a fish. The elegance and grace of snowy egrets poised in watchful waiting on the shore. More pelicans, transformed into ballistic missiles diving with folded wings to blast an unwary fish below the surface.

Porpoises and dolphins moving along in their undulating unhurried glide, or leaping from the water for the sheer sport of it. Once, the wheezing exhalation of a baby whale so close behind me that I thought it was an asthmatic surfer. A curious baby seal popping up at intervals like a puppy, eager to play but too shy to do so. A lone seagull or cormorant in full flight, pulling up slightly and readjusting its feathers by shaking its entire body like a person struggling to put on a balky overcoat, then flapping resolutely onward.

The crystalline aquamarine of a calm sea, the surface like rippling satin. The same sea a gunmetal gray pocked with raindrops that ride up and over the incoming swells.

It's all beauty and power and special magic that can't be experienced in any other place or in any other way. You have to be there, and you have to be there when it happens. It's not there for you, but you for it.

And now, for me that was all in the past. I was done. All I had left was memories. So I embarked on the next phase of my life.

PART III: CAST ADRIFT

1980: Abandon ship

As if it weren't bad enough that I was being forced out of the waves, I finally had to face the fact that my whole laid-back lifestyle was done for.

The Vietnam War was over, but it had left inflation and unemployment in its wake. The OPEC-induced oil shocks of 1973 and 1979 made matters worse. The US economy went into a weird flat spin. They called it stagflation – a stagnant, low-growth economy with high unemployment and high inflation. Rents near the beach began rising astronomically and rental cottages were being torn down to make way for condos. At the same time, schools were cutting back and itinerant teachers like me were the first to go. Suddenly, what remained of my happy little beach life was about to go under; it was time to abandon ship.

Someone suggested that I try a local business group that was looking for a new international director (whatever that entailed; no one seemed to know). Right up my alley, more or less. The immediate problem was that I didn't own a suit, a decent necktie, a dress shirt, or even a pair of leather shoes. I had gotten away with academic dress-down for too many years.

If I wanted to make the big time, a baggy tweed jacket, a ratty knitted tie, worn corduroy slacks and scuffed Hush Puppies with moth-eaten socks weren't going to cut it. But I didn't have enough money to buy all the stuff I needed.

My solution was used clothing, or what is euphemistically called resale clothing.

For a fraction of the new price I was able to get a full outfit: three-piece suit – *de rigueur* at the time – dress shirt, nice tie, shoes and even socks. The best part was the suit: some guy exactly my size had parted with a gray pinstriped number, tailor-made (MADE IN ROMANIA, the label proudly proclaimed) and a perfect fit. I was ready to make the big time!

That suit may actually have gotten me the job. It was summer, and the temperature in the Executive Director's poorly-climate-controlled office was hovering in the mid- to high eighties. The suit was wool. Thick, tightly-woven wool, excellent no doubt for harsh Romanian winters (I had visions of wolves howling hungrily outside the castle gates, beyond the drawbridge) but soporific on a warm and unusually muggy Southern California summer afternoon.

The Executive Director was given to making sweeping statements followed by long, expectant pauses, during which I sat stolidly in my chair, barely conscious, my brain empty of everything except discomfort, giddy with heat and silently praying for the ordeal to pass. He later told me the long silences were a test and the fact that I hadn't tried to fill them with nervous chatter had convinced him I was the man for the job. He also admired the fact that I had showed up even though I was clearly running a fever, as evidenced by the rivers of sweat pouring off my face. A man of courage, a man of resolve, a man not easily deterred!

I was hired on the spot.

I had just been launched in a new direction. And I was making a lot more money than I ever had before.

I was also stuck in a nine-to-five situation, but that was actually a good thing. The free time that teaching had left me to surf had become a dead weight hanging heavy on my days, like rotten fruit clinging stubbornly to a withered branch. It was time to cut myself loose and move on. I went international again.

Using my new job as a springboard, I got a series of public and private sector assignments that took me to Mexico, then Asia. I lived for several years in Korea and Japan with side trips to China and Hong Kong, Taiwan and Bangkok and Singapore. I was crisscrossing the Pacific at 39,000 feet and never once looked down to check the waves.

I had experiences that were fascinating and illuminating and amusing and tragic and exciting. Most of the time there was so much going on that I didn't feel as deprived as I would have otherwise. My first day in country in Korea, the street in front of the Embassy where I was assigned was a welter of riot police, demonstrators, flying stones and the occasional Molotov cocktail. Rioters hurled rocks and firebombs at the police in front of the embassy, right outside my office. Neighborhoods filled with tear gas.

In addition to the big stuff, there were small personal adventures. One night, returning from a picnic in the countryside, I came across a column of ROK soldiers milling around the road in the dark, one of their number writhing on the pavement while his buddies took turns kicking the motorcyclist who had run into their column in the dark. The evening ended up with me covered with blood from the victim as I carried him and two M16s – his and a random one that somebody had tossed into my car at the scene – into a hospital, which sent the staff screaming out the back door, convinced that I was a deranged Rambo berserker on a killing spree.

On a fine spring weekend I was taken into ROK military custody while running on a deserted beach which turned out to be a camouflaged ROK commando base. I wasn't released until the CO satisfied himself that I didn't have any American cigarettes for him to confiscate.

An anti-government demonstration turned into a riot, with me in the middle. The day I left Seoul we had to drive through a shower of stones hurled by angry student protestors who had closed the freeway to the airport. Never a dull moment.

Japan, my next posting, was tamer in some ways, but it had its moments. Radicals firebombed a railway station near my office. There were occasional home-made rocket attacks on targets like the airport and the US Embassy. The Yakuza used a samurai sword to slice up an American ex-Marine who dared to set up a flower stall without paying enough protection money in front of the station at the end of my daily commute.

All this was exciting, but none of it provided enough distraction to fill the void left by the loss of surfing. In Korea, I sought out rivers and streams, anything with moving water. In Japan I haunted the area along the shores of Osaka Bay and occasionally rented a small sailboat. Anything to get out on the water, or at least close to it.

No doubt I was seeking international adventures partly as a substitute, a vain attempt to fill a hole that kept growing no matter what I did. For a time, the tactic seemed to work. The life I was leading was so interesting – living overseas is not always fun, but you learn something new every day – that it distracted me from the aching void left by my forced separation from my childhood love. But increasingly I felt deprived. No matter how busy I was, I missed the water and the waves.

In addition, the intermittent excitement couldn't conceal the fact that the nine-to-five rat race still wasn't for me. This had nothing to do with the ocean; it was simply that although I could fit in, I didn't belong. I was still the square peg trying to conform to a round hole.

Meanwhile, my love life over the years had been like an extended country western song, filled with cheatin' hearts and lyin' eyes, faithless loves and breakin' up and movin' on down the road.

Finally this changed: in the skies above Asia a chance encounter introduced me to a woman who was intelligent, well-educated, multilingual and willing to put up with my aging ex-surfer-dude nonsense. Which was a good thing, because after a decade of trying to fit in to corporate and bureaucratic frameworks and stay away from what sometimes bordered on outright corruption, I realized I'd had enough.

1991: The sound of waves

In a fit of altruistic optimism, I took a job teaching bilingual courses in a town I'll call Alcachofa, at a tiny high school teetering on the brink of extinction. To stave off closure, the student body was augmented by cast-offs and rejects from nearby districts in order to keep enrolment above the district minimum of one hundred kids. I thought I was motivated by my love of teaching and doing the right thing; I suspect that being near the sea might have had more to do with it.

I was a long way from my lost paradise of teaching nights and surfing during the day. But it wasn't all bad. The Central California coast is beautiful, and magic struck at times like lightning, unplanned, unbidden, and without warning. Driving to Alcachofa to teach one morning, I was traveling south along the coast on Highway 1. The sea was shrouded in fog, and I could hear the muffled waves, as if from far away, as a background to the CD playing in the van.

As you approach San Gregorio Creek from the north, the coast highway curves slightly away from the ocean and goes up a hill; at the crest it turns again to head back down toward the narrow beach where the creek spills into the sea. Now the only sounds were the strains of a Beethoven piano concerto, which came to a crescendo just as I reached the crest of the hill and the rising sun hit the fog-filled valley below me and turned it into a swirling river of spun gold. It was like seeing the face of God.

•   •   •

Sometimes the face of God was too close for comfort, and after I had a couple of near-misses with death on the foggy two-lane coastal highway, we moved from Redwood City to a cabin in the redwoods up the canyon from town, with a V-shaped sliver of ocean visible a couple of miles away at the bottom of the valley. At night you could hear the mountains breathing as the wind sighed through the tops of the redwoods and the moon created strange radiographic images through lazy rivers of wispy clouds.

Alcachofa had beauty. It was drowning in beauty. The school was surrounded by fields of straw flowers in cheerful pastel shades of blue, pink, yellow. The coastline was rugged, the sea tumultuous and raw and wild. A creek flowing into the sea had created a region of dunes and a sandbar. As the creek washed down sand and sediment from the hills, the bar would thicken and rise until it blocked access to the sea. Behind this barrier a large lagoon would form, building higher and higher until a combination of pressure from the water and the action of tides and waves from the other side would weaken the bar. Then a portion of the bar would give way and millions of gallons of water would flow into the ocean, after which the entire process would repeat itself.

"Welcome to Brigadoon" they said when I was hired. They must have seen a different version of the movie. The actual situation was more like a combination of *Blackboard Jungle, God's Little Acre* and *Peyton Place*. Dealing with the school, the kids and the parents was like being an extra in a B-movie about self-destructive delinquents.

Before and after school, and in the halls between classes, pandemonium reigned. Chicano gangsta wanna-be's faced off with junior rednecks. In the hallway, one kid attacked another with a chain. One of the girl students moved in with her grandmother because she kept waking up in the night with her mother's boyfriend on top of her. An eighth-grade boy hit another kid over the head with a typewriter.

Two tenth-grade girls propositioned me.

"Your wife's a stewardess, right? We can come up and do you when she's out of town."

"What? Are you crazy? You shouldn't be talking to me like that! You're just high school kids."

They rolled their eyes and toyed with their hair and wiggled their tight little tenth-grade butts.

"That didn't stop the shop teacher."

Shop teacher? I thought. *What shop teacher?*

"The school doesn't have a shop teacher," I said.

They looked at me patronizingly.

"Well, duh! He's in jail for statutory rape."

As a teacher I was supposed to provide guidance to students. But what kind of guidance would work here? With these kids there was nothing off limits or out of bounds.

Another student – not one of mine, thank God – got a possible skull fracture when another kid jumped him and smashed his head against the floor, just like in the movies. One of my students got twenty-five to life for shooting his girlfriend to death as she held their baby in her arms. The local watering hole had a small patch on the front wall, marking the spot where a disgruntled drunk had exited the place, turned around and fired a single shot through the wall, killing an innocent patron at the bar.

Amidst all this mayhem the gaily colored cornflowers bloomed, the creek burbled happily within earshot of my classroom, and the surf roared and thundered against the nearby shore. The lagoon filled and emptied as it had for thousands of years. In the evenings, the eruption of Mount Pinatubo, seven thousand miles away, turned the sunsets into wild spectacles of color: neon magentas, brilliant purples, flaming reds.

There was mystery and menace and drama: when big north swells came rolling down from the Gulf of Alaska, huge waves – twenty feet or more in height – jacked up and broke on a deep reef half a mile offshore. Once on the beach I came across the corpse of an enormous leatherback turtle with a huge bite taken out of it by a great white shark.

None of this had any effect on the behavior of the locals. The kids used to ask me why I wasn't bored; I could only wonder how they could be so immune to the magic around them.

One of the kids wheelied his motorcycle out of the school parking lot, to the cheers of his friends, roared off toward the nearest crossroads at full throttle, and T-boned an ancient sedan full of young children. The middle-aged woman driving the car never saw him coming. She took the full impact of the bike as it embedded itself in the her door; the kid flipped over the roof and landed on a hillside above the road, startling a group of cows from their Zen-like contemplation of existence in the shade of a small tree. Both the kid and his victim were airlifted to the nearest hospital.

I could have been next.

One afternoon, driving up the winding road to our cottage after yet another frustrating staff meeting that ignored the failing educational process at the school, I found myself accelerating needlessly on the straighter stretches and coming perilously close to losing control on the curves. I envisioned myself keeping the pedal to the metal on a curve, maintaining a straight course, flying off the road and soaring over the fields below, finally crashing in a ball of flame. It didn't seem like a totally bad idea – maybe the self-destructive biker kid was onto something. Anything to escape the madness.

I ate more, drank more, exercised less. I haunted the beach in my free time, gazing at the water, letting the roar of the Central Coast surf pour into my ears, hoping it would somehow fill my soul. It wasn't enough. When we went to Davenport or Santa Cruz or Half Moon Bay and I saw people surfing, I got the same dead sick feeling that you get when you see your lover arm-in-arm with someone else, laughing and kissing and having a great time without you.

I knew I had reached a new low point when one night I found myself sitting outdoors beneath the moon, swilling cheap red wine out of a jug and taking random potshots at redwood trees with a .38. Something had to change before I cracked up completely.

In the morning I awoke to find that my perception had shifted. At school, I saw the kids in a new light. They were part of a tiny local subculture with its own internal logic that was, within its narrow confines, adequate. There was a sort of balance. Most of them were going nowhere and felt fine with that. The few who were going somewhere, young as they were, knew that all this was just temporary, so they rode it out. My best bet was to emulate them. Or get out.

I started scanning the *San Francisco Chronicle* for jobs.

My lifeboat was a teaching job at a college in Japan. Somehow my wife, by now a legitimate contender for sainthood, agreed to go along with yet another change. How can you thank someone who has been with you through thick and thin, for better and for worse? She could have refused, or simply abandoned ship. She wasn't searching or compensating or yearning or deprived. Luckily she knew Japan and liked it.

1992: Land of the Rising Sun, Part II

I was teaching at a private college in Kawasaki, across the Tama River from Tokyo. Feeling deprived, drinking beer and sake, eating *nikuman* and *takoyaki*, watching sumo on TV. Getting out of shape.

The Tama River, which flows into Tokyo Bay near Haneda Airport and separates Tokyo from Kawasaki and from Yokohama, was the closest accessible body of moving water.

Like most large Japanese rivers, it has been channeled and landscaped over the centuries. A central channel, fairly deep and not very wide, handles flow in normal times. Dotted with deeper pools and lined with natural riverine vegetation, it is a nesting and gathering place for all sorts of waterfowl and other birds. On both sides of this channel extends a broad area of varying width – up to a hundred yards or so in places – to handle extreme flood conditions. Because it is always at risk of being flooded, it contains no permanent structures. Instead, it is devoted to community gardens, soccer and baseball playing fields, and the occasional tennis court. The final feature is a pair of thick stone-clad earthen embankments, one on each side of the river, with paved paths on top for pedestrians, bicyclists, and joggers.

Within a week I had sought it out and spent as much time as possible haunting its banks. Every weekend morning I would ride my bicycle through the back streets and alleys of suburban Kawasaki to the river, where I would spend a good part of the day riding up or down stream according to my fancy.

Upstream featured more amenities: small, funky shoreline restaurants that appeared to be left over from the 1930s, and dams and even a place where one could rent rowboats for a couple of hours on the water.

Downstream was perhaps more interesting: there was a large baseball field where professional baseball teams sometimes practiced and a regulation-size track for exercising racehorses. If you went far enough you came to Haneda Airport on the Tokyo side, and the Morinaga chocolate factory on the Yokohama side. And if you knew how to follow the network of three-hundred-year-old barge canals, now converted to streams with footpaths, you could reach the Tsurumi River and go back a hundred years in time as you ascended upstream toward the mountains.

I was interested in my work, interested in my students. I loved Japan – the food, the language, the atmosphere, the way the entire country functioned smoothly and flawlessly and seamlessly, like an enormous precision timepiece. And yet, underneath I was bored and frustrated and feeling deprived. I missed the ocean, I missed surfing. At some point I might have tried going over Nachi Falls in a barrel if the opportunity had been presented in an attractive way. Anything to ride moving water.

1993: The Great Kawasaki Kayak Expedition

In this midst of this empty, surfless existence, I discovered that one of my students was in a kayak club. Instantly my mind began to whirl. Salvation! What was a river but an endless moving wave? What was a kayak but a clumsy, heavy surfboard? And no worries about back problems – you could paddle it sitting down! I dropped hints until I was invited to join the group for a weekend on the upper Tama River.

A week later I reaped the harvest of what I had sown. I had taken the train up to Tachikawa, then changed for the little two-car electric that ran up the mountain. The rail line climbed along one side of the narrow valley occupied by the river. Rushing water, pine-clad slopes, deep blue sky. The river was clean and sparkling and coursed along its rocky bed as cheerfully and energetically as a squad of Japanese cheerleaders. Like the country itself: orderly and chipper and moving right along. I'd been through a flash flood in Mexico, ridden gnarly waves on shallow reefs. This would be a piece of cake. The next best thing to surfing.

I reached the station. The one street of the little station village was filled with light and the scent of pines and the sound of the river.

The kayak club cabin was rustic. Sliding doors, tatami on the floor, one room for boys, one for girls, toilets and shower outside, like in a campground in the U.S.

The boys were pretty much like college-age surf rats in California. The tatami floor was littered with empty sake and beer bottles, and they spent the evening watching videos of extreme kayaking: going over waterfalls, descending raging rivers at full flood, braving rapids filled with massive jagged boulders, riding the wave above each boulder before breaking free and going on to the next. They excitedly oohed and aahed and cheered every radical drop and extreme move. I modestly refrained from sharing my own exploits with them.

The next morning I found myself in two feet of icy mountain river water, trying to cram myself into a kayak built for an average Japanese adult. That is to say, a person several inches shorter than I am. Well before my body settled into the seat, my feet had hit the inside of the bow. With an apologetic shrug to my student hosts, I started to raise myself back out of the hull. If the kayak doesn't fit, don't try to wear it.

But this was Japan, and the rules were different. The applicable rule, Japan's Golden Rule, the overriding rule in almost every conceivable situation, is simple, and it is programmed permanently and indelibly into the brain of every Japanese.

NEVER QUIT.

This means, among other things, that once you have agreed to do something, there is no circumstance, no act of God, no force of Nature that is compelling enough to override your commitment. Every agreement is a promise, and every promise is irrevocable. To express the Japanese Golden Rule another way,

DO OR DIE.

In ancient times, this was interpreted quite literally. Failure to carry through on a promise or obligation led to ritual suicide, *seppuku* in formal Japanese, commonly known to the West as *hara-kiri*. Even today, one hears of people killing themselves over a real or imagined failure to do their duty.

My students, bless their hearts, were not about to inflict such terminal resolution on me. Instead, they helped me honor my promise. Before I could extricate myself from the cramped kayak, a pair of burly kayak clubbers (rugby players, perhaps, or members of the judo team) grabbed my shoulders and jammed me down until I was seated.

My feet were being flattened against the forward bulkhead, the base of my spine was wedged into the seat back, my knees were crushed so hard against the top of the kayak that I thought I detected a bulge in the rigid plastic deck. I was in, and nothing short of dynamite or a wheel puller was going to get me out. At first the pain was excruciating, but within moments a paralytic numbness set in. I gritted my teeth and decided to go along with my hosts. Besides, there was no way I was going to be able to get out without help. Best stay on their good side until the ordeal was over.

At first we practiced paddling in the shallow backwater where we had launched. Because of my surfing experience I was used to sitting on a narrow floating object in moving water, so I progressed without difficulty to the next phase, paddling back and forth across a moderate current.

I moved as one with my craft – in fact, by now I was one with my craft, flesh fused with plastic. My feet, legs and knees were without feeling, and my hips and lower spine were starting to melt into blissful numbness. But my upper body was still functioning, and in the finest Japanese tradition I gave no indication that anything was amiss. Why bother? No one would have cared.

We moved on to the next stage: paddling laterally through the small wave made by the current rushing against a submerged rock. As guest of honor, I was invited to go first. To the applause of my students, I made it across and started back. Then – I choose to blame it on my inert lower extremities – I capsized.

In moments of intense experience, there is often an enhanced ability to perceive and remember detail. I'm not referring to situations in which time appears to slow down, although that phenomenon does exist. Rather, the mind divides and perceives more clearly the information pouring in. In other words, you pay closer attention to everything instead of filtering out the majority of what you perceive. It's like a digital camera set on maximum resolution – the higher the number of pixels in the image, the more you can enlarge without the image getting blurry. Something like this happened after I capsized.

There was a moment of confusion, followed by a crystalline clarity. I had kept my eyes open. My first thought was admiration at the amazing purity and transparency of the water. Huge boulders glided past me as I drifted slowly downstream, numb feet and legs encased in the capsized kayak. Mountain trout finned and undulated about, keeping a wary eye on me. They didn't seem terribly worried, perhaps because they knew they could stay under water longer than I could.

One thing surfing had done for me was get me accustomed to the experience of being held under water. Whether getting wiped out by a wave or getting caught by one when paddling out, on a big day you got used to involuntary oxygen deprivation as the roiling whitewater slammed you and churned you up and down like laundry in an industrial washing machine. It was no use trying to swim. The forces were too great and the bubble-filled water was a poor medium for swimming. Fighting it was just a waste of precious air. All you could do was relax, loosen up, and wait until it was over.

Now, in the river, I was able to keep calm and assess the situation. It was good that the water was cold. It would slow my metabolism and allow the oxygen in my blood to last longer. I wasn't concerned about drowning. Yet.

I tried to push myself out of the kayak, but the judo team had done their job well: I was jammed in tightly and every effort I made was not only useless but sent skewers of pain through my knees as they were forced up against the inside of the hull.

I floated majestically on, still inverted. Each boulder in the stream bed was outlined with a nimbus, a layer of diffraction created by the invisible compression of the current. Or was it the combined effects of hypothermia and hypoxia?

I wondered what the hull looked like from the surface. A floating blue log? The students knew that I was in there. By now, I was sure, they were paddling frantically toward me to effect a rescue.

But this was Japan. Rule Two of Japanese culture, a corollary of Rule One, was just as simple:

YOU GOT YOURSELF INTO IT,

YOU GET YOURSELF OUT OF IT.

I needed to concentrate harder on saving myself. I had kept trying to push up out of the kayak, but I couldn't get enough leverage to pry myself out. In addition, my arms and shoulders were weak from my years of enforced idleness and every shove sent needles of pain through my elbows.

I'd heard that Inuit and skilled recreational kayakers could right a capsized craft by bending at the waist, laying the upper torso flat against the top of the kayak and rolling to the side. I tried it, without success. Were you supposed to bend backward, or maybe sideways? I tried both of these but stabs of pain in my lower spine nipped my efforts in the bud. And by now oxygen was becoming a problem. I remained calm and quit moving to conserve my dwindling supply while I figured out what to do.

I considered trying to grab a boulder and somehow use it to push myself upright, but by now the boulders were rushing more quickly toward my face in the clear cold water, forcing me to bob and weave with my head, like a boxer. Technically, of course, my face was rushing toward them, but if we made contact the end result would be the same.

If I stayed like this much longer, I was going to end up with a boulder embedded in my skull. Or run out of oxygen, whichever occurred first. I felt a slight dizziness, accompanied by a sudden overwhelming urge to inhale. I was running out of time. It was now or never.

Putting one hand on each side of the cockpit opening, I put everything I had into one last mighty desperate shove and managed to slide my body out of the kayak like a foot sliding out of a too-tight boot. As I did so I felt my cartilage-challenged kneecaps being crushed against the underlying bone. It was like being stepped on by a horse wearing golf shoes.

By the time I freed myself and got some air into my lungs, I was standing in icy waist-deep water far downstream from my starting point. Here the river was rimmed by low cliffs, vertical but broken by clefts and ledges. Below I could see some serious rapids. The current made it impossible to wade upstream. I braced my feet against the boulders and clung to the kayak and the paddle. In spite of being half-numb with cold, my knees throbbed complainingly as the blood returned to them.

My students were staring at me from upstream. I had saved myself from drowning; surely now they would help me. After all, I was not only their guest, I was their teacher, their *sensei*.

Unfortunately, the Darwinian imperatives of Japanese culture were more powerful than mere social niceties or humanitarian urges. The overriding obligation was to remain true to the objectives of the group. Only the weak and the cowardly abandon the mission. The weak link shall be cast into the scrap heap. I had forfeited my rank in the hierarchy.

The students began to shout and gesture in Japanese. The distance and the steady rushing and burbling of the river made it impossible to make out any words, but their meaning was clear: they expected me to get back upstream to my starting point.

But how? No one could have paddled upstream against that current, and wading back in waist-deep water over round, slippery boulders of various sizes while carrying a kayak and a paddle would have been a major challenge for even a young super-jock. Which I was not.

The longer I stood there, the more their voices and gestures became ominously imperative, with overtones of irritation, impatience, and contempt. I was rapidly transitioning from guest and teacher to the most reviled of beings, the lowest of the low: a quitter.

Well, so what? From my point of view, their attitude was outrageous. Their demands were absurd. I was old enough to be their grandfather, and I had reinjured my surgically diminished knees, and they had provided me with a kayak that was far too small. Whatever happened to respect for elders, compassion for the handicapped, contributory negligence? They were damned lucky I had managed to get out alive. They owed me some assistance.

But inside I knew that if I didn't continue the ordeal, I might as well go sleep with the fishes, or throw myself on my sword. Something – maybe the Devil, maybe cultural insensitivity; I'll never know – made me say it anyhow.

"I can't," I shouted back in Japanese while doing my own pointing and gesturing. "I damaged my knees."

This only made things worse. When the going in Japan gets tough, the tough get going. They don't make excuses. Excuses are the refuge of cowards, weaklings, and scoundrels. The students turned their backs on me and began wading through the shallows to the launching point.

Despite all the evidence and all the experience I'd had in Japan over the years, my American mind still refused to accept reality. Instead of feeling abandoned, I was stupid enough to feel encouraged. I told myself that I must have misinterpreted their meaning. Obviously, they were going to leave their kayaks on the shore and come down to help me out.

As they left the water, shouldered their kayaks and began marching back toward the clubhouse, I realized that I was on my own. Natural selection in action.

Somehow I managed to clamber up the cliff, half carrying, half dragging the kayak, bracing myself with the paddle. By the time I staggered back to the clubhouse with the kayak, scraped and bloody and frozen, everyone had dried and changed clothes. As I approached the door they were talking and laughing, but when I came in silence filled the room, as heavy and thick as curdled soya milk.

Japan is like an enormous symphony orchestra and harmony is all important. Living in Japan is like playing a complex piece of music. If you've studied the score and practiced and learned the notes, the music flows effortlessly from your fingers, and you're part of the harmony. If not, you will be, as the Japanese saying goes, pounded down like a protruding nail. This can make your stay in Japan very unpleasant. The kayak club had taken another option. As a nail, I protruded so far and was made of such inferior metal that they simply yanked me out.

I knew my welcome was over. For me, it was time to go home. I dried off, changed clothes, shouldered my overnight bag and headed for the station. Better to leave than wait to be banished. The worst thing was that I had really wrecked my knees; they felt like they had been filled with ground glass. I had given my all to try to live up to the standards of the group and this was all I had to show for it.

I kind of wished I had just let the damn kayak go.

1996: Yankee goes home

On our return from Japan after four years in country, we lived on the Peninsula and I landed a full-time college teaching job. We joined a Redwood City sailing club to get out on the water. (My wife was no surfer, but she loved sailing and loved the sea.) We bought a small skiff with a little 5-horse outboard and I spent hours exploring the snaking sloughs and channels in the southwest portions of San Francisco Bay. I drifted past narrow mudflats surrounded by sedge, past herons and egrets and seals. I came under attack by terns nesting on a small sandy islet that they were determined to defend against all comers large and small. I felt the ebb and flow of the tides probing in from the distant ocean.

Once we took the skiff to Sausalito and launched it with the vague notion of going over to Tiburon to explore. There was a strong sea running that day and in the channel between Tiburon Point and Angel Island we encountered beautiful clean swells about six feet high. Once a surfer, always a surfer – I took off on a swell and we rode it through the channel. It was pretty dicey, and only a lot of well-timed work with the tiller and the throttle kept the boat from broaching and flipping both of us into the frigid, sharky waters of San Francisco Bay. I was smart enough to catch one swell and leave it at that.

On weekends we would drive our van over the Santa Cruz Mountains and park all day by the beach at Montara, backing up with the open tailgate facing the sea, and read and rest and drink in the salt air and the sound of the waves beating endlessly on the rocks. Or down to Pacific Grove to be by the shore, or even, on occasion, to Port San Luis where at sunset we watched the daily afternoon feeding frenzy in the cove – seals, dolphins, gulls, terns, pelicans and fish all roiling the water and filling the skies with frantic activity in one last attempt to eat or go hungry, survive or be eaten, before the sun came smashing into the sea and put a stop to the mayhem. And in the indigo evenings we would bed down in the van and camp all night on the dock, the breakwater teeming with barking seals and crashing surf, as the moon towed its net of shimmering stars overhead.

The sea was a constant point of reference. We went to the City and looked down at the roiling sea below Fort Funston. We drank coffee at the Cliff House, at a window table overlooking Ocean Beach, and watched endless lines of swell sweep in from somewhere in the Pacific and crash onto the submerged sand bars in great explosions of foam. We explored Pacific Grove and watched the windows in Santa Cruz across the bay turn to flame in the late afternoon light. We went to New Brighton and camped within sight and earshot of the surf and walked on the beach and watched the waves.

We spent a lot of time on and around the water, but for me it was never enough. But at least proximity to the magic and majesty of the sea inspired me to whip myself back into decent physical condition. My timing couldn't have been better.

Our next move was almost enough to make me believe in destiny or fate. I still couldn't surf, and I had no reason to believe I ever would. I was over sixty years old and I had been out of surfing for over twenty years. My joints were a mess. On bad days I had to use a cane to get around. But when my wife was transferred to LAX, I applied for a job at Santa Barbara City College, overlooking the sea, and when I was selected, I took it.

This was a very providential step.

PART IV: THE COMEBACK KID

2003, Santa Barbara: Comeback

I had been out of surfing for over twenty years. And for over twenty years, I woke up every day feeling that something was missing in my life.

I didn't fully realize how deprived I felt until we moved to Santa Barbara. When the surf came up the first winter, I was like a starving man watching a banquet from outside the windows of the dining hall. I hadn't surfed for ages but finally, driven by a big winter swell with pounding sets that formed a haze over the beach for three days, I knew I had to give it one more try.

After almost a quarter century away from surfing, I felt like Rip van Winkle awakening to a changed world. The changes had been going on around me, but because I didn't surf I hadn't paid any attention to them. I had never worn a full wetsuit, never put on a pair of booties, rarely used a leash. In a fit of optimism – or at least some very positive thinking – I bought a full set of gear.

I let the surf subside, borrowed a 9'6" board from a neighbor and gave it a try on a shoulder-high day. I was cautiously optimistic. I had been doing workout drills; I had desire; all I had to do was make it happen. I waded out into the water, waited for a lull, and started paddling.

Every motion sends ice picks stabbing into my shoulders. From time to time one pierces my elbow or my neck. I'm shocked – this was the last thing I expected. The weak link in my body was supposed to be my lower back. But I have no time to think. A wave comes toward me on a collision course, breaks just in front of me, turns into a mass of roiling foam. I take a deep breath and push the board through it. As I do I feel another burst of pain, this time from my elbows. The good news is that it keeps me from noticing the icy winter water slapping me in the face.

My sternum feels as if the bone were being crushed, slowly and painfully, by a vice-like implement from the Spanish Inquisition. The ice picks are still probing my shoulders, stabbing at my tendons, with an occasional random thrust somewhere between my shoulder blades. The easy thing, the pain-free thing, the sensible thing to do would be to quit. Pack it in, give it up.

Two hundred miles and over fifty years away, a young boy struggles to drag a heavy clumsy surfboard to the water.

I have come this far, I'm here for a reason and I am not going to back down now. There's been a gap in my existence and I have to make one last try to fill it. One wave, just one wave, and then decide whether or not to quit. I keep paddling. My right shoulder, where the end of the collarbone was removed after a bicycle accident, is starting to make a grinding noise. It sounds like ice being crushed under pressure. The sound is ugly, appalling, but so far there's no pain associated with it. Now both shoulders are emitting a rough grinding sound, like someone crushing gravel beneath a heavy roller.

The boy gets the board out past the small swells, turns it around so that it faces toward the shore.

I get past the impact zone, make it to the lineup, and sit up. The action sends a final stab through my shoulders.

As I sit there waiting for a set, I have time to think. This is insane. I'm sixty-two years old; I haven't surfed since I was in my late thirties. My knees and shoulders are a mess, my back hurts, and paddling out felt like some bizarre primitive ritual of self-inflicted torture. I want to surf, yeah, sure, I really do, but only if I can enjoy it. And this isn't enjoyment.

Today will always be special. Today the boy will catch an unbroken wave. The sky and sea are crystalline copies of each other, so that each incoming swell seems to slide down off the horizon into the water and then roll to shore.

I could be reading a book or sitting in a park, having coffee with my friends or just enjoying the day. And I've chosen to subject myself to unexpected pain and suffering in search of...what?

One of the approaching lines of water is slightly larger, which gives it a darker aquamarine hue. This is what he's been waiting for. The beach is deserted, the water empty of swimmers. He is alone with the approaching wave. Nothing else exists.

I had just about decided to paddle in, take the board back to my neighbor, and get back to my surfless existence. And then I saw it. Slipping down from the horizon, sliding toward me with the promise of happiness and joy and exhilaration, was the wave. The same wave that had picked me up and moved me into a new realm and onto a higher plane of existence over fifty years before, a wave that had been patiently circling the globe, waiting for me to give it one more try.

He lies down on the board and begins to paddle, straining to reach his arms deep enough into the water. He feels the tail of the board rise and an invisible force grips the board and he stops paddling and he is moving, sliding forward with no effort, gliding above the sandy bottom and the pure transparent water like a gull across the sky. It feels better than anything he has ever done in his life.

The wave arrives, I paddle, and somehow the spikes in my shoulders are forgotten. I feel the familiar magical surge, the mysterious force driving the board with no further effort from me. As I spring to my feet my wrists and elbows are pierced by red-hot spikes, but my upward momentum carries me through and I'm up. And then I'm riding the wave and turning and it's as if I never had been away. After years of limping and hobbling and canes and frustration I can move fast and free and unrestricted.

The only thing in the universe that matters is the feeling, the magical holy fluid sensation of movement without effort, without sound, without friction; the absolute perfection of natural forces in harmony, the dream of perpetual motion realized for a few eternal seconds.

I'm surfing! Gliding over the surface, soaring up and down the wave, in a moment beyond time and beyond age and physical disability. I'm ten, I'm twelve, I'm ageless and timeless and immortal. I've been released. After nearly a quarter of a century I'm free! I want to throw back my head and howl at the sun, dive into the water and kiss the bottom of the sea.

At that moment I know that whatever I have to do, whatever it takes, I'm not going to give this up again without one hell of a fight.

That night I have a dream. It's one that I may have had before, so long ago I can hardly remember when or where.

I'm standing on Mount Soledad, just below the top, on the side where the land falls steeply away to meet the sea eight hundred feet below. Above me the sky is a brilliant Hokusai blue. Below me is air, clear as crystal and summer warm. I rise to my full height, raise my arms, and soar upward. I quickly level out and glide in gentle arcs above the beach. The tide slips outward toward the blue horizon, hundreds of yards farther than I've ever seen it go. The wet sand gleams gold in the soft hazy light of early afternoon. Below I see small shapes, people eagerly running across the glistening sand, fanning out toward the horizon to collect the gold. I smile. Let them have it. I could swoop down in front of all of them, but I choose not to. I'm gloriously happy doing exactly as I'm doing.

I awaken in a state of pure blissful joy that lasts all day. I have been reunited with my true love.

Santa Barbara: Whatever it takes

When I got up on that board after a forced layoff of almost twenty-five years, suddenly time was erased and I was ten years old again, riding the same wave that had been circling the universe for fifty years, patiently waiting for this miraculous reunion. After years of deprivation, boredom, pain and frustration, I had been granted a second chance. I was reunited with my first love; I had my life back!

The road back was a little longer than that, of course. It took me a year to learn how to pop up without damaging a shoulder that was missing several parts and components, and without wrecking wrists that had a very limited range of motion due to prior injuries, how to crouch and move quickly on knees that had experienced a couple of surgeries each, how to paddle with elbows that had been repaired more than once.

Through trial and error and with the aid of a great physical therapist I figured it out. The next step was settling on the right board.

The first board I bought for my comeback was a Doyle 9-foot foamie. This was the grandfather of all foam boards, the ancestor of the sleek, brightly-colored popouts sold by the truckload at Walmart and Costco.

I bought the board because it was soft. I had been practicing popups at home, and a fairly high percentage of the time my bad shoulder would collapse before I could get my feet under me, causing me to fall straight down on my face. The backyard grass was very forgiving, but I knew a real surfboard would be a lot harder. The foam board could save me a lot of bruises.

For the first time in my life, I practiced surfing. In every other sport I had attempted – skiing, karate, tennis, golf – I had put in countless hours of practice working on basic moves. But not with surfing. In my thirties, my shortboard phase, everything seemed natural, and during my earlier longboard phase my main concern had always been to not lose my board. I had never worked on any surf moves or techniques.

Now, equipped with a leash, I worked on everything. I practiced late takeoffs. I practiced walking to the nose and smoothly walking back. I sought out ugly, slabby reef breaks and took off on unmakeable waves just to see how the situation would unfold. I worked on turning while popping up and remaining tucked in a tight crouch. I even rode the wrong way into collapsing barrels just for the experience.

Amazingly, I came to love that board. Doyle had really done a great job on designing something that was ugly and brutish but worked really well once you figured it out. Due to the boogie-board plastic bottom, it was very fast in the water, and whenever I took a couple of steps toward the nose, I could feel it accelerate. Turns were delayed, but once the board started to come around they were quick and tight; it was just a matter of getting the timing down and starting everything a second or two early.

On bigger waves – anything above head-and-a-half or so – I loved to relive the old '70s style: straight down the face, way out into the flat, then put the board up on a rail and feel the Gs in the knees as I cranked a carving bottom turn and roared back up the face. Once when I did this on a wave on a visit to Windansea I could see little wrinkles forming across the deck as the board actually acquired additional rocker due to the force of the turn. It had the same effect as reverse camber on a ski, and the turn was incredibly fast and tight and exhilarating.

2003, Santa Barbara: As good as it gets

You've been surfing, had a good session, gotten some good rides. It's a beautiful day. You're on the beach, feeling warm and tired and full of endorphins and happy feelings. You're enjoying watching others surf. You're immersed in the warmth of the sun and the sound of the waves, a boundless world of motion, blue water and white foam. If this isn't perfection, it's the next best thing. It's the way things are supposed to be. It doesn't happen after every surfing session. When it does, it's bliss.

I truly understood this for the first time after my comeback. We had driven the van down past Rincon to the small campground at Hobson for a weekend of relaxation. It was early spring and the weather was perfect: warm, glassy, not a cloud in the sky. Somewhat surprisingly for that late in the year, there was a strong north swell hitting, beautiful clean lines and overhead sets of up to half a dozen waves each. There was small "local" crew that surfed Hobson a lot in those days: four or five guys, all in their thirties, all really decent people. They made me feel welcome; they shared waves.

I had been back in surfing for only a couple of months, but the old muscle memory had come back and I had been working on things like nose-riding, which I had never really done much before my layoff. I was still riding the 9-foot blue Doyle foam tri-fin and I had gotten used to the board and figured out how to make it work.

After a few decent overhead waves I managed to hook into a really nice set wave, a right. Fade left, drop down and do a right bottom turn, come up into the pocket. Looking down the line, I saw that this was one of the best lined-up waves I had ever seen at Hobson; the face seemed to extend forever.

As the breaking wave was overtaking me, I took a couple of steps up to the nose and felt the board accelerate. From then on, it was a perfect ride: the wave and I stayed in the same relative position, the lip cracking over right behind me, an endless wall in front of me, and me in the middle, nose-riding a 9' Doyle foamie. I dimly heard a couple of guys paddling out cheering me on. Finally we got to the shorebreak, I kicked out over the back, and paddled in.

The session was good and the last wave was great, but paradoxically the greatest joy was afterward: changed into dry clothes, wetsuit hung up to dry, sun on my shoulders and the sound of surf in my ears, reliving my session and watching the other guys ride wave after wave after perfect wave. It doesn't get any better than that.

Flashback in the rain

I'm surfing Hobson alone, in the rain. It's a solid swell, with faces of eight feet and more. There's no wind. A steady rain falls in fat heavy drops. The swell is perfect: big, glassy lumps, surfaces dimpled by the rain, rolling in from across the Pacific, the rushing sigh of wind up the faces accentuated by the steady, soothing hiss of the falling rain. I can barely make out the shore through the rain; the horizon is obliterated. It's like floating in another sea, on another planet, and the wait between sets is, in its own way, as enjoyable an experience as the waves themselves. I'm enveloped in the dynamics of nature. I recall another ocean, another rain-dimpled swell.

It's 1964, and we're on our way from Spain to Tangiers on the midnight ferry.

We had waited for the departure in a small cantina in Algeciras, taking shelter from a relentless driving rain. An hour or so before midnight, a handful of young locals came in carrying a couple of guitars. Amid round after round of cheap wine, they played and danced exuberant, spontaneous flamenco in pure gitano fashion. When we tore ourselves away and went out into the night the sounds of the guitars and jaleo echoed down the narrow cobblestone street behind us, sounds from a world that has long since disappeared.

We're on the ferry, a small passengers-only vessel. As soon as we leave port I feel the heaving sea beneath the hull: a powerful, slow, rhythmic pulsing up and down, up and down again, like the surge and ebb of vital fluid in an artery. An hour into the crossing, the hard wooden benches are becoming uncomfortable and the odor of vomit from seasick passengers is nearly overwhelming.

I get up and step out onto the forward deck. The wind has abated but the rain continues. At first, the sea is blank and dark beneath a moon half-hidden by clouds. I take a step forward and flail for balance as the deck drops from beneath my feet. I recover and stop to adjust. The moonlight reveals an endless series of enormous, perfect swells, driving in from somewhere in the vast Atlantic and passing beneath me as they surge eastward through the Strait of Gibraltar and along the coast of Africa until crashing ashore in Sardinia or Sicily or Tunisia. With each passing there's a deep sigh of wind as the ferry is lifted ten feet or more, then dropped, lifted, then dropped again. Rarely have I been so aware of the power and majesty of the living sea.

I'm so lost in my reverie that I almost fail to spot the set looming toward me through the curtains of rain. The sight pulls me back to the present. I take a few quick strokes to set up further out, then wheel the board around and go. As I feel the wave start to drive the board I pop up and turn. It's a right that starts off as a lumbering mountain, then jacks up and peels off in a perfect, long line, the trough and face dimpled by the rain.

I'm still partly immersed in memory and for a few moments I visualize riding that big Atlantic swell somewhere in the Mediterranean. Then I'm back in the here and now. I turn on the face, cut back, do it again. In front of the breaking shoulder I take a couple of steps toward the nose and feel the board accelerate as it cuts across the wave, raindrops pounding against my face, the wave getting steeper as we approach the outer shorebreak. I have never felt more alive.

Santa Barbara: Prayer or prophecy?

So there I was, in my early sixties, back into surfing again. Teaching night classes at Santa Barbara City College, hitting the waves during the day, living a block from the beach within the sound of the sea, and within striking distance of Rincon, one of the classic point breaks on the West Coast. It was almost like the old times when I was a much younger surfer dude in the '70s, before my forced hiatus from surfing.

I explored up and down the coast from Santa Barbara, learned the reefs, the currents and the best swell directions, and found dozens of spots to surf, often alone in a state of creative solitude. When Rincon was crowded, I knew where to go to get waves that were almost as good, and had the advantage of being rideable without fighting for position in the lineup, getting dropped in on, and having to thread a slalom course through all the surfers on the inside.

I had a full wetsuit and a leash! No need to ever be cold or swim for my board again. Well, almost no need. When the water got down into the high 40s even a 4-3 wetsuit couldn't keep the chill from seeping in. And of course the wetsuit didn't keep your hands warm. There were a couple of times when I had to ask for assistance in getting my car key out of the key pocket in my wetsuit and into the door lock of my van – my hands were so cold after a session that I simply couldn't make my fingers work. But that was minor. The main thing was that I had my life back.

I met a great group of guys to surf and hang out with: Kemp Aaberg, Bob Perko, Frank Suttner, Sam Webster, Glenn Vargen. They shared their surfing fun and stories, and gave me the comradeship and inspiration and encouragement that got me through the inevitable setbacks of any recovery.

When I had to quit surfing, I had been riding a 7'0" and a 7'6". My plan was to start with a 9' board and work my way back down. I quickly realized that with a partially missing collarbone, plus all the other issues of the previous sixty-two years, I was not going to go to anything under 9'. So I was a long board guy again.

After trying a number of boards I settled on a 9'6" Infinity epoxy board, ultra light weight, that surfed like a 7'6". In some ways it was like having a longer version of my old Canyon board shaped by Rusty back in the '70s: paddled and surfed fast, quick on turns, and a great board for catching waves. Like the Rusty board, it was a great "two to ten" board, fun on anything from knee high to double overhead.

Back in the lineup in Santa Barbara, I reveled in my new life. And I remember murmuring something that, if not a prayer, was about as close to a prayer as possible: "*If I could just get ten more years of this, I would be eternally grateful.*"

In a way, that came close to being not only a prayer, but a prophecy.

Strategic withdrawal: La Jolla Cove

Shortly after my comeback I was down in La Jolla to visit old friends. I flew down, it was just for a couple of days and I was into traveling light, so

I didn't bring a board or a wetsuit. The Cove was breaking and I decided to bodysurf it using borrowed fins. No wetsuit, but hey, no problem – I never had a wetsuit when I was young, right?

I set up close to Alligator head; any surfers were farther north so my takeoff spot left me a lot of wave to work with.

The surf was a solid north swell, maybe eight to ten feet. I caught a set wave that closed out and left me quite close to the face of the low cliff and about halfway between the Cove beach and the notorious Hole – a rock cleft with no way out except through a small cave that led to even more turbulent ocean and surf-beaten rocks on the other side. Fine, no worries. I would wait for a lull, swim back out, and catch a better wave next time.

La Jolla Cove – John Ahlbrand photo

I started diving under successive waves, using their backwash to keep myself from being pounded against the rocks. One wave, two, three, half a dozen. The set seemed endless, and the waves kept coming, one after another. About eight or ten waves in, I felt myself running out of gas. The combination of cold winter water – maybe a wetsuit would have been a good idea? – and constant diving and breath-holding was taking its toll. Furthermore, the current was slowly pulling me away from the beach and toward the Hole. If I got swept in there, all bets were off. If no one saw me go in, I might well come out in a body bag. In that moment, I realized what would have been trivial at age twenty or thirty or forty was now potentially life-threatening or at least very hazardous to my health. In other words, I was getting too old for this particular set of circumstances.

The only solution I could see was going to require a serious effort: instead of waiting for a lull, I would burn all my remaining energy to head for the beach against the waves and the current. It wouldn't be easy, but it was the best option at the time. But almost the moment I put my head down and started to swim, my right calf was knotted up by the worst cramp I have ever had in my life.

There was only one thing to do: suck it up and keep kicking, cramp or no. By the time I got to shore, my leg felt as if someone had driven a railway spike into it, and I was so cold, weak and dizzy that I literally crawled out of the water and onto the sand.

Another spot was added to my "off limits" list, and my range of permissible activities got a little smaller.

Island magic, Part III

A year or so after making my comeback, my inner ten-year-old wanted to go to Hawai'i. Nostalgia for warm water and gentle offshore breezes grew and grew until it became too strong to resist. I had just retired from teaching; the springtime ocean in Southern California was its usually foggy, surfless self, and an airline was offering a discount fare.

Rather than bring a normal board and pay the exorbitant airline fees, I bought a Pope Bisect: a 10'0" board, shaped by Bruce Jones and manufactured by Carl Pope and divided into two five-foot sections. The board was held together by an ingenious latch and lever system that was foolproof and fast – I could break it down and put it back together in under two minutes. In its 5' x 2½' canvas carrying case, it looked nothing like a surfboard. I called it "exercise equipment" and the airlines never once questioned it or charged an extra fee. Once in Hawai'i, I never had to worry about storage, since I could take it apart and bring it up to my room in the elevator. It was the perfect size and weight for Waikīkī, and I got some of my most memorable rides on that board.

That board, plus the fairly slopy takeoffs at Waikīkī, extended my repertoire. One of my memories from my gremmie days was watching slightly older and much more talented guys take off on a wave, pop up, run to the nose while going straight off, then take a couple of quick steps back to crank a turn on the face. I started working on this at Queens and later at Publics. It was a great way to ensure getting into a wave early, before it got steep, especially with an offshore wind. At bigger days at Publics, this worked like a charm. And it got me one of the best rides of my life.

I'm surfing Publics on solid day, breaking outside at eight feet plus. It's raining, with a stiff offshore wind. The rain is making it hard to see my usual lineup points so it's all done by intuition. Luckily I've been surfing here a lot so I have a good feel for where to sit, even with nothing to line up on.

There's a pack of guys out on short boards, but with the wind they're having a tough time. On every set, everyone tries to take off, including me. As the wave starts to stand up, the combined force of the water rushing up the face plus the increase in offshore wind flow blows the shortboarders almost backwards. From the corner of my eye I can see them moving up the face and out of the takeoff zone. Meanwhile, my longer, heavier board has momentum and I'm still in the wave. When I feel the water pick up and drive the tail of my board, I pop up in a crouch and take two quick steps forward; this drops me solidly into the wave so I can step back and crank a backside left.

After a couple of these a bigger set comes through. Not a real cleanup set, but definitely above average. Due to the size the rush of wind and water up the face makes it even harder to catch, and as usual the shortboarders are struggling.

I paddle, pop up, take my two crouching steps to the nose. I find myself looking almost straight down; the wave has jacked and there's no way I'm going to be able to get back to turn. My only chance is to stay low, grab the rail near the nose, and use the nose rocker to turn the board.

Somehow, it works. I feel the tail slide down, then the nose rocker starts to bite into the steep face and the fins (2+1 setup) take hold. I slide down under the lip, and I've done it! I'm in the pocket so I just stay where I am as the wave throws out behind me and the barrel catches up to me. This is the most awesome ride I've ever had at Publics. In fact, it's my most awesome ride ever.

It's not over. Due to the chain of shallow and exposed reefs on the inside part of the break, riding the wave all the way in means risking serious reef rash and a trashed board, so when the barrel slacks off a bit I'm ready to go out over the back of the wave. Just at that moment, it jacks up and hollows out again. I'm so pumped that I stay where I am and try to make the next section. Suddenly I'm looking at bare reef inside as the water sucks out. The only hope is to stay high and hope the wave puts enough water on the reef that I'll be carried past it without hitting it. Luckily, that's what happens.

When it's all over, I'm sitting inside recovering and letting the adrenaline drain away. Truth be told, I'm kind of shell shocked. Did I just do that?

A local guy paddling out has a comment:

"Great ride, brah – you almost got barreled twice. How did you get that big piece of junk moving so fast?"

2004-2016: Have board, will travel

Surfing warm water with offshore breezes was so nice that I wanted to make it part of my life. We bought a small unit in a "condotel" – a mix of short-term tenants and more or less permanent residents. We would rent the unit out when we were not there, and use it as our own crash pad a couple of months a year. The renters would cover the nut and generate some surplus. I stocked it with shorts, T-shirts, rash guards and a folding bicycle, all locked away in a small closet.

It worked out perfectly! Back and forth I went, once a year, between the mainland – first Santa Barbara, then La Jolla – and the Islands.

In Waikīkī there was plenty to do when not surfing. I rode my bike up to Kapi'olani Community College bookstore and bought a couple of books on the Hawaiian language. I got into Japanese again, inspired by a Japanese-language column in the local paper. This, in turn, got me riding my bike to the Japanese bookstore in Shirokiya in Ala Moana, where I bought used Japanese-language paperbacks for a dollar apiece and an electronic Japanese dictionary to look up the words I didn't know. I took surf photographs and videos from the rooftop deck of my condo building.

Way back in the 1950s Hawaiian transplant Ronald Patterson had taught me to play simple versions of couple of slack key melodies on the guitar, and now I reignited my love affair with Hawaiian slack key music and started building a collection of slack key guitar recordings on CD. I made some new friends by going to listen to local musician Mike Keale play.

But surf always came first. One evening I had just gotten spiffed up to listen to Mike Keale and his group play Hawaiian music at one of the big hotels. Put on my best aloha shirt and my nicest shorts and sandals (or, as the locals would say, slippers). Got as far as the corner across from the beach and saw overhead sets rolling in at Queens.

Run back to the condo, change clothes, grab my board, run back to the beach and hit the water. The swell had appeared out of nowhere, totally unexpected, and there were only a dozen guys out, most of them local kids. The sun was just about to set, the conditions were perfect, and we were all pumped at having hit this surprise jackpot.

And then it got better!

One of the kids turned to his buddies and said, "We bettah go now, we gonna be late."

Late? Late for what? Who cares about late?

All the kids started heading for the beach. It was senior prom night and they didn't want to miss a moment of it!

There were only four of us left out there with all those waves, and we surfed until well after dark. Not much moon so it was hard to see the sets coming, but once they got close there was so much light from the shore that the faces were illuminated well enough to see where you were going. You just had to be alert for one of the few remaining surfers paddling back out after a ride. I can still see the water all lit up by colorful reflected light from the shops and hotels on Kalākaua Avenue, darkly glittering hollow wave faces curving up overhead in front of me, rushing through the night beneath a star-drenched tropical sky, surfing in a dream.

•   •   •

I would always jump on an unexpected opportunity like prom night at Queens, but since my dormant back and shoulder problems were still lurking I normally had to ration my surfing sessions – one or two hours max, and no more than once session a day. I made up for that by surfing every day. Once I surfed twenty-eight days straight and enjoyed every outing even though I was getting pretty drained by the end of my run. When my wife commented that it seemed to her that I was trying to get all I could while I could, all I could say was "of course!"

It was a good thing I did. I was changing and the reality of Hawai'i was changing even faster. Get it before it's gone. Because when it's over, it truly is over. Might as well quit with a lot of nice waves in the memory banks. But I wasn't just trying to beat the changes or make up for lost time.

The most important factor was novelty. In many ways surfing – with better boards, better gear, and a new thought process – was new to me after all these years. Since my comeback I was, for the first time, truly aware of what I was doing. Before, it had all been instinct. Now, I was thinking and planning and consciously adjusting. My eagerness to ride waves was as much discovery as it was a ravenous appetite after a long fast.

I had reconnected with my beginner's mind.

*My wave, haole f*ckah!*

When I started going to Waikīkī after making my comeback, I hadn't been there in over forty years. The changes were astounding. But the ocean was still the same: warm, blue-green, inviting. Same sea, same waves. But lots more people.

At first I tried, unconsciously, to recapture the feelings and experiences of my first visits as a teenager. And to an extent, it worked. Canoes still offered long lefts and rights, and the beautiful peak and right wall at Queens were still available. I could do a pre-sunrise dawn patrol at Queens and for awhile there might be only a handful of surfers in the lineup. I could even get lucky and find beautiful head-high waves at Publics with literally no one else there for half an hour or so.

But within a few years these things were no longer possible. There were not only more people, the attitude had changed. The famous aloha spirit seemed to be wearing a bit thin. My epiphany, as it were, came at Queens. It was a very intermittent long period swell, which meant long waits, and some of the sets consisted of just one wave. There was a pack of surfers on the inside, scrambling over each other for the smaller waves.

I was sitting outside, waiting for something to show up, when a huge Hawaiian paddled out. Ignoring my smile and nod, he set up just outside of where I was sitting. When a one-wave set arrived, he turned around to take off.

"I'll go left," I volunteered, knowing that he would want to take the good direction, which at Queens is the right. I was there first, but he was local, plus he outweighed me by a hundred pounds or so. I had been sitting there so long that even a short, mushy left would be better than nothing.

He fixed me with a baleful glare.

"My wave, haole fuckah!"

As I sat there and watched him sweep all the way across the wave, asserting his claim to the whole thing, I realized that my old favorite breaks were no longer working for me. From then on, no matter how tempting the waves looked at my former haunts, I stayed further east, toward Kapi'olani Park and Diamond Head.

Publics started getting crowded, so on bigger swells I shifted to surfing Cunha's, at the foot of Kapahulu Avenue between Publics and Queens. Cunha's has to be at least head and a half to break, and to be really good it needs double overhead. It can be a great wave, but for some reason even when Queens and Publics were packed there was no overflow to Cunha's. On many days you could have it all to yourself. There were long waits, but the solitude was nice. While you waited you could watch people riding Queens or Publics, and often a friendly turtle or two would come by to check you out from a discreet distance.

My change of venue gave me the chance to encounter one of the most impressive surfers I've ever met.

Waikīkī: Profile in courage

I was out at Cunha's on a very solid day with very long intervals due to an extremely long period swell. As happened often at Cunha's, I was alone. I'd gotten only one wave since I'd been out, and it was one of those days where just one other person in the lineup could have a serious impact on wave selection. So I wasn't the happiest camper when I noticed a lone surfer on a yellow board paddling in my direction from the far side of Canoes.

"*C'mon,*" I tried to project my thoughts at the intruder, "*Stay at Canoes. Stop at Queens. But don't come over here.*"

He paddled past Canoes and kept coming. The good news was that he was a really, really slow paddler. A wave came and I caught it. By the time

I got back out he was only reaching Queens. Maybe with a little luck I could manage one more ride before he arrived.

Before the next wave appeared he was past Queens and closing. Suddenly I realized why he was so slow: he was strapped to the board, lying very flat, and seemed to have a lot of trouble raising his head. He paddled up next to me and stopped.

"Hi, I'm a paraplegic surfer. Can you help me out by getting me set up right and giving me a push when a wave comes?" He added that although he could paddle, he couldn't arch at all and couldn't turn his head to look over his shoulder at the wave.

This, of course, changed everything.

"Sure, glad to."

I felt conflicted. If anything went wrong, it would be partly my fault for helping him do it. But how could I say no?

As if he had caused it, a set appeared on the horizon.

I helped him get set up for the first wave, gave him a push, and he paddled for it – but not hard enough, and he missed it. As his board settled back on the back side of the wave, I was secretly relieved; I couldn't see how he was going to make the drop on a ten-foot face with the speed that the waves had on that day. If he caught a wave, he would end up in the emergency room or worse, and it would be my fault. If he got flipped over, how would he get back right side up? I didn't want his death by drowning on my conscience.

I could see that the rest of the set was not a threat to him, so I took off on the next wave and got it. A nice left, lots of speed and good for some fun turns.

At the end of the ride I turned to paddle back out, and there he was, going straight down the face of the last wave of the set. I didn't get to see what happened when the wave broke, but I was sure he had been driven straight down. I stopped, sat up, and hovered over on the shoulder, waiting for him and his board to pop out of the foam. I was ready to sprint over and flip him back upright, give him CPR, whatever. But amazingly, he appeared inside, paddling back out around the shoulder.

When we got back to the lineup, he asked me for another favor.

"Can you help me get set up on my board? That last drop kind of pushed me forward. Happens a lot."

Sure enough, his entire body, even though strapped down, had slid toward the nose. Following his instructions, I slid off my board, got behind his board, grabbed his ankles, and pulled him back toward the tail until he was in position again.

We each got another wave, and then he paddled back the way he had come. As I watched him slowly and painfully work his way back toward his launch point, any problems that I had ever had seemed miniscule by comparison.

South Shore: Free-range surfing

After I abandoned my earlier breaks, I was happier. The waves I was now riding were often either less clean or less frequent, but there was no more racing to beat the crowd, no more jockeying for position, and no territorial vibe. Sometimes the crumbs from the table can be very satisfying, if consumed in solitude and at your leisure. And sometimes you end up getting far more than you would have if you'd stayed where you were.

Due to lingering lower back issues – aggravated any time I tried to carry a surfboard more than a block – I was still pretty much tethered to the area closest to our condo near the foot of Kapahulu. I had abandoned Canoes and I was evolving away from Queens, but I still would make the long paddle to Pops. My go-to breaks were Publics when it was small and Publics or Cunha's when there was a big swell.

Then the condo built board racks, eliminating the need for riding the elevator with a two-piece board, and I got Craig Angell of Ventura to make me a beautiful ten-foot board, a perfect size and shape for the long paddles and offshore winds in South Shore surf. I got a Carver board rack for my folding bike, and suddenly I had total surfing mobility.

I quickly unleashed my inner twelve-year-old. A board, a bike, a pair of trunks, and nothing between me and a dozen beautiful breaks. The world was all blue sky, warm water, golden white sand and surf.

Waikīkī is absolutely flat, so with a bike I could easily surf anywhere: all the way to Ala Moana and beyond or go the other way to Mākālei and Lēʻahi parks to surf breaks like Sleepy Hollow or Suicides. In theory.

But context is everything, and my mini surf safaris toward Ewa involved a lot of context that wasn't so good. I made a few forays to Threes and Kaisers; the surfing was great, but the difficult, sometimes dangerous and always stressful trip to and from the water tended to pollute the entire experience. One-way streets, horrific traffic and hostile traffic cops made the trip too risky and unpleasant, so I started going the other way, toward Diamond Head. From then on, my beat was Cunha's up past Kaimana Beach and the Elks Club to Sleepy Hollow. And my harmony quotient went way up.

I created a new routine: big swell, head out at Cunha's half a block from the condo. Otherwise, ride the bike past Publics and hit it if it was really good and not crowded. If it's not, keep riding to Kaimana Beach. From there I could check everything from Castle's to Rice Bowl. Often I would end up at one of the breaks near the Elks Club; on those rare days when there was no wind I would continue on past Tonggs, to surf the breaks off Mākālei Park. A bike meant freedom to choose any break with ease.

Waikīkī, Castle's: fatal attraction

I had been coming to Waikīkī for a couple of years and had never surfed Castle's. Actually, I had never seen it break very well – just a few intermittent waves with poor form. Of course, you can't just show up someplace for a couple of months a year and expect to hit it. It's all about timing.

One morning I'm up on the observation deck of the condo, sipping a home-brewed espresso and trying to decide where to surf. The swell is solid, and no matter where I go it's going to be good. A beautiful three-wave set shows up at Castle's and breaks in long, peeling walls, lefts and rights. There's no one out there. Must have been a fluke. Five minutes later, there's another. I've got to give this a shot.

Get the board from the rack, put it on the bike, head out. A few minutes later I'm sitting in the channel off Kaimana Beach, watching another set break at Castle's while I wait for a lull so I can paddle out. The channel is closing out and there are a number of people riding the breaks in front of the Elks Club. The waves there look great: solid, clean and well overhead. But I came to surf Castle's and it's still deserted, so I paddle out there, set up outside where I saw the last set break, and wait.

Keep in mind, I am not and never have been a big-wave rider. My comfort zone ends somewhere around double overhead, depending on the wave. And that's for what I would call "normal" waves, ones that have to cross shallow water like the continental shelf – losing power and mass as they do so – before arriving at the spot where they are going to break.

Waves like those on the North Shore – or Ocean Beach or Maverick's, or Tarantulas, or Puerto Escondido, or any number of other spots – are in a different league. At these spots, words like "fast" and "powerful" take on a whole new meaning. Even in Waikīkī, at any given size there's a world of difference between a swell breaking at Queens, say, and the same swell breaking at Rice Bowl. So even though I was generally comfortable with Waikīkī surf, I didn't really know exactly what to expect at Castle's.

When a set darkened the horizon, I took comfort in the fact that I seemed to have set up in a perfect spot. I was riding the 10'0" that Craig Angell had made for me and I was confident that it was the perfect board for these waves. Stable at speed and in bumps, solid in the offshore wind, quick to turn and a great nose rider.

As the set approached, it looked bigger than I had expected. I found myself experiencing one of those scenes they sometimes put into cartoons, where a character has opposing inner voices, often depicted as a little angel and a little devil, one on each shoulder, whispering conflicting advice.

"C'mon, do it."

"Don't do it!"

"Go on, don't be chicken!"

"Are you crazy? Don't be stupid!"

The first wave was big, and getting bigger. As it continued to expand I remembered a conversation with old-time Waimea surfer Kemp Aaberg. I had asked Kemp how he had adjusted from taking off on ten-foot waves on the west coast to taking off on twenty-foot waves at Waimea.

"Simple. You're not taking off on a twenty-foot wave; you're taking off on an eight-foot wave. It's only twenty feet after you catch it and it jacks up."

This conversation flashed through my head as the wave kept getting closer and closer, and bigger and bigger. It was like a cartoon wave that just kept growing, threatening to fill my field of vision. By now, just a few seconds from when I had to decide to go or not, it was easily the biggest approaching swell I had ever been in front of – nearly double overhead. And it was still an unbroken swell. With Kemp's words echoing in my brain, I had a very unsettling thought:

If this thing jacks, I'm gonna be on a 25 foot wave.

That would have been at least double the biggest wave I had ever ridden, and way out of my league. Now, this might not seem possible at Waikīkī, and normally it is not. But I had read Duke Kahanamoku's account of his epic ride from outside Castle's to somewhere in front of the Royal Hawaiian Hotel, a total straight-line distance of nearly a mile, and he was very clear on the size of the wave: well on the high side of twenty feet, probably closer to thirty. And this is coming from one of the most skillful, knowledgeable and capable Hawaiian watermen and surfers of all time. So it was, in fact, possible.

The moment of truth had arrived – it was now or never, do it or don't. For motivation, I taunted myself under my breath.

"C'mon, you dipstick, you're here to surf. Catch the damn wave."

I took a deep breath, turned around and went for it with long, deep strokes. As I did, I got a quick mental replay of the disaster at Dunemere in the '70s, when I slacked off while paddling and paid a hefty price. In response, I put everything I had into my paddling. I might get eaten up by the wave, I might get crushed, but I was not going to get pitched.

I saw the water in front of me change as surface water was drawn toward the wave now looming behind me, I felt the rush of wind and water coming up the face, and I felt the tail of my board lift and thrust forward as it caught the energy of the wave. This thing had some juice! Two more quick strokes and I was up, looking down the face. It was steep, but thank God it was nowhere near twenty feet – probably more like ten or so. Instead of jacking up, this wave grew as it rolled onto the reef, then pitched out and fell over forward behind me as I made my turn.

I was ecstatic. I had three quick thoughts in succession:

This is really fast!

This is really bumpy!

I'm riding it!

I was hooked on Castle's.

But the wave wasn't over. Castle's can be good on both the left and the right. I had gone right. The first part of the wave was a dream: drop down, glide back up, cut back, do it again. It was great to have so much wave face to work with; it seemed like I was going down a full floor in a building and then back up again.

After that the wave went over a deep spot and got a little more slopy, so I took a couple of steps forward for more speed and squatted, near the nose, for less wind resistance. Some guy paddling out flashed me a *shaka* sign as I slid past him. The offshore was pretty weak that day, so I had no trouble staying in the wave.

Then the wave started standing up again, so I took a couple of steps back, cut back shallow left in a sweeping arc and went down the face. Roll onto the right rail to turn right again.

Then another of my many "*What have I done?*" moments.

I had gotten myself into a reverse version of my big left at Publics on the Pope Bisect board, when I got caught up in the moment and had to ride across the inner reef. Now I had been so busy admiring my own handiwork that I had ridden all the way into a zone of shallow coral that the locals called the minefield. And the wave was now towering above me, hollow and fringing, ready to break. No way to kick out, too late to straighten out towards shore. All I could do was fill my lungs with air for buoyancy, squat down as low as possible, and roll gently off the board to the side toward the wave and back, extending my body flat and straight as I went off, trying to stay shallow.

I hit the water an instant before the lip came crashing down inches from my face. As I was pummeled and churned and dragged, all I could think of was waiting branches of razor-sharp coral reaching up from the ocean floor, ready to slash me to ribbons. A few seconds of serious turbulence – but no coral slashes – and we were past the danger zone. The only ill effects were some nasty little cuts on my hands from gingerly paddling my way to the nearest mini-channel so I could get out again.

This was not the last mistake I was to make at Castle's.

Castle's: Humble pie

In the meantime, Castle's had another lesson for me.

I was out on a big day. The channel in front of Kaimana Beach was closed out, sometimes even between sets, and it took me a long time to get out and over to Castle's, get set up and start catching waves.

It was a great day, still early morning and the trades were weak, making just enough offshore wind to give the waves some character. Today the rights were better than the lefts; although still a little gun-shy about rights at Castle's I had learned my lesson about not going too far. Settle for a shorter ride – it was less hazardous to your health.

I had gotten a couple of beautiful bombs and was waiting for the next set when I saw what appeared to be a *haole* guy on a boogie board coming out. He must have launched from the steps near the aquarium – a theoretical alternative to the channel but not one I favored since although there was no inside wave to contend with you had to go through some fairly shallow reefs. In addition, if you timed it wrong and got caught inside you would be facing the full force of whatever outside waves came through. I might consider getting to the beach that way in a pinch – although the coral heads made me nervous – but I wouldn't paddle out from there. And especially not on a big day.

Anyhow, that's what he chose to do, and he made it out. As he drew closer I realized that it wasn't a guy on a boogie board, but a *haole* kid on a kid-sized shortboard. He was really small, probably younger than I had been when I got my first unbroken wave, and a lot shorter. Small.

He set up a little inside me and to my right. I started thinking that this kid had some seriously irresponsible parents. First, his choice of launch points indicated that he probably wasn't local and didn't know the area or the break. Second, he was really small to be out on a day this big. Third, setting up in front of me indicated cluelessness about surf etiquette and safety issues. You don't want to take off in front of someone on a big day.

I started feeling a bit protective. Who was going to look after this kid? I scanned the beach and the area inside and saw no one. Was this some tourist kid who had gotten up and blundered out here on his own? What kind of parents would show such disregard for their child's safety?

When the next set came, my desire to surf overcame my virtuous outrage and I went for it. I couldn't babysit someone else's kid all day; I was here to surf. As I popped up, sure enough the kid was paddling in front of me for the wave and I had to call him off. I have to admit I was irritated. Here I had been worrying about the kid and he tried to snake me as if I weren't even there.

The wave, as waves always seem to, took away any bad feelings. It was a great ride, drops and climbs and big swooping turns and cutbacks and with the size and the swell angle I might have been able to go all the way past the point of my first-time mistake. Rather than push my luck I made one last turn and went out over the back.

I scanned the area to see if the kid had survived the set. Then I saw him. He was dropping down the face of a monster wave – ten or twelve feet but for someone his size easily triple overhead. And he wasn't just riding it, he was ripping it. Carving quick turns, sharp cutbacks, zipping up and down the face at will. It was like watching a snowboarder shred a steep slope. A very tiny snowboarder.

At the end of his ride, I heard a parental voice calling to him from shore. The kid's dad was by the steps waving his arms, signaling to the kid to come in. And the kid yelled back, in a heavily Aussie-accented little voice, "Not yet, dad, I wanna get some more of these set waves."

I should have let him drop in on me. In fact, I should have just given him my wave. He would have done a lot more with it than I did.

2000s – Why me?

My new life as a retired old surfer dude was like a junior high school grom's dream: living and surfing in Southern California summer and fall and winter, then spending the spring and early summer in Waikīkī, riding my bike to whatever break struck my fancy. I was able to do this for twelve years, and in the process I generated some of the best surfing memories of my life. I didn't catch the best waves ever ridden, and I sure didn't ride anything super big, but boy, did I have fun. The joy of pure, simple freedom.

We joined the Elks Club, and I could launch from there, surf anywhere from Tongg's or Rice Bowl to Castle's – actually I could have paddled past Tongg's but I was too lazy, and I could do it by bicycle anyway. Then back for a fresh water rinse off, lying in the shade by the pool, and lunch from the outdoor snack bar (until they took it away; if any Honolulu Elks read this, please get them to put it back!). Or launch from Kaimana Beach; same selection of breaks and a great place to hang out on a bench afterwards and watch people surf, or talk story with some of the great locals and transplants.

One of these transplants was a guy named John "Wheels" Williams, a marvelous old-time Aussie surfer from Bondi who had relocated to Honolulu back in the '60s. Amidst his many stories of surf adventures around the world, he solved a mystery that had baffled me for almost fifty years.

If you've read this book from the start, you may recall that during my first year in college I was beaten to a pulp in a boxing class by a football player acting on the orders of the coach. The reason for that was a mystery to me at the time, and it remained so for decades. Wheels and I were talking story about the past, somehow I mentioned the boxing incident at Pomona College and he told me the rest of the tale.

In 1959, there were only two students at the entire school who were active surfers. I was one; a kid named Bob was the other. Amazingly for a small school, I never met Bob and didn't know he existed.

One night before the start of the spring semester, the coach was awakened by a slurred voice shouting something from the street beneath his bedroom window. Outside, beneath a streetlamp but partly obscured by the shadow of a large tree, was a figure, carrying a surfboard under one arm and a half-empty jug of wine in the other hand. At intervals he would tip the jug to his lips and guzzle some wine. After each slug of wine he would bellow toward the window, "Hey coach, I wanna fuck your wife."

The coach's wife was indeed a cupcake, and no doubt many students – and perhaps even the odd faculty member or two, more lecherous than the average academic – shared this sentiment. But they had the good sense to keep it to themselves.

The coach didn't know Bob, but he knew me, and he knew that I surfed. That was all he needed to conclude that I was the culprit. Rather than confront me directly or seek some sort of disciplinary action through the school, he had devised a brilliantly simple and effective method of revenge. A guy kind of thing: have Cody beat me to a pulp. The only problem was, of course, that the real offender got off scot-free.

So how did Wheels know about this? Apparently Bob, who had moved to Australia, had told and retold the story, since he thought it was one of the funniest events of the twentieth century.

Who would have thought that just being a surfer could get you into so much trouble – and change the course of your life? I guess I owe Bob a thank you, actually. I wasn't really a good fit at Pomona anyway.

Santa Barbara: I'm so sorry!

Decades later I was still a magnet for bizarre situations. One of these occurred in Santa Barbara.

In Santa Barbara there lived a family of surfers; I'll call them the Wilsons. The brothers, both big surly guys, liked to use their size to intimidate. Like the three-hundred pound Samoan in the joke (*How many waves can a three-hundred pound Samoan ride?*) they took every wave they wanted. Looking back, I suspect that they were a lot tougher in the context of Santa Barbara than they would have been elsewhere; if they had acted that way in Ventura, let alone Hawai'i, they would have been shut down in short order. But in Santa Barbara they ruled the roost.

There was also a sister. She had the family genes for size, she was just as surly and intimidating as her brothers, and she also surfed.

A year or so after my comeback, I'm out at the local beginners' break on a small day, trying to learn how to switch stance on a wave. (I never did get it right.) I'm almost alone in the water – just one other person in sight, farther down the beach and nowhere near the peak.

I take off on a small, weak right. There's not enough power to do much except execute mushy, shallow turns. As I approach the only other person in the water, she takes off in front of me and goes straight off. To my horror, I see that it's the Wilsons' sister. There's no room to go around her, and if I hit her I'm in deep doo-doo. To offend this family would be like antagonizing the Mafia, or the Hell's Angels. I can't let that happen. I'm in my normal stance, but the wave is so small and weak that any kind of turn is painfully slow and if I try a kickout I may fall off and the board will hit her.

I try to turn straight off before I get to her. I get the board most of the way around but by now we're rail to rail. My momentum suddenly stalled, I start to fall toward her.

If I fall, I'll probably knock her off her board – more deep doo-doo. If I put out my arms or try to push off from her, I may push her over and in any case it will look like assault.

Instinctively, as our bodies collide, I wrap my arms around her for support! Now we're headed for the shore, boards parallel, bodies entwined. All I can do is repeat in her ear, over and over again: "I'm sorry! I'm so sorry".

No response. She just kind of froze.

I truly expected a reaction – a swift elbow to the ribs, a head butt, maybe some sort of jujitsu throw. After all, she was at least my size, half my age and no doubt stronger.

But in spite of all these advantages, she did nothing. Maybe she was enjoying the possibly novel experience of having manly arms wrapped around her, a husky voice whispering in her ear. Or, more likely, she was waiting to beat me up on the beach, or have her brothers do it for her.

Somehow I regained my balance, carefully released her from my embrace and turned my board a couple of degrees to port to put a bit of space between us. I rode straight to the beach, scooped my board from the water, fled to my car and made my escape. I managed to avoid all the Wilsons for weeks.

Coral Casino: Freeze-frame

Meanwhile, the ocean was cooking up some very special sauce. This time it was on a clear, dry pre-dawn morning in Santa Barbara. I had been getting up before dawn on days when the weather forecast looked good, ready to pounce on any swell that might appear. Santa Barbara can get great waves, but the swell window is tiny: swells are blocked by Point Conception to the north, and the Channel Islands form an effective breakwater to the west and west-southwest. On this morning there wasn't any significant swell in the forecast, but the weather had been good and I had the same feeling that I used to get when the surf was up or coming up. It's that special vibe where you just have a feeling that something good was going to happen.

I had spent the first year of my comeback learning everything I could about the bottom contours of the various beaches and reefs and points from Goleta to Ventura, especially in the area of Santa Barbara and Montecito. I had gotten a pretty good sense of what tide and swell direction would produce the best waves, and where those waves were most likely to hit.

This was before buoy information was widely available online, so you had to listen to harsh, crackly audio swell reports that you picked up on a special receiving device that you bought at a boating supply store. The reports were read starting from north to south, so before you could hear the one you were interested in you had to listen to a ton of other irrelevant information. If you let your mind wander, the read-out would go past your area and you'd have to wait while they got to the southernmost point on the list and then worked their way down from the top again. It was nothing like what there is today, but it was way better than pure guesswork or intuition.

On this morning, after listening impatiently as the report worked its way through Mendocino and other points north, they finally got to Point Conception. I knew instantly: Hammonds was going to be epic. The deep-water swell wasn't big, something like four to five feet on average. But that meant two things: the larger swells – the ones that would create sets – were going to be over six feet, and the effect of the bottom in shallow water would create faces at least a couple of feet bigger than that, so that the bigger sets would be eight feet or so when they broke. The best news was the swell angle: it was perfect for Hammonds.

No time for breakfast or even a quick cup of coffee – I had to hit this before conditions changed. My only hope was that no one else had figured it out.

I hastily suited up (4-3 wetsuit, booties, hood; the ocean temperature was hovering around 50°) in front of a space heater in the spare bedroom, then jumped into the van – my board already stowed and ready – and headed south along the coast. The atmosphere was mystical: ice on neighbors' roofs, cold stars glinting brightly in the predawn sky, a frozen moon working its way toward the horizon. Racing to the beach, I arrived before dawn, under a full moon. I could feel the waves crashing at Miramar when I pulled into the small parking area by the beach. No other cars!

I leaped out of the van, grabbed my board, and ran down the narrow dirt trail through the trees toward Hammonds. When I emerged at the beach end of the path, I was almost transfixed by the sight: a huge shining moon casting silver light onto the sea just as a head-and-a-half set peeled off across the reef. Each wave had a frosty trail of white just in front of the lip, the wake of a surfboard cutting across the face. I counted the waves. A six-wave set, and no one riding the last two waves.

I ran down the beach and leaped into the water just south of the break. The ocean was so cold that the first contact made my fingers hurt, but I barely noticed. I was full of excitement and adrenaline and pure surf stoke.

Just as I had thought: there were only four other surfers in the water. The eastern sky was starting to glow with a faint blue above the coastal hills, but it was still too dark to make out faces. It made no difference; we all shared the conspiratorial feeling of having made a secret discovery. As

I got closer, somebody summed up the situation for me: "You're never going to get it any better than this."

He got that right. We were like the sole inhabitants of an enchanted kingdom. It was set after set, short waits, absolutely clean and perfect waves, and plenty of rides for all of us. The takeoffs were quick, the barrels zipping perfectly, crackling in the cold air. As the sun came closer to rising we could see small dark shapes moving about on the beach.

"The party's over," someone said. And within a few minutes another half dozen or so had joined us in the lineup.

By today's standards, ten or twelve surfers on an epic day is hardly a crowd, and there were still plenty of waves to be had. But the spell had been broken. Nevertheless, the otherworldly feeling of that initial session had set the stage for what was going to happen next.

I had been keeping an eye on the next break to the north, Coral Casino. Due to bottom contours and orientation, Coral was a very different wave from Hammonds: thicker, faster, more powerful. A challenging wave on the right swell, at times it had a tendency to wall up and close out. Today the waves were breaking bigger there, and due to the nature of the break they were jacking up much faster and pitching and breaking harder than Hammonds. But they looked makeable – if you picked the right wave – and the lineup there was inexplicably deserted: not a soul to be seen.

As more people paddled out to the lineup at Hammonds, I made up my mind: I was going to give Coral a shot.

As I paddled away from Hammond's and toward Coral, the offshore islands seemed to hover above the sea in the predawn light.

I was riding the perfect board for the conditions: my 9'6" epoxy from Infinity, the one that surfed like a 7'6". It was shaped like a short board and was so light you could easily pick it up by grabbing a rail with one hand and lifting. The length allowed me to paddle fast and get in early and the shape and light weight meant quick turning.

As I paddled the three hundred yards or so to Coral, I watched the sets. What I saw confirmed my original opinion: pick the right waves, and I would be in for some epic rides.

When I got closer, I watched a set break and then paddled to set up a couple of dozen yards outside of the break. I lined up on the shore – the flagpole at the Coral Casino made a perfect marker against the hills – and sat through a set to see how the waves were working. Watch a wave come toward me, then turn to observe the back of it and see how it broke. The pattern was pretty basic: every wave that looked at all lined up would wall up and break across a wide front, impossible to make. The waves to catch were the ones that looked too narrow and peaky to be interesting; they were the ones that lined up steep and fast but makeable.

My analysis done, I went for the next set.

Paddling into a narrow A-frame wave, I popped up and cranked a right turn on the face. In the second or so that it took to pop up and turn, I found myself looking down a screaming overhead tilted half-pipe – no, make that a three-quarter pipe – that seemed to stretch all the way back to Hammonds. I pulled up into the pocket, put more weight on my front foot for speed, and blazed across the face. This wave was fast!

One idiosyncrasy of my board was that at really high speeds the skeg would hum. It didn't happen often; I had only caught a couple of waves that were fast enough to produce the humming sound. On this wave, the humming started right after I got into the pocket. Not only that, it rose to a high whine and then stopped as my speed exceeded whatever frequency was making the noise. It was like breaking my own little sound barrier.

As the wave curled over my head, I could see little white faces of the surfers at Hammonds – I was still in the shadow of the hills, but the rising sun had just lit them up – turned toward me in my barrel. It was like looking through a telescope made of water. I just had time to get in front of the edge and go out over the back before the wave walled up and crashed onto the cobbles close to shore.

I was beyond pumped or stoked. I was in another zone, on another level. To borrow a popular expression from pro tennis, I was surfing out of my mind.

Another set. Pick the narrowest wave and go. Launch into a searing right barrel. Ride it as far as you can, then either get out over the back, or get buried when the whole thing caved in; I was too stoked to care which. On every wave I broke the sound barrier: the fin would hum, then stop. On every ride I saw the faces at Hammonds, but no one made any move to join me. Between sets I could see a cluster of people on the street above the beach, most likely the local kids who usually would swarm this spot on a good day. But for whatever reason, none of them had paddled out yet.

Then it happened. A cleanup set arrived and I got into position to take advantage of it. I remember hoping that my wave selection formula would still work on this set, which was considerably larger. When a wave that had the right configuration arrived, I took a couple of deep breaths and went for it.

I felt from the first that this wave was different. Faster, more powerful, surging up and forward like a living thing. When I popped up there was a feeling of being elevated; as I turned the wave seemed to actively drive me through the turn and down the line.

All my senses were in overdrive; I was tuned to every nuance. As I accelerated I could feel the turbulence around the fins and behind the tail as displaced water rushed to fill the temporary disturbance created by the passage of the board. Above the crashing and thunderous rumbling of the wave breaking behind me, I felt and heard the rush of wind generated by the wave and my own forward motion. The humming sound of the fin reached a shrill, whining crescendo and died out.

As I rocketed across the face, suddenly the crashing of the wave collapsing just behind me stopped. For another second I sped along in an eerie silence, wondering what had happened. At the speed I was going, I wasn't about to look over my shoulder to find out. The wave was looming over me, curling out and over my head, and behind me it was caving in like a dynamited mine tunnel – and yet it was absolutely silent.

Then everything stopped as if frozen in a photograph, or a single frame in a video. No sound, no speed, no movement. Stationary. My rational mind knew that I was still flying across a very steep and hollow face, in the grip of a wave that was breaking very hard and very fast. And yet there was no sense of motion. It wasn't so much that speed had stopped, but time.

Probably every surfer has experienced the time compression that takes place on larger waves, especially in crowded conditions. The mind races like a computer, sorting masses of information and reaching multiple decisions in milliseconds. But this condition is more a matter of warp-speed thinking, during which everything is still in motion. The wave is still cresting and breaking, you and those around you are still flying. It's just that your mind is flying faster.

This was different. There was absolutely no sense of speed or motion. Yet my rational mind knew that this wasn't true.

It was like the short story by Jorge Luis Borges, about a prisoner facing a firing squad and regretting that he hadn't had time to finish a play he was writing, and suddenly time stopped – the soldiers pointing their rifles, the commandant's saber upraised, ready to fall on the order to fire, the cigarette smoke stopped in midair – and the prisoner had all the time in the world to finish, in his mind, the story he had been writing. And yet in the next instant the saber was going to fall and the rifles would crack and he would crumple over dead with the unsmoked cigarette still between his lips.

Like the protagonist of Borges' story, I had all the time in the world to deal with a situation that would be over in a few seconds. I was flying across the wave, in the midst of getting barreled, and everything – time, space, motion – was in suspension, frozen in place.

I had time to wonder if I should have placed my front foot a little farther forward to gain speed. (I decided I had the correct position.) I had time to wonder if maybe I should have been a little higher in the wave. (I decided I was okay where I was.) I had time to think about how bizarre this experience was. I had time to look down the tube of water at the cluster of little white faces, by now illuminated by the rising sun, looking toward me from the next break, a couple of hundred yards down the beach. I had time to wonder how long this condition could last.

Then it ended. Once again I was rocketing through a closing barrel and the dawn air was cold against my face and the wave was roaring behind me and on top of me and all around me as everything collapsed into a jumble of churning, tossing water and foam.

When the water hit my face it was as cold as ice.

I paddled back out, but not to Coral Casino. I returned to the original lineup at Hammond's, which by now was pretty crowded. The same surfer who had welcomed me when I had first come out an hour or so earlier, asked the question.

"Why'd you come back? It looked like you were getting some awesome rides."

I had no way to properly explain the experience I'd just had, and this wasn't the time to do so anyway. I wanted to preserve it just as it was – pure and raw, undiluted and undiminished. So I just smiled, caught a wave to the beach, and went home.

2006, La Jolla: Going home

After three or four years of surfing in and around Santa Barbara and Waikīkī, I realized two things. First, that my comeback to surfing was real. My daily workout using old recycled and adapted physical therapy routines was working. I had even been through a second shoulder surgery and gotten back into the water – albeit after a forced layoff of several months. I was more or less pain free, and I was surfing well – in some respects better than I ever had in my life. I had learned to nose ride – not as a hot-dog trick but with the original purpose of making the board go faster to get through a critical section before it broke or to keep up enough speed to make the wave. I was making late takeoffs, doing crisp cutbacks.

The credit for this wasn't mine, of course – I owed most of it to having a leash, which encouraged experimentation by removing the penalty for failure. And I owed some of it to having a full wetsuit, which allowed for more surfing and longer sessions, plus freedom from the pervasive clumsiness that comes from being too cold. And I had a dynamite epoxy board, the Infinity 9'6" that surfed like my old Canyon 7'6" and was so light I could pick it up from the top rail, like a short board.

Second, although the Santa Barbara area boasted great waves, from local semi-secrets like Hammond's and Miramar and Coral Casino to destination breaks like Rincon, the season was all too short: steep north swells were blocked by Point Conception and many of the remaining points of the compass to the northwest and west were blocked by the Channel Islands. There was also the issue of water temperatures which, in winter, could dip into the high 40s. I wanted more waves and warmer water. My annual pilgrimage to O'ahu every spring was giving me a taste of that, and I wanted more.

It wasn't practical to move to the Islands, but we could move to La Jolla. More consistent surf, warmer water, and about the same distance to LAX so my wife's commute would be roughly the same. And I was nostalgic. After all, the main reason I had left La Jolla was because I was no longer able to surf. Now that I'd fixed that problem, why couldn't I go back and pick up where I left off?

So we moved back to La Jolla, the place where I first fell in love with surfing.

Porpoise escort

As we prepared to leave Santa Barbara for our move to La Jolla, I got in one last session below the cliffs at Shoreline Park. I loved that spot, mostly for the solitude. Only a few hundred yards from the more accessible – and therefore more crowded – Leadbetter's, it was like another world. The waves there could be outstanding; on this day they were small, maybe shoulder to head high but clean and perfectly formed. The weather was gorgeous: clear, warm for the season, no wind. I got a few little rides and paddled back out for what might well be my last-ever wave there.

So, feeling happy and optimistic and nostalgic all at the same time, I took off on a nice little right, popped up, and cranked a turn. Suddenly, I didn't know what was happening. I knew all the reefs and rocks at that spot, and there was a large boil in front of me that shouldn't have been there. No, two boils. This was cause for concern.

The sand at that break is more like silt and it gets stirred up at the slightest swell so that the water is never very clear if there's any surf at all. This prevented me from seeing what was causing the boils, which could have been almost any sort of flotsam or jetsam: submerged logs – I had encountered them before – or some piece of junk from a freighter plying the channel between the shore and the Channel Islands.

Just as I was about to turn out of the wave to avoid whatever it was, two frisky porpoises broke the surface, riding the wave just in front of me. I felt a wave of relief that I wasn't going to run into an uncharted obstacle after all, followed by a surge of pure joy at having a porpoise escort. Then, hearing a huffing sound behind me, I looked back to see two more. I finished my very last Santa Barbara wave surrounded by surfing porpoises. Either they were giving me a symbolic sendoff, or they were celebrating one less surfer to contend with.

Strategic withdrawal: Horseshoe

After moving back to La Jolla it didn't take long for me to realize that my old home break, Windansea, wasn't really viable anymore. Sure, it still had the great summer rights, with the inside reef adding a bit of spice to a long ride, and the big winter left bowls with a shoulder that just kept appearing and cracking out of nowhere, so that you could get blitzed even though the wave looked like an open door. But the number of people was absurd and the attitudes made things worse. Being an Older Guy – hell, by now I was a bona fide Old Guy – and having surfed there before the current crew (or their parents) were even born, was no help. Too many people; too much 'tude.

No problem: La Jolla is full of breaks so I picked one that was less crowded. I didn't have to go far.

Horseshoe isn't far from Windansea; you can see it from the Windansea lineup and in high school and college we would often paddle the half mile or so up there just for a change of pace. It needs more size than Windansea to break properly, and when it does it jacks up quickly off a very steep reef, and breaks hard and fast. If you dawdled you might find yourself paddling straight down through empty air as the wave stood up and hollowed out. And Horseshoe broke hollow.

In addition, Horseshoe is a bowl where the swell wrapping around the reef focuses the energy like a radar dish. This makes Horseshoe a fast, nasty and generally unforgiving wave. You have to get in early, get up quickly and make your turn (left or right) instantly. No time for stalling, fading or indecision. Most of the time you can't do a bottom turn because by the time you hit the trough the wave has already jacked up and pitched, and will bury you. The hold-downs are brutal and long: one of the old Windansea crew who rode Waimea in the '50s told me he'd been held down longer on a ten-foot Horseshoe wave than on a twenty-foot Waimea wave. In short, on a big day you have to bring your "A" game on every takeoff.

On big days at Horseshoe we would watch an almost-set-wave roll beneath us, hump up – sometimes the back of the wave looked almost bigger than the face – and smash itself onto the reef with such force that the white water being blasted up through the back of the collapsing tunnel blew upward like a waterspout, much higher than the original wave itself. And someone would comment on how glad they were not to be inside of all that. So Horseshoe kept the crowds down for two reasons: the predominantly left break was avoided by a lot of regular-foot surfers who didn't like going backside, and the speed and power, not to mention the hold-downs, were intimidating.

I rode Horseshoe a lot for the first couple of years after moving back to La Jolla. I lived just a few blocks away, and it was the first place I looked at every day when I set out to surf. I loved the paddle out. Instead of going out over the reef like the shortboard guys did, I launched from the long sand beach at Marine Street, just to the south. Once you cleared the shorebreak there, you had a leisurely paddle of a couple of hundred yards to the lineup – plenty of time to get warmed up and get a look at the waves and how they were breaking.

The regulars there were focused on surfing rather than on competition, so if you were there and not getting in the way or being greedy or putting them at risk they accepted it. As a bonus, they mostly preferred to go left since that was where the most extreme rides and best barrels were to be had. That worked out perfectly for me; as an old guy I wasn't looking for extreme anymore and I was happy to go right. A win-win for everyone, and it got me into the steepest wave I have ever made.

I had surfed Horseshoe a lot in high school and college, so it had the benefit of being a known quantity. I had done a fair amount of diving there, too, so I knew the reef pretty well. And when I moved back, I made a point of going out at Horseshoe on small days – there's nothing better than to ride an intimidating break when it's small, to get a feeling for the place and remove the fear factor. So when the surf got big, I was ready, riding a 9'6" diamond tail made for me by Craig Angell, a board that had a bit more drive and was more solid in turbulence than my previous Infinity epoxy.

It was a three-day swell, a big southern hemi event that grew and grew. The evening before, the forerunners were very long period and the sets were head high or a bit more. The first day of the real swell, the waves were well overhead. I got all the waves I could handle, and had a great session. No blunders, got both lefts and rights, and had a great time. Getting back to shore was a bit dicey since the reef shadow, which usually allowed for a fairly shorebreak-free exit from the water, was ineffective due to the swell angle, and I ended up getting trounced when I tried to get my footing on the sand. Luckily, no damage to self or board.

The second day was pushing double overhead with larger sets breaking on the outer reef, standing up and pitching with great energy. I had to wait quite a while for a lull long enough to get past the shorebreak. Paddling out and across to the lineup I could see what this session was going to be like: set up outside, pick your wave carefully, paddle as hard as you ever have in your life, pop up fast, and turn on the face. Nothing fancy and no delays today or you would be hammered.

The first wave I caught didn't work out, but it wasn't a disaster, either. I had decided that my chosen direction was going to be right, since on a longboard I really wasn't up for ending up in front of the rocks, which is where the left would take you. The rights were usually much shorter but on a big day like today you could get a nice line that took you into a second section that might or might not be makeable, depending on the wave. The end of the ride was in front of a sand beach, and usually you could easily get to the channel and use the rip to paddle back out.

The wave almost went as planned: quick paddle, pop up, turn on the face...it was already breaking in front of me! I barely had time to straighten out and hurl myself prone onto the board, so that I could soup in until the wave calmed down. Luckily my momentum had driven me far enough into the flat in front of the wave, so that when it broke the lip came down behind my board. If you took a direct hit, it could easily snap your board, maybe even injure your spine.

I was riding prone toward the shore, trying to angle toward the channel, getting buffeted by the massive, roiling wall of foam but hanging on and congratulating myself on having dodged a bullet, when the foam ball hit the inside reef and blew up again, sending me skyward. Suddenly I was in the air and doing a spectacular front flip, board and all. For the first time in my life I had gotten pitched, while prone, on a wave that had already broken! In the dozens of times I had proned out as a kid and later, nothing like this had ever happened. It was an indication of the power and speed of the waves.

Back out to try again. I set up a little farther outside, and was soon rewarded. The set of the day loomed up on the horizon. I considered waiting for the second wave since it would probably be bigger and maybe better than the first one, but on the other hand this wave looked perfect so I went. When I turned to paddle, I could hear the shortboard guys inside hooting.

Again, a few quick strong strokes, pop up, turn on the face. I found myself staring south down the line of a concave vertical face that seemed endless. It was one of those "*What have I done?*" moments. The wave was already too steep for any hope of turning straight off, so the only thing to do was keep going and hope I made it. I had recently made the switch from old-school single fin to 2+1, and those thruster fins saved my life. All the way across the face, the only thing holding me into the pocket was the uphill thruster fin and the hard down rail near the tail. The rest of the board and the other two fins were touching nothing but air. I could feel the board twitching and quivering as it started to lose its grip on the water, then recover itself.

The face seemed interminable, but I made it – by far the steepest face I've ever made it across in my life. In front of me was the next section, and it was evident that I wasn't going to make it: it was still several yards ahead of me, and it was already fringing. So when the first section slacked off a bit I managed to go up over the top and out, just in time to feel the rush of wind as the rest of the wave broke.

What I saw next really took my breath away.

The second wave of the set, the one I decided not to wait for, was a monster – much bigger than the one I had caught. It started to fringe and it was clear that no matter how hard I paddled, I was not going to be able to make it around or over that wave before it broke. So I stopped where I was, waited while it broke, then took a couple of deep breaths to oxygenate and dove for the bottom before the towering, churning mass of white water arrived. I went down keeping my head oriented toward the horizon, grabbed two big fistfuls of eelgrass and hung on with my body straight and pressed against the reef as best I could. I could see the swirling, tumbling tornado of white water coming at me, and I could see that it reached all the way to the bottom. A moment later, it hit and all hell broke loose.

I now got to learn what it was like to be caught in one of those nasty, spitting, bone-crushing waves we used to talk about.

My grip on the eelgrass lasted less than one second. The eelgrass tore off like wet tissue paper as the wave reached down with a gigantic twisting hand, wrenched me loose, yanked me up just far enough to get some momentum and then slammed me back down on the reef. Luckily, being La Jolla it wasn't coral or lava and it was covered with eelgrass, but it almost knocked me hard enough to force out some air. And I was going to need all the air I had.

After that it gets a bit blurry. It was way past the common comparison of being like a washing machine; it was more like a very energetic washing by scrubbing and twisting and beating on rocks, as done by people who have no washing machines. Massive pistons of water and foam punched me down flat, grabbed me and shook me, twisted me from side to side, dragged me back and forth. In terms of sheer violence, this was by far the worst hold-down I had ever experienced. It was relentless. I felt like a chew toy being demolished by a pit bull. I was getting rag-dolled in all directions; I could feel my arms and legs and body flapping wildly, like one of those creepy, inflatable arm-flailing, body-contorting, neck-rolling tube men outside of car repair places and furniture stores where a sale is in progress. I tried everything: relax, float like a jellyfish, roll up in a ball, try to straighten out and use my body like a plane to ride the energy toward the surface. None of it worked. I had no control at all.

By this time I was running out of air. It occurred to me to grab my leash and try to climb it to the surface. After all, my board was up there somewhere. It wasn't possible – I was getting whipped around in all directions, so violently that I couldn't manage to make contact with my own ankle. I began to see little twinkling flashes and I was just about to give up and inhale when finally I popped to the surface. After taking a couple of gasping breaths, I tried to reel in my board and I discovered that I couldn't move my left arm. I had gotten some sort of whiplash that temporarily deadened the nerve.

Luckily on the rights the wave and the current at Horseshoe will push you south, off the reef and into the channel. As I floated in the channel with my board, waiting for the sensation in my arm to come back and luxuriating in all the air I wanted, I realized that big Horseshoe was now officially out of my league. I was, as they say, getting too old for this stuff.

Horseshoe: Out of my league

The third day of the swell was even bigger, so big that even without my little mishap of the previous day I wouldn't have gone out anyway. I spent the day watching other people get bombs and get crushed and break their boards, while congratulating myself on my good fortune and my good sense. A guy has to know his own limits, and you have to know when to quit. At least I had my epic, personal "steepest ever" to remember – and my personal "nastiest hold-down" to go with it.

Meanwhile, my annual pilgrimage to Waikīkī gave me a chance to conduct an experiment.

Mr. Science: Box jellyfish

One fine morning I was surfing in front of the Elks Club near Diamond Head when I got stung by a box jellyfish.

This sort of thing was a problem that had not existed when I first came to the Islands in the 1950s. Box jellies are not native to Hawaiian waters. They seem to have been inadvertently introduced sometime in the 1970s, mixed with the bilge water of one or more ships, perhaps from the Caribbean. Their initial range in Hawai'i was limited to the area near the harbor in Honolulu, but since then they have spread and even reached other islands in the chain.

The good news about box jellies is that they only appear once a month, about a week after the full moon. In a few days, they are gone again. Some infestations are much more severe than others, and sometimes the jellies fail to appear at all. As yet little is known about this cycle, other than the fact that it exists. The lifeguard service puts up signs when the jellies are swarming, and also maintains a calendar showing when future events are expected to occur.

I managed to get stung on a "safe" day. Jellyfish are not good about keeping track of schedules.

I was sitting in the lineup when I felt a sudden sharp pain low on my right thigh, just above the knee. It felt as if I had been stung by a wasp, and reflexively I smacked the spot with my open palm. Looking at my leg, I saw a glistening substance and a few small black spots, like black sesame seeds. There were more of the same in the water. Box jellies have tiny black eyes. I knew I had been stung.

The previous year I had been surfing Publics with a local Hawaiian who had a huge scab, like a healing burn wound, all over one forearm. He had been stung by a couple of box jellies at the same time. Was this what I had to look forward to?

I considered heading for the beach, then thought better of it. I was here to surf, the waves were clean and overhead, there was almost no one out yet, and by golly, I was going to surf. Besides, to my knowledge nothing would neutralize the neurotoxin of the box jellyfish. There are a million different suggested treatments for box jelly stings, each one contradicts the others, and none of them work. It was going to hurt no matter where I was, so I might as well be surfing.

It occurred to me that this was a great chance to run an experiment. People talked about how bad a box jelly sting hurt, but perhaps there was a natural way to minimize that. After all, this was not the really nasty Australian variety with venom so potent that it would cause an agonizing death. The Hawaiian kind was more localized, like a blowtorch aimed at your skin.

When the area around the sting started to turn red and burn, I tested my theory: by padding around instead of just sitting on my board waiting for the next set, perhaps the activity would increase blood circulation, thus drawing some of the toxin out of the affected area and reducing the effects.

My theory worked! The area around the sting on my leg was reduced to a low-flame burning that was more of a distraction than a crippling burden.

After a few waves, however, I discovered the downside to my procedure. I started getting a feeling of unreality, coupled with an increasing lack of wave judgment. Before long I was seriously buzzed. I took off too late and got blitzed. When I caught a wave my turns were sloppy. Apparently I had redistributed the neurotoxin so well that it was affecting my brain. Time to go home!

Riding my bike back to our studio condo with my longboard on a rack, it was all I could do to survive. My balance seemed okay, but I was prone to terrible decisions.

Car pulling out? No worries, I'll just swerve around him...ooops! Damn! That was close. Hey, don't yell at me, brah, I'm in the bike lane...

Hmmm. Can I make it across the street in front of that tour bus? Of course I can, plenty of...holy crap! He almost ran over me! How did that happen?

After I got home, I made a quick foray next door to the ABC for some alleged remedies, including vinegar and Benadryl. None of it had any effect. After that, I spent the rest of the day in the condo, afraid of what disaster I might blunder into if I went out, my head feeling stupid and heavy and dull, with a nagging headache. By the next day my head was okay but I had a large scab on my leg, much bigger than the initial area, that lasted for a couple of weeks.

My verdict: with Hawaiian box jellies you can keep surfing, at least for awhile. Then the fun begins.

2005 –2019 : Have camera, will travel

My dual focus on Hawai'i and Southern California provided ample material for a new activity: digital photography.

I had gotten into photography in the film era, with a Mamiya Sekor with a 55mm lens, but only to document my trip to Brazil. Since film was by my financial standards expensive, I shot sparingly and never took a single surf-related photograph. All my film shooting was people and places in South America, and after I got back the camera ended up in a closet. It was subsequently stolen by a vindictive ex-girlfriend, and to be honest I never missed it. I often used to think that if you couldn't remember an event without a photo of it, then maybe you should have paid better attention at the time.

But when the digital camera era came in, I gave photography another chance. Boy, am I glad I did. It not only taught me how to see things with beginner's eyes, it gave me a new way to interact with the ocean when there was no surf – or if I couldn't surf. I made my reentry modestly, with a point and shoot digital camera with a built-in zoom lens. Suddenly, with no film to buy and no developing cost, the act of taking pictures was free.

I went berserk. I roamed all over La Jolla shooting everything that moved and a lot of things that didn't. I shot seals, huge waves, backwash, surfers, shorebirds, beach rocks, seascapes. I got into video. I relearned the habits of paying attention to lighting, context (AKA "composition"), perspective, timing. I started to see details that I had previously overlooked. And the telephoto capabilities of my little camera got me to pay attention to the way things looked at different sizes, and where the center of the action really was in different situations.

In Hawai'i I used the camera to immerse myself in my surroundings. I shot waves, boats, surfers, sunsets, neighborhoods, picturesque characters, mynah birds, slack rope walkers, street people, Hare Krishnas, jugglers, hula classes, tai chi practitioners, moonlight scenes, rainbows and buildings old and new. Basically, it was a version of "get all you can while you can": I was capturing everything I could before it changed or went away.

Within a year or two I wanted to take photographs in the water. GoPro was still pretty primitive, so I got a little waterproof Canon D10, put it in a neoprene Walkman belt with a lanyard around my waist in case the camera came out or I dropped it, and paddled out to surf. I would catch a wave, pop up, and then do a quick draw kind of thing so I could shoot pictures while surfing. Paddling out, I would get shots of people riding waves. In the lineup, I stuck the camera beneath the surface and took pictures of fish. Everything was fair game. The camera wasn't all that good and the lens had a tendency to fog up due to multiple temperature changes as the camera went in and out of the water, so any decent photo was a matter of pure luck. But I had fun. It was another way to capture the magic of being ten years old again.

An added bonus was that instead of wanting every wave I saw, I wanted other people to catch them so I could take their picture. Their joy was my joy, and that made a big difference. In addition, on cloudy days and days with no surf, I could go back over the images on my computer and it was the next best thing to being there.

As cameras got better and I got better, I started tuning my eyes to get the precise best moment on the wave. I learned that the cliché surfer-in-the-barrel head-on photo, spectacular as it may be, isn't always the best one. Even better, for many people, is that moment when something is about to happen. A surfer poised on the lip of a steep wave or dropping toward a section that is about to break, the kind of will-he-make-it-or-not moment that we've all had on countless waves, actually has more drama. For isn't surfing really more reliant on what is about to happen than what's happening at the moment? You're riding in the moment, but each instant requires anticipation of the next, like a film where each frame creates anticipation of what's going to occur in the next. And that, I think, is where the thrill and the heightened awareness come from: anticipation.

I was in my late sixties before anyone took a photo of me on a wave and I was really happy to get it. (Luckily, it was a nice ride and the photo made me look good.) So it occurred to me that maybe others would appreciate having a photo as well. I started by taking pictures of friends surfing, and then extended the gesture to people I didn't know. *I think I got a good shot of you; I'll send it to you if you like.* At times I shot video as well. It feels good when someone's eyes light up with pleasure after getting their first ever – or, depending on the surfer and the wave, best ever – shot or video clip of them on a wave.

As a bonus, by capturing the best moments and focusing on the most critical parts of each wave I got to view and interact with thousands of waves vicariously. And I still can: whenever I look at those images and videos, I participate in the experience. Their rides but, in a sense, my waves.

2013, Castle's: Prophecy fulfilled?

Castle's had become my go-to spot when it was breaking, and today looked like it could offer an epic session. The swell wasn't the cleanest, but it had size. All night I had heard – and felt – the crash and rumble of a serious swell hitting Waikīkī. Up before dawn, get the board on the bike, and head for the channel at Kaimana Beach.

There's something special about hitting the water before the sun comes up, an expectant pause before the day asserts itself. It's like surfing in another world.

There's already enough light to get out to the break and find my lineup spots. It takes a while to get out because the channel is closing out, but patience does the trick. Due to the size, I set up outside of where I normally would. There's a stiff offshore blowing, which is going to make things a little tricky. If I set up too far outside, the wind will make it much harder to catch the wave while it's still slopy. I confirm this by missing the first set that comes through because I can't keep enough speed to catch any of the waves.

After missing the last wave of the set, which almost feathered underneath me, I stay where I am instead of going back outside. If I start from here, I'll surely be able to get a wave. But I've got to be quick, and allow for the fact that the wind will hold up the waves, making them steeper, while simultaneously making it harder to drop down the face.

My change of position pays off: when the next set comes, I get a beauty. Sure enough, the wind holds me up near the lip, and threatens to get under my board. I have to crouch down and push one hand down on the front of the board, in front of my feet, to keep it tracking across and down the face. The wave is a real thrill ride, a backside left that towers and crashes right behind me, the lip dancing and whipping in the wind. The energy is electrifying.

Paddle back out, set up in my new spot, wait for the next one. When it comes, it's a carbon copy of my last ride: big, thick, powerful, fast, steep. I make the same almost-late takeoff, pop up in a crouch. I feel board trying to go airborne so I put my hand down on the nose to steady it.

Castle's 2013

The next thing I know, I'm free-falling down the face, my back to the wave. The wind has taken the board. Okay, no worries, I've been in this spot before. Stay tucked, keep my feet together, arms in, try to defend against getting hit by my board when the wave breaks.

Suddenly, something doesn't make sense. An unseen force violently yanks my right leg straight out and up and I see my foot going up over my right shoulder. I hear and feel a sickening crunching sensation in my hip, like someone ripping the leg off a roasted chicken. Before I can react, the wave breaks and smashes me into the water, churns me around. But at least the horrible pull on my leg stops.

I come up gasping, almost in shock, trying to fathom what has just happened. My board is floating next to me, but there's no time to grab it because here comes the next wave. I turn toward the onrushing white water and dive down to go beneath it. As I extend my legs, I feel a paralyzing pain in my right hip. All I can do is curl up in a ball and let the wave beat me up. This continues until the set has passed. Between waves, I manage to get the leash off my right ankle and onto my left, to avoid further damage to my hip.

I get to my board and try to climb back onto it. Impossible. I'm destroying my right hip. Is it dislocated? I don't know. I lie there in the water, clinging to my board, trying to figure out what to do. The sun has yet to come up, there's no one around. The good news is that the waves, even at this size, aren't carrying all the way to the beach, so there's no danger of getting beaten up on the seawall. The bad news is that I can't use the soup to push me any closer to shore.

I hear a voice:

"Dave? What are you doing?"

It's a local surfer, Pat, paddling out to catch some predawn bombs at Castle's.

"I dunno. I think I dislocated my hip."

He tells me to hang tight; he'll try to get in contact with Ocean Rescue. I can only hope that there's someone on duty at this hour.

As he paddles back to shore, I make a couple of more attempts to get up on my board to paddle myself in to the beach. No luck: whatever has happened, my efforts are only making it worse.

Meanwhile, the big surf has generated some very strong currents. I find myself being swept sideways along the shore, then pulled out toward the horizon. I get to a point outside of Publics. Way outside. There's a guy on a surfboard sitting there. My heart sinks. This means that waves are breaking way out here.

Sure enough, a set approaches. The surfer looks at me hanging from the side of my board with both arms and makes a generous offer:

"Hey, uncle, you don't want this wave?"

I tell him thanks, but no thanks; I think I've dislocated my hip. Immediately he goes into rescue mode.

"Don't worry, uncle, we'll get you outa here." He tells me his name is Bryce.

We make several efforts to get me back on my board, without success. Finally we decide to see what happens if I just float flat, as high as I can, hanging onto his leash, while he tows me. No luck: the current is so strong that we're making no progress, maybe even going backwards.

Finally I make a supreme effort and manage to get up onto my board by lying face-down in the water behind the tail, reaching as far forward as I can, grabbing both rails and pulling the board beneath me, tail first. My leg feels as if it's going to fall off, but it doesn't. I feel strangely light-headed.

We start to paddle with Bryce in the lead. It's tough going. I feel weak and at times things get blurry. At one point I drift off to sleep and only wake up when I run into Bryce.

"Sorry, I kinda lost focus there for a minute."

So far things are not going well. I can make out a handful of surfers at Pops. We're drifting in that direction; maybe if I can last long enough to get there we can borrow enough firepower to help me get to the beach.

By now we've drifted farther, to somewhere way outside of Cunha's. There's a surfer out there, a local kid I've spoken to before.

"Hey, uncle, nice waves today."

If he's here, there are waves here. From my point of view, not good. Just then a long, dark line appears on the horizon. It's a set and it's a big one. The kid starts paddling out to keep from getting caught inside. I realize that in my condition that is not an option. I'm getting weaker, I keep having little white-outs and I'm having trouble understanding where I am.

I slide off the board into the water. I figure if the set does break, I'll use my previous tactic from inside Castle's: curl up in a ball as best I can and ride it out. At least the waves will push me closer to shore.

As the set approaches and the first wave starts to jack up, the first rays of the rising sun catch the lip. The spray blowing from the top of the fringing wave turns to gold, then lights up with all the colors of the rainbow. I'm awestruck at the beauty of the scene.

I turn my board sideways to the wave so that hopefully it won't get broken in half, and push it away from me so it won't hit me. It slides smoothly across the water, then begins to ascend the face of the wave. As the wave goes vertical and the speed of wind and water rushing up the face accelerates, my board is lifted and tilted skyward. Then it leaps from the water and launches up through the rainbow lip like a great leaping fish, trailing a shower of diamonds that refract all the colors of the rainbow. It's the most awesome sight I've ever seen. In my befuddled mental state all I can do is wish I had a camera.

Cunha's 2013.

I survive the set, along with my board.

By now the sun is up. I can see people on the beach. A helicopter comes over, shooting scenes for the local news TV. Bryce takes off his rash guard and waves it at them frantically as a distress signal. The chopper slows, banks, comes around past us again. Someone in the chopper waves gaily back at us (*Look at those two down there! I'll bet they're having fun!*), then the chopper straightens out and flies off toward Diamond Head, looking for more stuff to shoot. So much for distress signals. I feel like a character in a Gary Larson cartoon.

After the set has passed I try to get back on my board again, but by now it's not possible. It isn't about the pain – although there's plenty of that – but about my certainty that any serious attempt to get back on my board is going to cause massive, permanent, irreversible damage to my hip and leg. In addition, I feel increasingly fatigued, drained of all energy, and the slightest exertion makes the outside world grow hazy.

We make it over another, smaller set. I start to fall asleep again. I dimly realize that if I do, my head will droop, my face will go into the water and I will drown. For some reason, I don't really care.

I'm roused by the faint engine whine of a jet ski rising above the pulse and rumble of the waves. Pat must have made contact and sent help. There's only one problem: due to the size of the waves, they can't see us, and judging from the sound they're searching the area where I was last seen, inside Castle's in front of the aquarium. I can only hope that they don't conclude that somehow I made it to the beach on my own and exited the water via the ramp at the aquarium.

Luckily it occurs to them to follow the current, and finally they come in sight, two lifeguards on a jet ski, roaring up and over a set outside Publics. They get to us, unhook my leash, drag me up onto a sort of toboggan sled that's attached to the rear of the jet ski.

The ride back is a nightmare. Instead of doing what I would have considered the normal thing – stay outside the surf line, head for the channel, and either wait for a lull or head for the beach between waves, which would have been easy – the driver takes a route inside the reef, following the shoreline and the seawall. Thanks to a combination of surge and backwash, this produces a bouncing, pounding ride so rough that it takes all my strength to hang onto the two rope loops that are my only connection to the sled.

The sled is so short that my feet and legs are dragging in the water. My feet and legs are flapping around in the wake and my body – especially my hip area – bounces brutally on every bump, making it feel as though my injured leg were coming off at each impact. A couple of times I consider letting go – no matter how that worked out, I couldn't imagine that the damage to my hip and leg could possibly be worse than this – but for some reason I hang on and we make it. I wonder how much additional damage has been done.

Once on shore they got me to a bench and the lifeguard filled out an incident report. Date of birth: 1941...

"That makes you seventy-two."

"That's right. Seventy-two."

"I thought you were sixty-two."

I was, but every year I got older. But all I said was, "Nope. Seventy-two."

"I'm surprised you were even out there, then."

Under different circumstances I would have argued this notion. I had been surfing stuff like this at various breaks out here for ten years. He knew that; he had seen me doing it. Suddenly, now that he had a number to attach to me, I was too old? What was the cutoff point – last year? Five years ago? "Too old" is when you physically can't handle it anymore, like when I ran into trouble bodysurfing the Cove or when I got caught inside and thrashed on a big day at Horseshoe. But this was a freak accident – it could have happened to anyone. In that moment I decided that if at all possible I would go out here again on a big day, just to prove my point.

But I wasn't in any condition to argue or make future plans. My leg and hip were killing me, I felt weak and everything outside me was vague. I wanted to get off this bench and somewhere I could lie down.

I toyed with the idea of letting my body heal itself. This had always worked before, and after the experience of the jet ski rescue I wasn't eager to subject myself to any more first-responder treatment. But even as addled as I was I could still tell that this injury was different, so after some hesitation I decided I needed professional care.

Don't worry, we're here to help you

My experience with unorthodox rescue modes was just beginning. Once the ambulance arrived, I was sure that things would be handled quickly, efficiently and professionally. I had been present at a couple of surf injury rescues on the West Coast and I had seen how things were done: ask a few questions to establish tolerance to anesthetic, give a shot of morphine, immobilize the affected area, get the patient onto a gurney and into the vehicle, and provide a quick ride to the hospital.

Boy, was this different! No questions, no morphine, no attempt to stabilize. Get me to my feet – one foot, actually; I was totally incapable of putting any weight at all on the other – hop me to the ambulance, heave me inside. Then we were off!

Lying there in the back of the vehicle, trying to think good thoughts, after a few minutes I notice that we're not moving. We've stopped! We must be at the hospital. Now someone will surely do something to fix my hip. Yes, we've stopped. We are stopped. We are still stopped.

In the front, my two saviors are arguing about some mundane issue. No attempt to get me out and into the building where help awaits. Something must be amiss.

With great effort, I turn my neck – I'm lying on my good side – and lift my head to look out the rear window. Behind me I see a long procession of stationary cars and trucks, with Diamond Head in the background. We're on the H1 freeway, which in our lane is jammed to a standstill, although the other lanes are moving. And we've hardly covered any of the distance to the hospital. It occurs to me that from the time they tossed me into the vehicle, I haven't heard any siren.

I clear my throat, tentatively.

"Excuse me, why are we not moving?"

They both turn to look at me surprised. They seem to have forgotten that I was in their care and custody.

"Road repair, brah. Or maybe some kinda accident."

My quick glimpse out the window had showed me that the lane next to ours was moving, and I could hear the cars moving past.

"Well, could you use the siren to get us out of this lane?

They roll their eyes. Man, these haoles can be so demanding!

"We don't think your injury was life-threatening. No need the siren."

Oh. OK. Whatever. *How about leg-threatening, dude? That works for me.*

I can only think it; I'm in no condition to argue with a couple of guys who see their job as something akin to hauling trash or delivering a case of beer to a convenience store. They get back to their discussion and I cease to exist again.

The ride is interminable. I can feel my leg swelling to the bursting point, and the pain is off the charts. I decide that if the ambulance catches fire, I'll just stay put. Whatever happened, it would be less painful than right now.

In my mentally scrambled state, I think of the saying that you can't make an omelet without breaking a few eggs. Except in my mind, "eggs" is "legs." For some reason I find this uproariously funny and I start giggling to myself.

The two Hawaiians in the front look back at me, then look at each other and shake their heads. Crazy haole. Mo bettah deliver beer.

At some point, still the same day, we back up to the ER entrance. I know because I can see it through the rear window. Finally, salvation!

We stop. We're stopped. We're still stopped. I tune into the current conversation in the front, which seems to be about cell phone usage.

"No, brah, that's not da way."

"What you sayin', brah, you don't know how to use 'em."

"Gimme dat brah, you gonna break 'em."

I pray that somehow, someone will get me out of this vehicle and inside. Hand me over to someone else. Anyone else.

Finally the back pops open, and after a few more exchanges they get out and wheel me into the ER. On each side of the room, a row of narrow hospital beds with rails, separated by curtains.

The ER nurses, a couple of ex-corpsmen or medics, are great. Off the gurney and onto an ER bed. Quick check, a few questions, and then it's IV morphine. Finally my leg stops trying to fall off. My blood pressure is only 80/50, which even I know is marginal, so they hook me up to a second IV with something else; I'm not sure what. A doctor comes in, asks a few more questions and checks my leg. He says he's going to order an MRI and could I please be patient as they're having a busy morning. No worries, doc. Just keep the pain down and I have all the time in the world.

I spend the morning in the ER, listening to what goes on beyond the lateral curtains, and watching the tiny slice of the room that I can see past the foot of my bed. At intervals a doctor comes in to see how I'm doing. There's been a shift change so the doctors are different.

About three beds down toward the door, judging from the sounds, they've brought in a drowning victim and they're trying to get the water out of his lungs. The gasping and gagging and choking sounds are horrendous, as if he were being waterboarded.

"Hang on there, buddy, we're almost done on this side."

They turn him over and start on the other lung. I thank God that I'm not the one going through that. I'd rather have my leg injury.

Right next to me, on the other side, they install a middle-aged woman. She looks totally fine when they wheel her past the foot of my bed. The doctor comes in to ask his questions.

"What brings you in here today?"

"I have a headache."

That stops him cold. If there is such a thing as a surprised silence, that describes it. Finally he manages to speak.

"A headache."

"Yeah, it hurt when I woke up and I took a couple aspirin but when that didn't work I figured maybe I oughta come in here and see what's wrong."

They give her some extra-strength Tylenol and send her on her way.

The morphine is working and I'm getting drowsy again, just like I was in the water. I'm dreamily watching the monitor attached to a person in the bed across the aisle. There's something soothing about watching the little green line bob up and down, rhythmically, to the tune of a series of soft beeps. The nurse has her back to it, busy writing something down.

"Beep...beep...beep...beep...beep...beep...beeeeeeeeeeeeeeee" and the line stops bobbing up and down. The patient has flat-lined, but the nurse doesn't seem to notice. I decide to say something.

"Excuse me? I think your patient is having a problem."

The nurse turns toward me, clearly irritated at being disturbed. She probably thinks I'm hallucinating. I point toward the monitor.

She looks at it, then goes into full emergency drill mode. She picks up a phone, says something. A team bursts in from somewhere in the hospital and swarms around the patient, administering whatever treatment it is that they do. The monitor starts to beep properly again, accompanied by the dancing green line. I feel like a hero. Nobody says thank you.

Still no MRI. They need space in the ER, so they put my gurney in a hallway.

"Sorry, but we don't have any beds right now. As soon as we get a room free, we'll put you in it."

The hallway is, well, a hallway. At the end there's a large wall clock, so I can keep track of time. As if it made a difference. I count the little dots on the acoustic ceiling tiles, just like I used to do in primary school. People bustle past: doctors, nurses, orderlies. Everyone is on a mission. I see one of the doctors who checked up on me in the ER, a very kind person. I lift an arm as he approaches.

"Hi, doc."

He walks past me, no eye contact and no sign of recognition, as if I didn't exist.

When later this happens with another doctor, I realize they are completely focused on their current mission. Finish with one patient, on to the next. When you're taking off on a wave, or riding one, you don't distract yourself by thinking about the last wave you caught. Be here now. Anyhow, it's been a crazy day. I have no way of knowing how much crazier things are going to get.

By the time they wheel me to the elevator and up to a room, it's dark outside. From the window I can see the calm, park-like grounds of a cemetery studded with white tombstones. Overflow from the hospital, perhaps; it's certainly convenient. I missed the meal service, but although morphine appears to be an appetite suppressant, I haven't eaten since yesterday and I'm hungry. The nurse who sees me into the room is kind enough to get me some fruit and a muffin from the staff cafeteria. It's the best thing I ever ate.

Later a couple of doctors come in to take a look. They carefully jab the sole of my right foot – the injured leg – with a pin.

"Do you feel that? Do you feel that?"

I feel it. They confer in low tones. Before they leave, they tell me what to do.

"Every time you wake up during the night, we want you to use your left foot to tap against the bottom of your right foot. If you can't feel it, push this button right away, because we'll have to operate."

Naturally, I'm curious. Operate like how?

"We'll have to amputate. Otherwise you'll get gangrene."

And on this cheerful note they bid me good night.

I spend the night frantically tapping one foot against the other and thinking about whether or not they make artificial feet that you can surf with. I'm also kept awake by increasing pain in my right hip, the one I thought I had dislocated. It keeps intruding through the morphine.

Finally, the next day, they tell me what my problem is. I have ruptured a large vein in my right thigh. The entire time I was in the water, and for sometime thereafter, blood that was supposed to be going back to my heart was instead being pumped directly into my thigh. This is why I started to white out and fall asleep in the water, and why my leg was swollen and tight as a drumhead. If the bleeding hadn't stopped, the pressure inside the leg would have caused irreversible nerve and tissue damage.

But this explanation doesn't address the problem of my possibly dislocated hip. The nurse says she'll get someone to look at that.

Before long another doctor swaggers in, an overweight guy with a self-important air. He dispenses with small talk, puts his hands on my injured thigh, closes his eyes, and just stands there without moving, as if feeling the vibes. It's more like a laying on of hands than a medical assessment. He seems to be in some sort of trance, an aging hippie witch doctor tripping on his own imaginary powers of divination. Finally he brings himself back to the real world, then straightens up and turns to drift from the room.

I stop him.

"Excuse me? I have some really bad pain in the back of my right hip, the one that I wrenched and tore."

He looks at me, irritated at my presumption.

"That's just normal cramping."

Normal? As compared to what? This guy is a total loss.

"I never got my MRI; maybe that would reveal something?"

His irritation turns to contempt.

"I canceled your MRI. Waste of time. Wouldn't tell us anything."

I'm reminded of the old joke: *What do you call a guy who graduated at the bottom of his class from a third-rate medical school? Answer: "Doctor."*

I wait until he's gone, then call a nurse and tell her that everyone has focused on the thigh and ignored my hip joint. Once again, I request the MRI that I was supposed to get. This time I'm insistent. I suspect that these guys get paid more for not doing tests.

When I finally get the MRI, it reveals that I had torn the medial hamstring muscle completely off the bone. This means that I am going to have to be very careful for months, and that I am going to have trouble walking properly for a long time after that.

But the bleeding inside my leg did stop, and they sent me home. Or rather, I sent myself home, after one more Looney Tunes episode.

It had been decided that I should stay one more night in the hospital, just to be safe. "Safe," I soon learned, is a relative term.

After dinner, my IV machine started acting up. Every few minutes it would start buzzing frantically and a red light would start flashing to indicate a malfunction. I would push the call button, a nurse would come in, fiddle with the machine, and find nothing wrong. Reset. Repeat. After a few go-arounds the nurse decided to spend a little more time to try to fix this thing once and for all. As I watched her fussing and tampering with the machine, tipping it this way and that, suddenly I saw that the IV line, which was still attached to my arm, was filling up with air instead of liquid. An endless chain of elongated air bubbles raced gaily down the clear plastic tube, heading toward my arm.

"Stop! Stop! Turn it off! It's gonna pump me full of air!"

The nurse was undeterred. In fact, she was totally indifferent.

"I've just about got it, be patient."

I had visions of myself going into spasms as a huge air bubble rode down the tube, into my vein, and up to my heart. Or maybe I would be inflated like a gigantic balloon. Outside the window, in the dark, the gravestones in the cemetery leered white.

After all that I had gotten through over the previous couple of days, there was no way I was going to let it end like this. I reached over with my other hand and crimped the tube below the air bubbles, stopping the flow.

The nurse ignored me and continued to futz aimlessly with the equipment, disconnecting and reconnecting tubes.

"Hang on...okay, let's try it now," she said cheerfully.

Cautiously, I released my grip on the tube.

The chain of air bubbles quivered, hesitated, and then started to retreat back up the tube, pursued by a vigorous flow of rich, red blood. She had hooked the pump up backwards and we were now pumping blood out of me and back toward the IV bag.

I quickly grabbed the tube and pinched it shut again.

"Get this thing out of my arm, now!"

She was shocked – a patient giving orders to a nurse? – but she complied.

"I don't know why you were so upset in the first place," she huffed grumpily as she disconnected the tube and removed the needle from my arm. "No one has established how much air can go into a vein before it kills you."

My point exactly.

I had had enough. All I wanted to do was get out of this madhouse and go home. I got dressed, grabbed the walker they had put in my room for my eventual departure, and headed for the door. It hurt like hell to move but anything was better than this.

The nurse put herself between me and the door, blocking my passage.

"You can leave but you haven't been discharged so you can't take the walker."

This was starting to feel like a hostage situation. I abandoned the walker, dodged the nurse, dragged myself along the wall to the elevator, and somehow got outside. When a taxi came to drop someone off, I gingerly slid in – half sitting, half lying sideways, on my good side – and made my escape.

Waikīkī: Mea culpa

Back in the studio condo, I was immobilized. The morphine had long since worn off, my hip area hurt like hell – they hadn't issued me any pain pills – and so did my thigh, which was black, swollen and still as tight as a drum. After two days – or was it three? I had lost track of time – of the cartoonish ambulance ride and the ER and the witchdoctor mumbo-jumbo and technical malfunctions, no one had actually done anything to help remedy the damage to my leg and hip, and I was going to have to heal on my own whether I liked it or not. At least I had been able to smuggle my bedpan out of the hospital with me.

For the next few days I lay on the bed all day, coddling my right hip. Luckily the condo was small and the fridge was next to the bed so I could access it without taking any steps. Just ease myself up carefully on my good leg, open the fridge door, grab something to eat and fall carefully back onto the bed to eat it. Standing was not only painful, but I could practically feel the blood trying to open up the ruptured vein again, so cooking or heating up any food was out of the question. I just ate everything cold. With the pain and all the rest of it I didn't have much appetite anyway.

Then the food ran out.

And this is when I got the epiphany of my life: I saw my own oblivious lack of empathy.

One of the guys I had met at Waikīkī was a surfer who went by the nickname of Diamond Jim. Originally from San Francisco, he'd had an incredibly interesting life, including running illegal after-hours clubs in the City and owning a ranch near Mt. Diablo where he gave parties with guest lists featuring a variety of well-known musicians of the era. Now he was a transplant to Honolulu, and he had Parkinson's. He had it bad and it was getting worse, but he still tried to surf. He kept a big foamy board in the board racks by the police station at Canoes. He would accept no help in getting the board to the water and paddling out, even though it was clearly a painfully laborious chore. He gamely tried to catch waves, and sometimes succeeded, although he was past the point of being able to stand up.

So what was my sin? As I lay in my room, unable to walk and out of food, suddenly I realized how the simplest things, like going to the store, could take on tremendous significance to a person temporarily or permanently impaired. And I realized that although I had sympathized with Diamond Jim, and offered to help him with his surfboard, and encouraged him in the water, not once had it occurred to me to ease some of his daily burden by offering to go to the grocery store with him or in his place. It would have been so easy; we lived within blocks of each other. I had fumbled, dropped the ball, just as surely and shamefully as I had when I was failing at team sports as a kid.

Oh, sure, I'm the kind of guy who helps people in distress, pushes a wheelchair-bound person up a difficult ramp, grabs a stranger's loose surfboard so that it won't get pounded on the rocks, stops a kid's ball from going into the street. Anyone does that; we all do that. In Mexico I had helped patch up the car crash victims and get them to shelter and safety. But that is all spur-of-the-moment stuff, almost reflex action. It's quick, it's usually pretty easy, and it requires little thought and even less commitment. One and done. The situation with Diamond Jim – and anyone like him – was none of these things. Of course, he might have declined my offer. But I never gave him the chance to make the call.

Maybe that's what my injury was supposed to teach me. I hope I've learned the lesson.

Castle's: Aftermath

Months after the injury, back on the mainland, I was still unable to walk properly. Under the watchful eye of local waterman Jake Grosz I had tried a slow, relaxed snorkel session on a calm day but when I tried to exit the water I could barely walk. My injured leg was numb and almost completely paralyzed. I went to a doctor and was advised to avoid a repeat, for fear of nerve damage.

Some days later I was sitting on a bench above the beach, looking at the water and feeling sorry for myself. I recalled the times, decades ago, when I would go skin diving at this spot. Get into the water at the north end of the beach and drift south, riding the prevailing current in a few feet of water, looking for corbina, halibut and the occasional white sea bass. Would I ever go diving – let alone surfing – again?

As I sat there, gazing at the clear, blue-green water, I remembered how it was to be in it and beneath it, drifting silently over the rippled sand. And then, somehow, I was. I could feel the cool water all around me, supporting my body; the gentle current carrying me south along the sand, the rise and fall of the waves, the sound of my own breathing through the snorkel. I was on shore, gazing at the sea, and the experience I was having felt exactly like it had years ago. I took this as a good sign.

There were times when I thought I would never walk normally again, let alone surf. But the year after my injury I had recovered enough to consider paddling out and trying to ride waves. To give myself every possible advantage, I opted for warm water and flew to Waikīkī where my board and folding bike were still waiting for me at the condo.

I was in for something of a shock.

One of the people who lived in the condo building was a local surfer, a transplant named Monty. We never surfed together – he coped with crowds far better than I did – but we enjoyed watching the surf and talking story up on the rooftop deck in the late afternoon, and I always looked forward to seeing him again. On the same day that I had gotten hurt surfing Castle's he had been hit by a board and suffered an injury similar to mine: the rupture of a major vein in his thigh.

Monty was still young, and he was a tough guy – he worked in construction in some capacity – so he kept up his normal routine as long as he could take it. By the time he couldn't take it, his leg was in bad shape.

They saved the leg, but his convalescence was a lot longer than mine. When I graduated from a walker to cautiously shuffling around the building on my own, he was still in a wheelchair. In fact, he was still in a wheelchair a month later, when I was finally able to fly back to the mainland.

When I got back to the condo and went to check on my board, I noticed that Monty's board was not in the rack. Probably out surfing somewhere. But the next day, after he had failed to answer his door and his board was still missing, I asked the guy at the front desk if Monty had gone back to the mainland.

He gave me an odd look. Hadn't I heard? Monty had killed himself. No note, no reason, no explanation. Was it because of his injury, which might have been even worse than anyone had thought? Was it something else? No one knew.

I went up on the rooftop deck and gazed at the sea and let the impact of Monty's death subside. It was the strangest feeling, like something you would experience if you went under a wave next to a friend and you came up and he never did. It defied logic; it made no sense; it wasn't right. But it had happened.

This trip to Waikīkī was already a mission of sorts for me: one of my goals had been to go back out and surf Castle's, if only for one wave, so that I could leave it on my terms. Now I got it into my head that I would do this for both of us, for me and for Monty, to somehow put things back in balance.

As luck would have it I got the opportunity and when a big swell arrived I went out to surf Castle's again. As I paddled out I thought of a lot of things: my injury and recovery, Monty's death, the precariousness of everything.

When I caught a wave, all that was swept away. I had expected a lot of emotions: apprehension, nervousness, triumph, elation, whatever. After all, Castle's was the site of the worst injury I'd had in years and by far the worst injury I'd ever had in the water. What I did not expect was what I actually experienced: the usual happy rush of surfing. Beyond that, nothing. Not fear, not elation, not anything special. It was just another beautiful day, surfing a beautiful wave.

At the same time, that wave was a lot of other things. It put events in perspective, and it helped me put Monty to rest. It also marked a personal watershed: it was my second comeback to surfing, this time at age seventy-three. And it occurred to me that the injury at Castle's had occurred precisely ten years after the time I had asked the universe to give me ten more years of surfing. Coincidence? Maybe. Or maybe it was a self-fulfilling prophecy. Either way, I didn't tempt fate by requesting another ten years. One year at a time.

Photo by John Ahlbrand

Part V: Water Music

What goes up must come down

After my second comeback, I was still game to continue my periodic migrations between the mainland and Hawai'i. But the Islands continued to change and what had been an annual adventure became a chore.

My non-surfing routine – arrive, get my stuff in order, get the rust off of the bike chain and inflate the tires, bike to the supermarket for groceries, repair or replace all the things that the vacation renters had broken, lost or stolen – was still the same but nothing else was. Every year the surf was more crowded, every year another of my hangouts was converted to more touristic use. It was getting to the point where the benefits no longer made up for the hassles. And – who knows? – maybe I really was getting old.

So a couple of years after my return to Castle's, we decided to sell the condo, and in the spring of 2016 I flew over to Hawai'i, sold my boards and my bike and cleaned out all my stuff. I never even considered surfing while I was there; I was done.

The timing, as it turned out, was perfect since my surfing life was soon to take a very different course.

My leg had fully recovered from the disaster at Castle's and things were looking good. I was back in La Jolla, doing a lot of surfing and feeling great. But you never know what's coming next.

I had paddled out at North Bird on a solid day – not Maverick's by any stretch of the imagination, but respectable local waves that jacked up fast and broke hard. The sets were running maybe eight feet and the bigger

259

sets were above that. After a couple of decent rides, I took off on a nice set wave and got hung up at the top just as I popped up on a backside left.

I found myself free-falling through space down from the lip, on my back. I could see my board suspended above me, clinging to the lip as if trying not to fall. All I could do was curl up and cross both arms in front of my face for protection while thinking – maybe even whispering – "*Please don't hit me with a rail.*"

Then the lip came crashing down and drove me down and bounced me off the reef on my back. I was braced for an impact from my board, but it never came.

After getting churned around for a while and diving under two more waves of the set, I was able to crawl back onto my board and get to the channel. I had avoided getting hit by my board but I had landed pretty hard – I was later told that it sounded like a watermelon hitting the pavement after being dropped off a building – and I was a bit stunned.

To be honest, I was feeling pretty shaken, and I was tempted to call it a day, but then I got mad at myself for considering it. I had blown a takeoff and wasted a beautiful wave, and there was no way I was going to quit on that note.

So I made my way back out and set up on the outside, a few dozen yards beyond the handful of guys surfing there that day.

I don't know if it was intuition or dumb luck, but I was in the perfect spot when a cleanup set appeared just minutes later. Everyone was inside and no one was anywhere near being in position to get these waves.

Sometimes you surf better when you're a bit angry after a screw-up; it makes you more intense. I tend to be pretty laid-back and casual when I'm surfing, and now intensity was just what the doctor ordered.

The first wave approached and I went for it. It jacked up fast and I barely had time to pop up before I found myself flying down a very steep face, frontside right. It was too late to turn on the face, and I could see that a bottom turn wasn't going to be feasible because the wave was square, with almost no slope transition at the bottom. It went from hollow to vertical to flat and I would either pearl or the board would just stop when we hit the bottom of the face. So instead of a normal bottom turn, I focused all my energy and attention on the nose rocker, working to get the board just enough up on the rail to allow the rocker to carve a shallow turn when we reached the bottom of the wave. It worked.

Later I was told that the guys inside were cheering me as I took off (excited about another watermelon drop?) and Big Island transplant and North Bird regular Andy Yuen was encouraging me even while paddling furiously up the face a few yards from me as I came plummeting down past him. I had been so focused on the wave and the board that I didn't hear or see anything else.

I go into this in some detail because it was such a shocking contrast to what happened the next day.

The surf dropped and North Bird was no longer breaking, so I went out at a nearby reef break in waves that were somewhere between shoulder and head high. Oddly, in this smaller surf, which should have been more user friendly, I felt off-balance, incompetent, as if trying to do gymnastics on a water bed, or surf standing up on a surfmat – and an under-inflated one at that.

Eight takeoffs, eight falls. I didn't fall off, either. I just fell. As in fall down. I fell like a drunk on an icy street; I fell like a little kid learning to stand up without holding onto the furniture. Face plants, butt plants, a forward collapse ending in a spectacularly splashy somersault on my back, collapsing legs, toppling over, you name it. Finally I gave up and paddled in, wondering if I had suffered a stroke. At seventy-five you tend to have such thoughts.

After three doctors and a ton of tests, no stroke. Just vague general "equilibrium issues often associated with aging" – in other words, who knows? I suspected the problem might have something to do with my high-impact fall at North Bird the day before my fall-down day, but on the other hand I had made the next wave after that. At any rate, there was no way to be sure, and right now the issue was getting back into surfing.

Optimism is being seventy-five, having serious equilibrium issues, and ordering a new surfboard but that's what I did. I had sold the Infinity epoxy (too light in bumps) and I had sold my Craig Angell boards in Hawai'i. My current board wasn't exactly a high performer, and I wanted to give myself all the advantages I could.

Old dog, new tricks

But first I had to solve the equilibrium problems. I considered physical therapy, but decided that it would be more interesting and more relevant to take up an activity that specifically required balance on the water. So I bought a standup paddle board. I wanted something that I could ride waves on, and I wanted something that would fit in my van. I ended up with a 9'4" – actually a bit shorter than my "real" surfboard which was 9'6", but of course a lot thicker and wider – with an egg outline shape that provided a lot of stability.

I took my new SUP board out for a test drive on the nice flat water of nearby Mission Bay. One nice thing about being on the bay was that there would be no need for the slight extra hassle of a leash. No waves, nothing to separate you from your board. Right.

My initial efforts gave a whole new meaning to the concept of "learning curve." Over the years I had put in countless hours surfing, skiing, skateboarding and even ice skating, and none of it did any good.

My first foray lasted all of fifty feet before I went over backwards in a classic "banana peel" type fall, involuntarily kicking the board forward. I happened to be going downwind, so the board, driven by the breeze, sailed briskly away, leaving me floundering in the water clutching the paddle. I then discovered another problem to be solved: how to swim and hold a paddle at the same time. I ended up throwing the paddle like a javelin in the direction of the board, swimming to the paddle, and throwing it again until finally I was able to reunite me, the paddle and the board. From that day on, no matter how dumb it might have looked to an observer, I always wore a leash in the bay.

Remember how it was when you learned to ride a bike as a little kid? You were obsessed with it, and no matter how hard or how many times you crashed, you got back up and tried again.

That was me: paddle a short distance, feeling wobbly and excited and determined at the same time, fall off, crawl back onto the board – wet and more than a little embarrassed (as if anyone really cared what some old fart was doing) – and try again. It was a humbling experience.

The next couple of sessions were the same, and I was beginning to wonder if I had been too ambitious. But then I started to internalize some different feelings, and before long I was paddling hundreds of feet at a go without falling, and then I "got" it. In a few months – I am not a fast learner – I was up to a mile a day with no problems and no fatigue.

I started to make a point of picking times when there would be water ski boats roaring around, so that I could practice dealing with the chop and small swells that they created. I even started trying to catch the wake waves as they headed toward shore, and a few times I managed to keep up with them through constant paddling. The next best thing to surfing!

Now that I had worked up to paddling a mile without any serious hitches, and felt at ease with boat wake, it was time to give the ocean a try.

Back to square one! The ocean was filled with swells, cross swells, bumps, chop, backwash and assorted currents and eddies – all unnoticed and largely irrelevant when on a surfboard, but incredibly hard for me to negotiate on a SUP board. All the water movement was far faster and more powerful than any boat wake, and unlike the boat wake, stuff came from all directions at irregular intervals.

After only a few yards, I was totally burned out and had to drop to my knees before I fell over. If learning to SUP in the bay was like learning to ride a bicycle, learning to SUP in the ocean was like learning to ride a unicycle – at the age of seventy-five. I did a lot paddling sitting down, as if in a canoe.

Meanwhile, I bought a new 9'6" foamie surfboard so I would have something soft to fall on until I got my mojo back and could ride my new Ellington.

Look out for the old guy!

During all of this, my objective was to get back to surfing, so after I had worked on my balance with the SUP board for a few weeks, I tried riding my new foamie surfboard. It didn't go well. After a few fall-offs and no successes, I gave up and souped in. Back on the beach, somebody told me I was getting famous.

"Famous, like how?"

"The guy who came in just before you did was telling everyone: 'Look out for the old guy.'"

This was not exactly encouraging. But there was a positive side to it: like a lot of long-time surfers, I had been getting pretty bitchy about the crowds and especially the hordes of newbies – kooks, actually – who were surfing areas where their obvious incompetence was dangerous to those around them. Now, at least, I could take solace in the fact that no matter how bad they were, no matter what sort of blunder they made on a wave, they were still doing better than I was.

Now all I had to do was figure out what was wrong with my own game, and fix it, and get back to surfing.

By the end of my seventy-fifth year on the planet, I seemed to have recovered from whatever it was. The week I turned seventy-six, I took my new Ellington board out for the first time. It was a beautiful day, clear and glassy with an uncrowded lineup. A small long-period northwest swell was creating long, clean lines.

When it was my turn I took off on a nice head-high wave, faded left, and cranked a hard right. My previous board had been functional, but not very responsive, and I anticipated that even with a lot of power in the turn

I would end up sliding down the face and doing a bottom turn more out of necessity than design. That's just the way that board was.

Instead, my new board whipped into a tight 180° turn high on the face. This was the way a board should ride! The wave seemed to go on forever, filled with sections and cutbacks and drops, until finally it came to an end all the way inside. I had a ton of time to realize how much fun I was having, and as luck would have it surf photographer Scott Darran caught the best moments.

2017: Ellington board – Scott Darran photo

Make my day

Being back surfing again didn't mean that anyone was going to cut me much slack. Not even the birds.

I'm out alone at one of my favorite breaks. It's a beautiful morning: clear skies, glassy, nice little medium-period swell, the lines straight and clean. The kind of swells that a pelican can ride for half a mile on the updraft created by the motion of the wave.

A set comes; I catch the first wave (normally I would wait for the second wave because the first wave is often the smallest, but on this day I'm going with a simple philosophy: if you can catch it, catch it). I'm up, doing a backside turn on the slightly overhead face to go left. And suddenly, just yards in front of me, comes a squad of pelicans, six or eight of them, riding the wave in the opposite direction.

The squad leader makes eye contact with me – no one gives stink-eye better than a pelican – and that baleful glare tells me that they are not going to give way. They caught this one before I did and it's their wave. Pelicans are big birds and when they're this close, in full glide mode with wings outstretched, they're even bigger. I barely have time to drop lower in the wave and duck my head as they rush past just below the crest, so close I can hear the air in their feathers and feel the wind of their passing.

The rest of my ride was pretty nice, I think, but what I remember are the pelicans.

The opportunity to interact with local wildlife in the lineup, up close and personal, has always been one of the big attractions of the ocean in La Jolla. In contrast, my aquatic experiences in Waikīkī were quite different, and most of the marine activity – spinner dolphins, whales, terns, frigate birds – took place a long distance. The occasional monk seal on the beach hardly counts; the ones I saw just lay there by themselves, with none of the energetic interaction that you see in a seal or sea lion colony. The main exception to this dearth of up-close wildlife was turtles and even then they tended to keep their distance. This was fine with me, since turtles are known to be a favorite food of tiger sharks, and tiger sharks are known to nip arms from unwary surfers and take bites out of snorkelers.

Clearly there are more fish out farther, in deeper water and in more isolated areas. But I had no car and I wasn't a deep water guy. I did do some snorkeling in Waikīkī and toward Diamond Head, but it seemed like it was always right after some hapless snorkeler had been attacked by a tiger shark somewhere on one of the islands. As a result I spent all my time trying to snorkel while looking behind me for predators, which detracted from the experience. I soon quit trying.

There were, of course, *humuhumunukunukuapua'a* and other reef fish in the shallows, but their habitat was sharply reduced by widespread coral death. On land I enjoyed watching the comical antics of mynah birds, and the gentle cooing of the local doves, but that was about it.

I never once encountered a seal or dolphin up close in the water as I often did on the mainland. And I missed the raucous, disorganized cast of characters in the shallow waters along the Southern California coast: the pelicans, ospreys, herons, egrets, terns, cormorants, Brant geese, sea lions, dolphins, garibaldi, leopard sharks and other creatures – including the occasional baby gray whale – that made thing so interesting both on the beach and in the water. Wildlife can provide a context that, whether you notice it or not, makes a great difference in your enjoyment of a place. Without wildlife, even the most beautiful area can seem lacking, even sterile.

Bottom line, for me: Waikīkī offered warm ocean, better weather more often, more waves, better surf conditions, more dramatic landscape. La Jolla had more accessible marine life and more birds above, on and under the water, including great masses of migratory birds. While I could still surf, it was no contest: Waikīkī won hands down. But times change and what works for you at sixty-five doesn't always work for you at seventy-five. I'm grateful to have had the chance to enjoy a dozen great years on the waves at Waikīkī; I'm fortunate that when that ended I had a perfect location for a change of orientation and priorities.

It only hurts when I paddle

For a time I got some good rides and had memorable experiences in the ocean, but again it was all about to come crashing down. Somehow, all the falls I had been taking had injured my bad shoulder. And this time, there was no surgical option that would allow me to continue surfing. My shoulder had been seriously trashed twice before and it was beyond repair.

Time for physical therapy.

PT was a humbling experience. Any previous PT had been for rehab after surgery, when I was simply trying to get back to peak performance. But this time peak performance was clearly a relative concept. There were people in there doing stuff that I would have had trouble doing on my best day – were they really there to fix things? At least a couple of times I couldn't resist the temptation to ask super-jock-looking people, both men and women, if they were training for some specific event.

Nope. Trying to get over X or recover from Y or fix chronic Z.

And then there was me. It was like junior high all over again, with nicer people.

I would love to report that a few months of PT fixed the problem, but it did not. I'm still working on it, but it's doubtful that I'll ever paddle prone again. Knee paddling for any distance is too hard on my back, so that's out. The only thing left is SUP.

I'm certainly not the first person to be in this situation; I've discovered that a lot of SUPsters are former surfers who had to abandon regular surfing due to physical problems. Some of the stories are pretty amazing.

One guy was surfing at an isolated break in Baja, got slammed onto a reef feet first, and broke one foot in half. Every single bone in his arch, all the way across, broken.

He had to crawl out of the water and across hundreds of feet of rocky desert to get back to his vehicle, then drive – using only one foot – miles to get to a hospital. After they patched him up it was weeks before he could get back to San Diego.

On his return, X-rays revealed that the repair job had been totally botched, so they had to open up the foot, re-break all the bones and use screws and rods to align them properly. Even after recovery, popping up on a surfboard was painful and risked even more serious and crippling damage to his foot, so he had to switch to SUP surfing.

He must have been a damn good surfer, because he rips on some pretty big waves on a SUP board, bad foot and all. It's inspiring to see what he has accomplished. And he sure put my problems in perspective for me.

Imagine that: Big air at Publics

During PT, someone suggested to me that it might be helpful to use visualization: imagining myself performing whatever action I was trying to recover. It was further suggested that I do this at night while falling asleep, to lock in the mental construct of the target activity. This sounded somewhat like stuff from the old hippie era, but what the heck. Can't hurt, and it might help.

It occurs to me that I might raise the bar: instead of just visualizing paddling, why not fall asleep visualizing surfing itself? I like the feeling of it. Each night I'll doze off reliving various waves I've ridden: seeing them, catching them, riding them.

Let's remember a ride – a short one, to make it easy.

I'm out at Publics on a solid eight-foot-plus day. It's cloudy, and dense curtains of rain hang like a shroud in Pālolo Valley but no rain yet at the beach. The offshore is very strong.

At Publics, as at other breaks, the peak moves according to swell size, swell direction, currents and tides. Today the usual peak has shifted toward Ewa; there's a secondary peak toward Diamond Head that today is actually better on the sets. I set up there.

I catch a wave, drop in, cut left. I'm heading for the usual peak, hoping to slide through before it breaks, so I'm well out in front of the breaking wave behind me. It's actually kind of slopey on the outside; Publics can be that way. I realize I'm not going to make it through so I crank a cutback and head back the way I came. Of course that's a dead end but I can go up the face and over the top.

But I don't have the good sense to just go out over the back; there's one more thing I want to try. I turn straight off and shoot down the face, then power a bottom turn and jet back up the face again. The wind and the water rushing up the wave combine to catapult me up and over the lip just before it breaks. The feeling is awesome, a perfect parabola down and up the wave and into the sky, perfect assistance from wind and water, perfect everything.

Except for one thing: the height of my catapult plus the trough behind the wave leaves me suspended in space like Wile E. Coyote after one of his brilliantly stupid stunts. I'm eight or ten feet above the water, tethered to a heavy longboard, and nowhere to go but down. All I can think of is not landing on the board, and hoping that the board doesn't land on me. Somehow I manage it so that we hit the water side by side.

That's the ride, but maybe the last part won't be conducive to restful sleep and happy dreams. So I select just the smooth parabola part, gliding down and shooting back up and flying up into space. I drift off to sleep feeling that part of the wave in my entire body. When I wake up in the morning, I have to remind myself that I didn't really surf Publics yesterday.

Look, Ma, I'm standing!

. Maybe I managed to re-awaken the feeling and muscle memory from my Publics ride. A couple of days later, I'm so encouraged by my stand-up paddling progress that I decide to try to catch a wave standing up, just like the big dogs.

I've been working on SUP in the bay for nearly two years, with periodic forays to the ocean. I'm getting better at balance in the combination of mixed swell and mild backwash, but it's still quite an effort. Old dogs can learn new tricks, but it's not easy.

I'm riding my 9'4" egg. Gentle nose rocker, concave to flat to V, 2+1 fin setup. Very stable, paddles pretty fast.

I launch from a flat sand beach and paddle up the coast a hundred yards or so to get away from the people. I'm not seeking solitude; I just don't want to hurt anyone if I fall off or careen out of control down a wave.

It's a small day, shoulder to head high. Beautiful clear blue sky, no wind, warm air, water maybe low 60s. This is a perfect spot for a novice: the waves are gentle, round, slopy. Actually everything is quite similar to the day I caught my first ever unbroken wave on a surfboard. Will that bring me luck?

I get to a suitable setup spot. I've seen the occasional wave hump up here and the form looks good. There are a lot of people at the breaks on both sides, but this spot seems to be more inconsistent so it's empty. This means I won't put anyone at risk, except maybe myself. It's an easy day to try to ride: decent period, not a lot of cross swell, minimal backwash.

I sit on the board while waiting. More experienced paddlers stand on their board while waiting, but I find that my legs get too tired too fast when I try to do that. Then fatigue makes balance more difficult. Maybe over time I'll habituate, or become more efficient. Meanwhile, this is how I do it.

Every time I think I see a set coming, I get to my knees for a better view; if it looks promising I pop up to my feet. After a couple of false alarms, a viable wave arrives. I'm still getting the hang of where to set up with a SUP – farther out than I would on a surfboard – and how soon to start paddling. Start too soon, and you use up too much runway, ending up with the wave breaking on you. Each SUP stroke can burn up several yards.

I take three strokes, four...I feel the tail lift and the board start to drive forward, propelled by the energy of the wave. I take half a step forward with my front foot, lengthening my stance for stability and getting my weight farther forward to ensure that I drop into the wave.

I've done it! At the moment the wave takes over I get a taste of the same thrill I had when I was ten – the sense that something magical has happened. Beat up and jaded as I am, it's like being kissed by the sea all over again. We've been through a lot together, had our ups and downs and fallings out – but I'm still in love.

I shift my back foot a bit back and toward the rail, and turn right. No fancy stick-the-paddle-in-the-wave type of turns for me; I'm riding this thing like a surfboard. It turns beautifully! I'm totally stoked, like a grom with a new shortboard. I shift my foot again, cut back, then turn back right again, going down the line, high in the wave.

What the heck, why not: I take a couple of steps toward the nose and ride a few yards. Everything works perfectly. Two steps back, turn out of the wave, struggle for balance and put one hand down on the deck to keep from falling. Then sit down before I fall down.

Some guy paddling out says, "Nice wave." I don't care whether he's sarcastic or sincere or just being polite. For me it's one of the best rides I ever got in my life – right up there with my first ever unbroken wave.

It's the only standup takeoff I get that day – although I do catch a couple of kneeling takeoffs – but it's baked into my memory. I want to do it again.

That wave was so much fun that I almost quit worrying about getting my prone paddling back. But it's not over until I decide it's over, so I keep doing the PT. After all, prone paddle or not, the PT is keeping me in better shape for SUP and for general life.

Imagine that: Cunha's through Queens

I keep up the visualization thing, catching and riding waves. I decide to get fancy. I go to sleep remembering the time I rode from Cunha's all the way through Queens, something that was made possible by a big southeast wrap that generated some of the best waves seen in Waikīkī for many years.

I'm at Cunha's alone, possibly because on this particular swell the interval between sets is far longer than at anywhere else nearby, and nobody wants to endure the wait. After a couple of OK waves, finally I hook into a bomb and go left on my Craig Angell 10'0".

Drop in, big bottom turn, come up the face, slide into the pocket. The swell, sweeping in around Diamond Head, is really driving the wave from right to left and me with it. It's not the steepest wave ever ridden at Cunha's, but it has a lot of juice and speed. We get to a slightly flatter spot and I take two steps forward and crouch for better speed. Then the wave stands up again.

Suddenly I see a little knot of surfers in front of me. For a moment I'm confused: this doesn't seem right. What are they doing? Where are we? I realize that they are in the lineup for Queens. I've done something I've often thought about: I've ridden all the way to the next break.

The wave jacks up as it approaches the reef outside Queens, so there's no time to waste contemplating my little triumph. I almost get barreled as I rocket through. I see that the wave is going to close out, so I edge the rail into the face and just barely manage to go out over the back before the whole thing comes crashing down.

That's such a nice way to drowse off that I want to do it again. The next night I pick another two-break ride, from my time in Santa Barbara, when I took off at some ugly, hostile-looking no-name reef in front of Shoreline Park and rode the wave through the next break, Leadbetter's.

After a bad start in big surf (got pitched on the first wave after starting to paddle too soon and continuing to paddle long after I should have sat back) I figure it out and take off when the wave is fringing, with an ugly shallow reef making a vicious-looking boil in front of me. Turn right, off to the races.

It's a wild ride, filled with suck-outs, jack-ups, weird sections. Things are happening so fast that it's like being in a speeded-up movie. Go up, go down, scoot under a slab, shake off the white water from a section that breaks on my head. No cut-backs on this wave; all I can do is try to make it past the next surprise. Ride right through the next break just inside a cluster of surprised faces in the lineup; continue on past the point and toward the sand beach; kick out before the shorebreak.

On my way back out, one of the guys in the Leadbetter's lineup sums it up: "Looks like that was worth the wait."

Even if I don't get any shoulder recovery benefits from all this, I'm reliving some of my most beautiful experiences on waves. If I can't surf, this is the next best thing. As they say, it's almost like being there.

Water music

Since I had to abandon surfboards for a new life as a SUPster, the drama content of my experiences has dropped off, well, dramatically. I can't cope with the bigger stuff anymore, I have trouble dealing with bumpy water, and there's not much drama on the bay. But life isn't all about drama and excitement, fun as those things might be. I'm finding the secret beauty of common things, and there's excitement in this process of discovery. The adventures I'm having now are a lot shorter and lack risk, but they're no less compelling for that. It's all a matter of perspective.

Beyond that, and perhaps more important, is a heightened awareness. I feel that I'm recapturing the old magic, the wonder I felt about the sea and the shore when I was a kid. SUP has been a real eye-opener in terms of ripples, bumps, cross-swells, odd backwash and general random events in the ocean. The subtle music of the sea.

On a surfboard, or in the water as a bodysurfer or skin diver, they weren't that obvious, and I simply never needed to pay this much attention to them. Suddenly, it's like walking through an area filled with activity that was barely perceptible to me before. There is water moving in all directions. The added height of standing on the SUP board makes it more obvious, and the balance required makes it imperative that I be aware of every subtlety.

Another bonus: SUP in the bay has put me in closer contact with shorebirds and waterfowl of all types, some migratory, some not: curlews, sandpipers, plovers, snowy egrets, the occasional blue heron, ducks (mallards, canvasbacks, teal), Brant geese, grebes and others. Once even a pair of black swans. For some reason, they allow a person on a SUP board, paddling slowly and rhythmically, to approach much closer than they would a person walking, paddling a surfboard, or in a boat. So I can observe their behavior at close range, often only a few yards.

Beneath the surface, made easy to observe by the height and angle of view provided by standing upright – rather than sitting in a kayak or lying on a surfboard – there are various kinds of rays and fish ranging from minnow-sized fry to two-foot mullet. One can feel surrounded by nature, immersed in it, in ways that simply weren't otherwise possible. Or maybe I had just forgotten them.

In the upper reaches of the bay the restless music of the waves is muted, attenuated until it is imperceptible: the water in the middle of the bay appears uniformly flat. But at the shoreline small surges reveal the swell pushing in from the ocean, sliding for miles around corners and through channels, deflecting off of islands and spits of land to arrive. At extreme high tides they make their active presence known. As the water reaches the previous high tide mark it seems to hesitate, probing. Insistent pulses urge the tide higher. A foam-flecked finger of water caresses the dry sand as if to see how much farther it can go. Small silvery liquid tongues insinuate themselves into low spots, withdraw, move farther in. The water swirls in lazy gentle eddies, deepening hollows, carving small channels as it reshapes the contours of the sand.

I realize that here I'm still experiencing the ocean. I don't have to be on the waves to feel them. And I don't have to keep going back to my personal Golden Age for inspiration and memories. I'm making new memories every day, each one beautiful and unique, and I should embrace them. Otherwise I'm living in the past.

Great expectations

A friend of mine who has been facing a series of physical limitations suggests that the best solution to avoid feeling deprived is to lower one's expectations. Sounds very buddhic – *All suffering comes from desire* – but I'm not convinced that's the only solution, or even the best one. Instead, one can simply learn to appreciate different things. The expectations aren't lower, just different.

I realize that at some point my priorities have shifted. I'm still doing exercises that might allow me to get back to paddling and riding a surfboard, but what I'm really focused on is getting better at balancing while doing stand-up ocean paddling. Things change, and you have to change with them. Besides, learning anything new keeps you from getting stagnant.

At the same time I'm getting more and more enjoyment out of stand up paddling in the bay rather than trying to SUP surf in the ocean. It's not just laziness; I'm not just trying to minimize effort. I'm learning to take more pleasure in the simplicity of it. SUP surfing adds layers of complexity – equipment, technique, more complicated situations – to what can be a direct, natural experience. Contending with waves and managing the SUP board in bumps, let alone trying to get out through breaking waves with a bulky board and a paddle, can be a distraction.

On flat water none of that gets in the way. I don't have to think about the board or my technique; paddling on flat water has become as natural as riding a bike, almost as natural as walking. That leaves me free to be aware of my surroundings.

So I'm not reducing my expectations, more like refining them. Or, to paraphrase the famous military anecdote, I'm not retreating – I'm advancing in another direction.

Little kids want to get better at crawling, standing, walking, running and riding a bike because it is a challenge. They are driven by an innate passion for growth and development, exploration and competence.

My return to surfing in my sixties let me be a ten-year-old kid again. And now – accidentally and contrary to all my expectations – SUP is doing the same thing. That was true when I started, and it's still true. When I do choose to SUP in the ocean, I find myself looking at tiny waves that I wouldn't care about on a surfboard, but because they match my current SUP surfing level they're just as intriguing as they were when I was ten years old.

The entire experience has been truly rejuvenating. And it's been gratifyingly humbling, too. You have to be willing to fall down a lot.

Meanwhile, there are still lots of interesting things to see.

Bat ray fever

The adventures now are shorter, but that doesn't make them any less intense. The behavior of rays, tidal flows, a huge silvery school of bait fish – countless thousands of them, flowing like a river beneath my board – all the ebb and flow of life. Short and sweet and sometimes as intense and as vivid as anything anywhere on the water. You just have to adjust the focus.

Beyond all that, there is still the sheer joy of being on the water, seeing the bottom shimmering with diffracted sunlight, great piles of cumulus clouds reflected in still water.

No waves, bumpy ocean. I break out the SUP board and hit the bay. The water is crystal clear, no tourists – or much of anybody else – on a weekday morning, and today the shallows are teeming with life: crabs, bait fish, the occasional school of mullet or corbina. Also lots of stingrays of several types, plus a few bat rays and even a couple of small butterfly rays, which I have never seen in the bay before. It's not Steve Irwin (*"Crikey, mate!"*) but it's nice to see things thriving despite the periodic invasions of ski boats and party boats and cabin cruisers, plus the seasonal inundations of tourists.

Today I got another unexpected bit of magic: a large group of bat rays, ranging from about two feet to four feet across. I was paddling along the shore, enjoying the day and the clear water, and suddenly there they were beneath me, gliding along in the same direction.

I've seen a lot of bat rays in the bay, but never this many at the same time and never such a mix of sizes. I quit counting at twenty, but there have to be at least two or three dozen, swimming in a group along the shore in about four feet of water. Usually rays are skittish, darting off into deeper water as soon as a SUP board gets close. But these are strangely accepting of my presence, making no attempt to move away from me or even to change course.

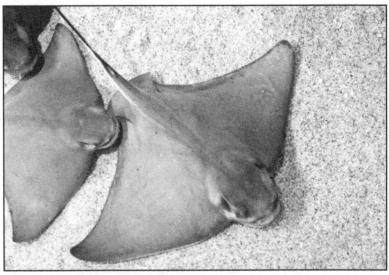

Bat rays can measure over six feet and two hundred pounds.
Photo: Martin Holst Friborg Pedersen

Taking slow, shallow, gentle paddle strokes so as not to disturb them, I study them. It's like flying above a squadron of stealth bombers: the dark gray color, the hump of the bulbous head and thick body, the tapered wings. Their swimming is effortless and graceful: just slight undulations of the thin fringe and tips of their wings.

I feel privileged that they allow me to accompany them and observe them like this. After a couple of minutes they slow down, as if to allow me to get ahead. I continue paddling alone for another half mile, then make a U turn and retrace my course, hoping to encounter them again, but they're gone. Once again, Nature makes the call.

When I get home I look up the correct term for a group of bat rays. It's a "fever."

New directions

It's a beautiful Southern California winter morning: clear sky, not a breath of wind, temperature in the low 50s. On a day like today, the first order of business is a SUP paddle in the bay. When I get to the bay, I become aware of a dull roaring, mixed with intermittent bursts of thunder. It sounds like a squadron of jet fighters taking off and firing their afterburners for extra speed. It's waves. We've had days and days of big surf from a series of storms in the Gulf of Alaska, but this sounds like it's way more than we've had. For a moment I feel a twinge of nostalgic deprivation, almost like I used to feel at Pomona College when I was trapped miles from the ocean.

I shake it off. Nothing I can do about it anymore.

I launch from the north end of the bay and paddle toward the sound; maybe when I get to the west side of the bay I'll haul out and walk the couple of blocks to the beach, just to see.

Sure you will. Just do your paddle.

I started maybe half a mile from the source of the sound. Due to some quirk of acoustics, as I get closer the thunder dies down to a murmur.

I get back to noticing my immediate surroundings. As I approach a small pier, a lone pelican stops preening and eyes me with suspicion. The area is full of migratory birds: Brant geese, mallards, canvasback ducks. A flotilla of geese sees me coming and alters course, swimming at half speed. Each one leaves a tiny wake of ripples. The flotilla splits into two groups, as if preparing for some sort of naval maneuver. A flock of ducks sweeps over low and tight, checking out the landing zone. One duck separates from the group, peels off and lands on the beach to go for a waddle. In my mind I'm back to the hours spent near the shore when I was a kid, enjoying solitude, nature and the motion of the sea. There's no perceptible motion in this water, but two out of three isn't bad.

On the way back, the pelican ignores me. As I get farther from the ocean, the thundering noise increases again. I'm reminded of our epic day in Baja during the hurricane, the endless crashing and roaring of the hurricane surf. Those days are over, but at least I can go check this out.

Driving to my favorite break, I start thinking: *I've got fins and a wetsuit and a bodyboard in the van. I can get some of these waves. Recapture the thrill of big surf. You're only as old as you think you are.*

When I arrive, I see how absurd that thought is. The surf is huge, easily ten to twelve feet, and the outer reefs are breaking even bigger than that. There are no channels; everything is breaking. I had expected a crowd, but there are only two people out at one of the breaks, a couple more at another, and no one in sight anywhere else. It's easy to see why: in addition to the size, the waves are continuous. I sit there watching for maybe half an hour and in that entire time there isn't a single lull. Just wave after pounding wave.

A guy takes off outside and gets eaten up by the wave. His board pops up and starts coming in, leaping and spinning as it's tossed and dragged by the foam. Broken leash. He's in for a long swim. A bodysurfer – or maybe a knee- or bodyboarder who has lost his board – is trying to get to shore, but the surge and push from the two main breaks keep driving him into a massive rip current that has formed in what on smaller days is a channel. The waves are powerful and the white water is pushing him shoreward, but the rip is stronger. Even with fins on he's barely making progress, and if he lets up at all he's going backward.

Any sense of deprivation evaporates. This swell is too much for good local surfers half my age, let alone a worn-out journeyman like me. In my prime I would have tried to paddle out; if I made it I doubt that I would have made a single wave. I've done plenty of swimming in my life; let someone else have their turn. My SUP session in the bay was beautiful, relaxing, life-giving. I'm happy.

Taming the great white shark

My wife sometimes says that she wishes she had met me a lot earlier.

"No," I tell her, "you really don't."

When I was younger I felt like a pelagic fish: an albacore or marlin that needs to keep moving or sink; a great white shark that must move forward or suffocate. I had an inner need to be in constant motion, see other countries, experience new things, ride new breaks. I felt driven to surf and ski and play tennis and do martial arts and take day-long solo bike rides; learn languages and guitar; get into drawing and metal sculpture; experience a thousand places all at once. Immerse myself in the great multi-dimensional richness of the world. Maybe to make up for all the incompetence, clumsiness and isolation of my early years as a late-blooming nerd.

Nowadays they might say I had ADHD. Whatever it was, it put me into some crazy interesting situations, gave me some great experiences now turned to memories.

My wife has been wonderful at putting up with my aging-surfer-dude nonsense, but that's nothing compared to the scattered frenzy of activity that was the old me. The watered-down version is more than enough for anyone else to cope with.

I may never become a true reef fish, but I'm not as pelagic as I once was. I'm not sure how much of that is choice and how much is chance;

how much is maturity and how much is just being worn down and subject to physical limitations.

In the past few years I've had to turn down two surf trips to Nicaragua, one to mainland Mexico, and a couple to Baja. Why? It just wouldn't be smart. My lower back can go out at any time, and even in my own home with a carefully-selected mattress and the backup of a good recliner, I can easily be laid up – housebound and hard-pressed to get from one room to another – for several days. In addition, traveling itself is a chore: I end up stiff and arthritic, with swollen feet. I'm still good for the occasional trip to Hawai'i, but even then...

Can a great white learn to be a reef shark, or at least learn to act like one? So far, it seems to be working.

My life was once a constant adventure, now it's looking more like a chore. But it's still a voyage of discovery. It's like a really long coast trip, one that lasts for years: monotony, struggle, setbacks, boredom, frustration, drudgery, discomfort – punctuated by incredible episodes of magic and joy and wonder that leave me breathless. One of the most blindingly beautiful experiences I've ever had occurred while I was bleeding out into my own leg. You never know when or where or how magic will strike, and that's what keeps you in the game. All you need is faith that there will be a next time.

Life is sometimes like the Baja flash flood trip: you luck into one great adventure, then stumble into another. Mostly, it's just showing up. If there are waves to ride, maybe you ride one. Meanwhile, there's nature, there's the sea, there are people you enjoy and care about and love.

Life can be like going to a great break expecting surf – even if you have all the modern reports and forecasts, there's still no guarantee. On the other hand, you might simply go with no expectations and be blown away by what you find. You never know.

Over the years since my comeback at age sixty-two, I have watched as people I knew from surfing – some older than I, some younger (occasionally much younger) – had to drop out due to injuries, chronic conditions, illness, or even death. I have felt incredibly lucky to have gotten through for as long as I have. And I guess I started to believe that it would always be that way, that maybe I could be like Woody Ekstrom, who just sort of faded out of surfing or Rabbit Kekai or any of the other old-time surfers who were riding serious waves into their eighties and finally quit just because they didn't care that much about surfing anymore.

Now that I'm facing the high probability that my prone paddling days may well be over, I'm actually glad that I had equilibrium problems that drove me to get a SUP board. Why? Because otherwise it never would have occurred to me to do it. Now, even though I can't paddle prone I can still get on a SUP board, paddle it kneeling if I have to, catch the wave, pop up and surf. So I still can just fade away when I choose to.

Through it all, I've been incredibly fortunate to have encountered people who have been generous, encouraging, helpful and more. Pat in Hawai'i might well have saved my life by contacting Ocean Rescue before dawn; Bryce kept me afloat until they showed up. Closer to home, and on less extreme terms, I've been figuratively buoyed up by a wonderful group of friends and fellow surfers in the Bird Rock area. Actually, by now I'm not sure if I'm a friend or a mascot. But at this point in my life, I'll gratefully accept whatever I can get.

Message from the past

Note to the reader: I recently came across this comment, written by me when I was in my late sixties and surfing as much as I wanted both in Southern California and Hawai'i. Now, at age eighty, I think the younger me understood my situation pretty well.

I don't know how much longer I will be able to continue my rekindled love affair with the waves. On good days I tell myself it will last as long as I do. At other times I realize it may end tomorrow. Either way, I don't think I will ever take any of this – surf, nature, seals, birds, waves, endless lines of energy coiling and uncoiling from beyond the horizon – for granted again. I certainly hope I don't. I shouldn't. Like life, it deserves to be appreciated and celebrated on a daily basis while we are in it, and remembered with joy and gratitude when we are not.

I have no way of knowing how long this run is going to last. Of course that's true of anyone at any age, but when you're younger and on top of your game it's not a concept that seems real.

Once in Japan I read an article discussing the attraction of eating *fugu*, the blowfish that delivers a fatal poison if improperly prepared. One diner stated it as an incomparable thrill, the *frisson* of knowing that each bite could be your last. I'm trying to look at each wave that way. To appreciate each ride as possibly the last one I will ever get. Which of course it is.

The day I fell in love with surfing was an incredible organic high. The moment it took hold of me is burned into my memory so deeply that today, over half a century later, I can still close my eyes and recreate it – both the feeling and the entire situation – at any time. The ineffable, magical moment when the wave takes over and the board is impelled and gliding without force is intoxicating.

Every pilot knows a similar feeling, and every sailor. It's the moment when lift overcomes drag and the air that was an obstacle now becomes a magical force invisibly lifting the aircraft, the ground falls away, gravity loses its grip, and a psychological and sensory experience that had to wait for over one hundred thousand years of human existence is yours. The moment when you've hoisted the main and the slight wallowing and luffing gives way to the billowing of the sails and the heeling of the boat as the sky reaches down to pull you forward.

It is as if the hand of God has gestured earthward and worked unknowable magic.

What you do with it from there is up to you.

Why am I so infatuated now, far more than ever before? Perhaps, in part, because it's the only challenging physical activity I have left. But there's another reason, much deeper and far more important: to pursue anything with passion affirms life, overrides pain and infirmity, supersedes age.

Maybe the earth really is flat, and when you've traveled far enough you go off the edge and disappear into the abyss beyond. I can't see the edge yet, but at times I can almost feel it, like a river rafter intuits the distant misty breath of a great waterfall.

But when I'm on a wave, this perception disappears. I'm not 67 nor 30 nor 12. I am ageless, timeless and without form. I am so caught up in the process, so lost in the wave and in the extended moment it creates, that I do not exist. I become an expression of the terms and conditions imposed at this particular time, in this particular place, by this particular wave. And in this sense I become, for the few seconds the ride lasts, a participant in a dance of universal forces, a part of nature.

Life is a balancing act performed on a wire. The older you get, the higher the wire and the smaller the net, until finally the net disappears and the wire rises to infinity and melts into the clear blue space between the stars, and you're off on your final journey, a wave headed for a distant shore. But until the end, you always have the choice of which way to fall, if fall you must.

What could be better?

AFTERWORD

In spite of what I may have thought at times, my lifetime affair with the sea was never just about the waves. It was about the waves and more:

Golden orange garibaldi, bright against the dark green eelgrass, lurking and circling lazily around their chosen territory in the reef.

Seabirds flying underwater with quick, short movements of their stubby wings. An osprey hovering and diving and coming up with a shiny struggling fish in his talons.

A pod of porpoises charging down a huge face, bodysurfing directly toward me, only to veer off at the last minute as if testing my fitness to be in this ocean with them.

The sweet sound of slack key guitar played to the accompaniment of the waves – the color of the sky detaching itself from the sea at dawn – the clean exalted feeling of throwing myself into the shorebreak after digging ditches and breaking concrete all day – the otherworldly calm and quiet of the sea floor twenty feet down – the perfect shape of a breaking wave seen from the side – lobsters lined up beneath a ledge, warily eyeing an intruder – a cormorant popping to the surface with a glistening, wriggling fish – a string of pelicans hugging the surface of a swell, passing so close you can hear the hissing of the wind through their feathers – the sheen of the sea on glassy afternoons – surfing in a frigid offshore wind, the sea dark against a backdrop of snow on distant peaks – a baby whale coming to the surface between me and the shore – fishermen setting out at dawn from Mazatlán – a familiar shore seen from the sea for the first time – the gentle chattering slap and ripple of water under the nose of a SUP board when paddling upwind – a tiny fish skittering across the surface of the water – the ebb and flow of tides – the waxing and waning of sand along the shore...and it's not over yet.

My personal horizon is a lot closer than it used to be, but I haven't fallen off the edge yet. I'm still here and there are still new worlds to discover.

If you don't believe you have a future, you start living in the past. The past is a source of a lot of things, and it's a great place to visit but you don't want to live there. Build on the past, embrace the present, believe in the future.

Sometimes people say they wish they could go back to the past and do everything over again, knowing what they know now. In a sense, they can. By being ten or twelve years old again, you revisit the past in terms of attitudes and outlook, willingness to experiment, explore and discover. In the process, you create a future-oriented outlook: what new challenges will I face, what new discoveries will I make, what new adventures will I have?

For now, it's paddle the SUP board, catch a wave or two, take some pictures, hang in there with the PT. Especially the PT: it's part of my belief in the future. I'm like one of those old kung fu masters who keep practicing every day, maintaining the highest level that they can, both as a way of life and to be prepared just in case they need to do it for real.

I don't know if I'll ever be able to ride a wave on a surfboard again, but if my wave – the one that got me started when I was ten, the one that powered my comeback when I was sixty-two – ever shows up for me again, I'll be ready.

BACKSTORY

E very story has a backstory – the various events, experiences and factors that shape the main narrative and inform the motives and actions of the characters. The main narrative may be straightforward, but the backstory is more subtle and more complex.

The backstory provides valuable context and perspective, but it can be a distraction. Rather than interrupt the narrative flow I decided to break out the principal backstory elements and put them here.

1945: Destiny

Pearl Harbor got me into surfing. After World War II – which I spent absorbing Spanish in a mostly Hispanic trailer park while my dad served in the Navy – my parents weren't about to leave sunny San Diego for the dust storms and blizzards of our prewar home in Kansas, so instead we ended up a block from the beach in the sleepy little town of La Jolla, where my dad was sure he could somehow make the big time in postwar Southern California.

I had loved the trailer park – olive trees to play in and lots of other kids to play with – and since I was still learning to talk, Spanish came just as easily as anything else. But if the trailer park was great, this was super-great. Our house was on Kolmar Street, near what was then the very modest south edge of town. There were still plenty of vacant lots to play in, and a couple of blocks to the south, streets and houses gave way to dirt and wild grasses and sagebrush. There were quail, dove, rabbits, hawks, skunks, possums and the occasional coyote. On warm summer evenings there were swarms of fireflies, which we could catch and put into glass jars and watch them pulsing with glowing light as we drifted off to sleep, the sound of the sea in our ears. What a paradise!

The known world ended at the horizon to the west of our house, the drugstore on Nautilus Street to the north, La Jolla Boulevard to the east, and the sagebrush-covered lots and dirt paths to the south of Palomar Street. Everything else was terra incognita, a nebulous semi-presence. The beach extended beyond view; streets other than ours were known to exist, but all this was more alien and mysterious than ancient Cathay or Africa to medieval Europeans. The horizon – hazy, hanging from the sky, sometimes decorated with a ship or two, source of waves – was the farthest thing I could see, and it was the source of everything that followed.

Our house was only blocks from the reef break at Windansea, and when we went to play in the vacant lot across from the beach we could see mysterious forms – surfers! – blurred by the ocean mist, poised gracefully on long redwood planks, gliding smoothly toward shore. To a five-year-old they were beyond cool. I wanted to be like them.

If not for Pearl Harbor, I might never have seen them – and I might never have fallen in love with surfing.

1945: Hiding from the Japanese

One of the lingering effects of Pearl Harbor was a fascination with Japan. This started when I was four years old and the Second World War was still raging in the Pacific. I was with my mom, driving downtown to pick up my Navy dad at the base, when I noticed that we were under a huge sort of fish net, thickly festooned with countless scraps of green and brown cloth, stretched across old Highway 101.

"What's that?" I asked, pointing upward.

"That's so the Japanese can't see us."

My four-year-old brain had to digest that. We were invisible! Obviously not to each other, because I could still see my mom and all the people on the sidewalk, but to the Japanese, whatever that was. I was filled with curiosity and a desire to know what the Japanese was and why we were hiding from it. My mom sounded unconcerned; maybe it was just a game, like hide and seek. Not at all scary, but definitely mysterious. Intriguing. I tried to see if I could spot the Japanese somewhere above the netting, but since I didn't know what to look for I didn't have any luck.

So Japan and I go way back, and that was one reason I went to Japan in 1961 and so many times thereafter.

1946: Forbidden fruit – the tsunami of 1946

Even without surfers, the ocean was special to me from a very early age. Some of that had to do with the tsunami of 1946, which caused great destruction and loss of life elsewhere, but luckily for me missed San Diego.

When I was five, the news came that something called a tidal wave (a tsunami) might strike the coast. I presume my parents heard about it on the radio. All I know is that my seven-year-old brother heard them discussing it, and from the way they spoke it sounded very important. We weren't about to miss anything, so we went out and walked the short block and a half to the beach and sat in the sand to wait. We had no idea what we were looking for, waves happened every few seconds, but we assumed that if this one was so special we'd know it when we saw it.

Young as we were, we went prepared. Some snacks in case we had to wait a long time. And we departed after naptime. For something this momentous, you had to be well-rested and alert. Plus my parents wouldn't let me out of the house after lunch without a nap. At the ripe age of seven my brother had reached a nap-optional phase of life, but he generously waited for me. Or maybe—like the Californians in the joke about changing a light bulb— he just wanted someone to share the experience.

In those days child rearing was pretty loose. We ran around unsupervised and played outside wherever we wanted; the only hard and fast rule was "be home by dark." So no one asked where we were going or why.

At some point my brother got tired of waiting and wandered off somewhere else. But at the tender age of five, I already had all the attributes of a surfer. Curiosity, desire, patience, persistence, determination. I was going to see the wave of the day if it took all night.

At dusk, in response to a parental grilling, my brother reported that I was at the beach waiting for the tidal wave. I probably would still be sitting there waiting for it, but my dad dragged me off the beach, took me home and gave me a real thrashing.

Since the tidal wave never did show up, the experience was mostly wasted. But it left a general impression on my five-year-old mind, I mean besides the thrashing. Whatever the wave thing was, it was so special that kids weren't qualified to participate, or even observe. It clearly was something reserved for adults. Sort of like sex. I could hardly wait to grow up and find out more.

1946: Wagon surfing!

The sight of my first surfers led to my first really reckless action.

Little kids can be quite impressed when they see older people doing really cool stuff like riding motorcycles. Or riding waves. I had seen surfers at a distance, and I wanted to copy them. So one day I pulled my little red wagon – a Radio Flyer, I think it was – up the hill to the top of our block, pointed it down the sidewalk, climbed in and launched. The objective was to stand up and ride down the hill, just like the surfers rode waves.

I did manage to get to my feet, but steering that type of wagon – done by using the hinged pull-bar connected to the front axle as a tiller – was hard enough if you were sitting in it (they were prone to veer sharply, which made them flip over) and steering while standing was totally beyond me. The wagon swerved and I fell out, landing on my head, getting knocked out and suffering my first concussion. I have no memory of getting home – I was evidently on auto-pilot – but I do remember being in a darkened room with a headache and a sort of sick feeling of unreality while the doctor (who was also our next-door neighbor) conferred with my parents in hushed tones.

I never tried to stand in a wagon again, but my crash confirmed the cachet of surfing. These guys had a mysterious skill – golly, not even my older brother or my dad could surf! – and now that I had tried and failed I realized how tricky it was. More than my dad or my brother, surfers became my role models.

So as a little kid I had fallen in love with the sea, and I had become at least vaguely aware of the magic of surfing. But before going further I had a lot of growing up to do and there was a lot of random kid stuff to occupy me in the meantime.

1946: Mexico!

My first exposure to Mexico – the real thing, not the trailer park version – had quite an impact on my future. My parents were trying to renovate a house – a real fixer-upper, one of the old-style Mediterranean types that were on the verge of coming back into style – and my mom would drive to Tijuana to get the best prices on the wrought-iron lamps and railings and other stuff that was considered fashionable at the time. Baby-sitters cost money, which my parents didn't have, so I got to go with her.

Talk about magic!

1940s Tijuana was an incredible blend of everything: street-wise little kids – even smaller than me! – some almost too young to talk, selling tiny packets of *chicle* and impassive Indian ladies selling paper flowers; a guy with no arms, barefoot, weaving straw hats with his toes; a guy with no legs and a hunched-over torso propelling himself through the filthy streets on a small wooden platform with wheels, a sort of human furniture dolly; fifty thousand people living in cardboard boxes in the dry river bed (you drove past them and above them on a narrow old concrete bridge to get from the border into town); tiny stalls selling coconut candy, cactus candy, dried fruit, fireworks, woven finger traps, walnut shells hand-crafted into tiny pigs with moveable ears that wiggled as the beetle or fly that had been imprisoned inside struggled around trying to find a way out; pushcart vendors; the tortilla factory staffed by the same sort of impassive Indian ladies who sold the paper flowers, nimble hands patting the *masa* into tortillas and slapping it onto the hot cooking surface, quickly turning each tortilla over with their fingers – how did they do it without getting burned? – to cook the other side and then dropping it onto a clanking chain-driven conveyor belt that cooled the tortillas as they were transported to a table and dropped into a pile to be hand-wrapped in paper.

And from living in the trailer park I knew enough Spanish to get a sense of what was going on; at the same time at the age of five I was blown away by all this. It was like nothing I had ever seen or imagined. I was hooked on Mexico.

1940s: Growing up in Paradise

The circumstances of one's formative years have great influence on later life decisions and attitudes. Growing up in what was still a village by the sea certainly shaped mine.

By the time I was old enough for school we had moved again, closer to the center of the village. My world was expanding, and given the freedom that kids had in those days I was able to explore it.

All the places above the cliffs where you were absolutely not supposed to go because you would fall off and get killed and they would probably not find your body for days. So of course we went there anyway. And to all the places our parents didn't know, like the narrow trail that led down a sandstone cliff to a narrow slot filled with cobbles (and sometimes with piles of kelp) that the plank surfers who rode the Cove when it was big called the Hole, but of course we didn't know that yet.

All the paths and alleys and shortcuts between different blocks, the long series of steps beside the Valencia Hotel that led from Prospect Street down to the Cove Park and the sea. The endless flight of white wooden steps that went from a wooden foot bridge down a cleft in the cliff face to the enormous broken boulders of Devil's Slide. The mysterious series of caves in the cliff; the small, narrow clefts at the Cove, dark secluded coolness right next to the heat and beachgoers at the Cove on a summer day. The natural stone arch that formed a bridge to Alligator Head, but the lifeguards would always stop you if you looked like you were about to go across.

When I look back at that time there is a jumble of dozens of memories and images. Little green-painted gazebos at intervals of several hundred feet, all along the beach. Scores of cormorants perched on the hundred-foot cliffs above the caves. Nasturtiums, succulents and other wildflowers blooming in profusion after a rain. Fishing skiffs tied up to iron rings set into the concrete of the seawall at La Jolla Shores. Purse seiners anchored offshore. Waves, foam, sunshine, fog, salt air.

Even on weekends the beaches were more or less empty of people. You could ride horses on the beach; you could drive your car on the beach; people camped overnight on the beach. Residential neighborhoods were mostly modest, one-storey houses and in many parts of town were liberally sprinkled with vacant lots, dilapidated wood garages and the occasional old barn. The sprawling, canyon-furrowed hill above the town (823 feet high and rather grandly named Mount Soledad) was virtually devoid of houses, and was mostly sagebrush, cactus and narrow dirt roads carved out by the military after Pearl Harbor.

All this was marvelous, but it was still secondary to the sea. We weren't just near the sea, we were on a point and practically surrounded by the sea. No matter what part of town you were in you weren't far from the ocean. Walk down most any street, and you'd end up either at the ocean or in sight of it.

Our exposure to the sea started early: in the first or second year of elementary school we had field trips to the tide pools, walking the few blocks to the shore in single file, hand in hand with a designated partner or two, a couple of teachers herding us carefully across streets that in the 1940s were always nearly devoid of traffic.

And what a sea it was, with every type of marine environment possible: beaches where the sand fluctuated from several feet deep to totally exposed rock, depending on the seasonal swells. Long, sandy beaches and secluded coves; cliffs, caves, rocky points and headlands; sand bars, reefs, cobble areas, flat shallow stretches, steep drop-offs to deep water; beaches of gentle swells and areas with powerful surge and pounding shorebreak; rip currents, a submarine canyon, kelp, eelgrass, and an astounding variety of marine life.

To a young kid, the ocean was a wild and wooly place, with all kinds of exciting stuff going on. When the surf was up, you could hear it roaring and thundering all night; when it was calm you could hear the sea lions barking below the cliffs at Devil's Slide. Once when I was six years old, a pod of orcas attacked and killed a gray whale in the shallows between La Jolla Cove and La Jolla Shores, just a few dozen yards from the bluff and cliffs.

When I got older and started to interact with the ocean, I discovered that it was populated by big, round purple and white jellyfish, bat rays, butterfly rays, leopard sharks, moray eels, sardines and barracuda. Octopus and lobster and abalone. Seals and sea lions, sea urchins and seahorses. Tide pools filled with sea anemones, hermit crabs, nudibranchs, sea hares and various tiny fish. The sea produced hatch covers and round glass Japanese fishing net floats that appeared on the beach after storms. Once, the morning after a storm revealed a small fishing boat swept up onto the beach by winds, waves and tide during the night. Never a dull moment. An abundance of magic.

The outside world was at best a vague blur, more like a rumor than a reality. There was no reason to go anywhere else; everything a person could possibly want was here.

1947: Shorebreak 1, Me 0

Sometimes a single childhood experience can affect you for years. At least that was true for me – and it hit me in my most vulnerable spot.

On many Southern California beaches the depth of sand rises and falls according to the swell direction. Swells from one angle remove sand from the beach, and swells from the contrary direction redeposit it. This change can be dramatic. Often several feet of sand will be carved from the shore in just a couple of days or even over night, leaving sand cliffs several feet high. As kids we had great fun running and launching ourselves onto these cliffs, sliding down to the bottom and scrambling back up to do it again.

One of these sand cliffs was to have a major effect on me and my surfing life.

My parents had taken us to a beach party put on by one of their friends, with mostly adults in attendance. It was early evening heading into dark, and everyone was gathered around a fire, chatting and eating while a small swell rumbled and hissed on the darkening shore. I got bored with all the adult stuff and wandered off toward the ocean, drawn to the waves like a moth to a flame.

When I got to the sand cliff I sat down and slid to the bottom, but to my great surprise I ended up on wet sand, right where a small but consistent shorebreak was nibbling away at the base of the sand cliff. I turned and tried to climb back up. But every attempt I made just brought more sand crumbling down and I would slide backwards to the bottom. I tried and tried again, while little tongues of swirling foam from the waves would lick out to undercut the bank and make the cliff steeper.

A larger wave grabbed my ankles and pulled me off my feet. I scrambled to my knees and tried to get to the cliff, but the next wave knocked me down and dragged me toward the sea as it slid back down the steep incline of the beach. I struggled to my feet against the powerful pull of the backwash and ran back up to the sand cliff to try again to escape.

By now it was dark, with only a partial moon for light. I could see the flickering light of the beach fire casting a dancing glow on the tops of the palm trees at the far edge of the sand. It looked warm and inviting and very far away.

Between waves, above the hissing of the surge and backwash on the sand, I could hear the cheerful mindless gabbling of adult conversation. But since the sand cliff was a good two feet taller than I was, no one at the party could see me and they had no idea what was happening.

Over and over I went through the same fruitless routine: scrabble frantically at the face of the sand cliff and get a couple of feet up only to slide back down to the wet sand, where fingers of shorebreak grabbed at my ankles to pull me down and toward the sea.

I have no idea how long this grim little struggle went on, but by the time someone at the party noticed my absence and my dad came to fish me out, I was a sodden, shivering, semi-conscious lump. As my dad unsympathetically put it, I looked like a drowned rat.

It hadn't occurred to me to cry or yell for help; I was focused on survival, which was probably a good trait to learn early. The bad news was that this incident left a sense of fear and foreboding deep within my psyche: I associated waves and dim light with disaster. It would take many years for this to finally fade away.

1949: Surf mat vs. plank

As I got older and my universe expanded, I got my first lesson in surfing etiquette and a couple of other things.

In those days a common beach item was the surf mat, a stubby, thick inflatable air mattress about four feet long and two feet wide. Made of rubberized canvas, with red and blue stripes running lengthwise, and equipped with a rope that went between two grommets on one end, it could be inflated to drumhead tightness using the air hose at any gas station. In fact, many gas stations near the beach sold surf mats in the summer.

We had great fun riding waves, first launching into the soup of already broken waves, then – imitating older kids – trying to catch waves just as they broke.

My first interaction with a surfboard came via my surf mat, when I was about eight years old. Windansea (one of La Jolla's best-known breaks, and the one nearest La Jolla High School) can be quite mellow on small days. One feature on small to medium days is a reef on the inside right that forms a second section for waves that have broken on the reefs farther out. For kids, it can be a takeoff spot in its own right, and at lower tides you could take off by standing on the reef holding your surf mat and jumping toward the shore on your mat just when the wave hit. So it was that on a beautiful warm summer day, with a small south swell, I was working to catch waves on the inside right. Finally, success! A wave stood up on the reef just as I launched, and I was in it! Unfortunately, so was an Older Guy on a surfboard, who had been riding the wave from much farther out.

In those days there were still a lot of surfers riding planks – big, heavy boards, seventy pounds and more, made of redwood and spruce, with little to no rocker, round noses, square tails and primitive – if any – skegs or fins. The standard riding style was to take off at an angle, get up and get trimmed, and cut across the face in a straight line. There were some guys who did drop-leg turns, something like a telemark turn on skis, but many riders didn't even do that much maneuvering, and at some breaks they just rode straight off. In fact, if we're to believe Eugene Burdick, author of *The Ninth Wave*, at some breaks it was considered cowardly to turn or take an angle before the wave broke. Real men, apparently, went straight down the face.

If the surfer on "my" wave – actually his wave, but in those days few people thought in those terms – had been on a more modern board, he might well have been able to get around me – or he might have kicked out into my head.

As it was, his plank went sliding under my surf mat, and I took him out at the ankles, sweeping his feet out from under him, after which, still oblivious, I rode happily to the beach with his board bouncing in the white water beside me. If his board had gone over my mat instead of under it, I might have ended up in the hospital or in the morgue.

Instead of yelling at me or worse, the surfer I had swept off his board taught me two lessons at once. First, he gently and patiently explained to me why it would be much better for everyone if I would check to see if there was anyone on the wave already. Sort of like looking for cars before crossing the street. The second lesson was what he didn't do: he didn't mention "his" wave or his rights or me getting in his way. He also didn't lose his temper; instead, he educated me. So I learned two valuable things at once. What a kind and decent approach!

This was my introduction to Bill McKusick, an excellent surfer and an all-around great human being. Later, after I got a surfboard and started surfing Windansea, he was a mentor and an example in many ways.

McKusick was something of a local legend. Born in Minnesota in 1930, by 1945 he was living in La Jolla and surfing Windansea, soon moving up to ride big, gnarly breaks like the Tijuana Sloughs in the '40s and '50s. Like many Windansea surfers he was also a skier and spent a lot of time on the slopes at Sun Valley. McKusick, who was one of the first to experiment with foam as a surfboard-building material, was an all-around athlete in the mold of Jim Thorpe. I mention Thorpe because McKusick, like Thorpe, was a Native American and, also like Thorpe, as solid as a rock. Although he was kind and patient with kids, and good to his friends, he was tough as nails. His nickname, "Truck" was bestowed after some guy made fun of his Native American heritage and McKusick responded by challenging the guy to a fight. After it was over, someone remarked that the other guy looked like he had been hit by a truck. From then on, McKusick's nickname at the beach was Truck. But for me, he will always be the Older Guy who was nice to a dumb kid on a surf mat.

Late 1940s – early '50s: Alternative surfing

One of the great things about the time and place where I grew up was the almost absolute freedom to explore, experiment and innovate. Even at the risk of life and limb.

Fun in the surf continued and evolved for me as I got older. While I was still in elementary school, someone's dad picked up a four-man inflatable life raft, complete with collapsible aluminum oars, at the Army/Navy surplus store. A group of us had insane fun with those things. We'd push them out past the surf zone at La Jolla Shores, pack in as many kids as possible, and catch waves. Given the design and construction of inflatable life rafts and the total lack of expertise on our part, every wave resulted in us getting pitched spectacularly. If the wave was more than three or four feet high, the raft would flex and then snap forward, so that the resulting force combining with the breaking wave would literally catapult us through the air in a tumbling mix of kids, oars, raft and water. Then we would collect ourselves, go back out and do it again. Miraculously, no one ever took an oar in the mouth. This all seems pretty mindless, but in the process we were also learning about waves, wave energy, and how it all fit together. And every once in a while we actually managed to catch and ride a wave until we broached and got flipped over.

We kept finding new ways to surf. One feature of the still-undeveloped hillsides above the Shores was an abundance of wild mustard plants. After blooming luxuriantly golden yellow in the spring they would die, leaving large stands of pencil-thick stalks several feet tall with more or less the crumbly consistency of balsa wood with dry rot. Someone got the idea of trampling the dead stalks down to make a runway so that we could slide down the hill on flattened cardboard boxes. This was a rough ride but great fun. Standing up was way beyond our capabilities so we rode the cardboard sitting down.

The major drawback was that when you hit a small rock, it would tear the cardboard and give you a nice bruise or scrape in the process. This problem disappeared when we were given some large strips of linoleum or vinyl sheeting from someone's kitchen remodel, just the right size to use as dry-land surfboards. Just sit down, grab the leading edge and hold it up to avoid "pearling" in the dry weeds, and launch. They were a marvel of technology: far more durable than cardboard, and much better protection against the rocks.

And they were fast! We now had blazing speed that made even a short descent an experience in totally out-of-control insanity. The smallest bump would send you airborne, and every one of us had the heart-stopping experience of hurtling down the hill toward the end of the run, realizing that in a couple of seconds the slick path of broken-down stalks was going to end, leaving the rider to a lurching, grinding stop in sagebrush, dirt and, if you were unlucky, cactus. The only alternative was to bail off, but none of us ever did. Even at that age, it was death before dishonor. It was the dry land version of inflatable life rafts, and nothing could have been more fun.

1950s: Stone-cold killer

When I got into skin diving I had great fun and got some good eating fish, but one incident was shocking to me. I had speared a good-sized butterfly ray and lugged it up onto the beach, still wriggling on my spear. The plan was to kill it, fillet it, and pan-fry the fillets. Before we got to step one, the ray began a series of spasmodic convulsions and began to give birth right there on the wet sand – tiny baby butterfly rays, delicate little things that emerged rolled up like little tacos and then unfurled on the sand, fluttering and flapping weakly, as their mother died in a pool of her own blood and body fluids. I felt like an assassin, a baby-killer. I never speared rays again.

1950s: The ideal teacher

After catching my first unbroken wave on a surfboard I had the commitment to make the transition from wave rider to surfer, but I needed a teacher, and I had the best one there is.

I was not an outcast as a kid – more like a reject. For one thing, I didn't fit any of the usual categories. There were science dweebs (even in elementary school) but I wasn't one of those. There were kids who were into yo-yos, or collecting bottle-caps, or listening to the World Series on the radio. Most of that stuff seemed – well, not exactly dumb, but I just didn't get the appeal – so I didn't join in. Within a year or two, of course, all the kids who had been into whatever it was moved on, so that they no longer cared about it, either. But instead of being perceived as prescient or ahead of the curve, I was remembered as the dork who didn't get into whatever it was. You can't beat the past and you can't outlive it. Whatever happens, there it is. The past is a survivor, the original survivor. And it clings to you like a leech.

Beyond all that, of course, was the issue of competence. Already in elementary school the kids who could hit a baseball or drill you with the ball in dodge ball were looked up to. They were the winners, the leaders. On the other end of the spectrum was me. The nadir came the day they were choosing up sides for baseball and I was, once again, the last one picked. Or should I say, not picked. The team that should have been stuck with me decided that they would rather play short-handed. They reasoned, correctly, that they would do better without me than with me in the way. One less sure strikeout, one less useless fielder dropping easy fly balls or making wildly off-target throws. If memory serves, they won that game, proving their theory to be correct.

Some kids had dads who would play catch with them in the back yard, or hit fly balls to them in the park, to help them develop skills. My dad, alas, was not one of those. The beach became, in a sense, a surrogate parent.

With a surf mat, even a clumsy elementary school kid could ride waves after they had crested and collapsed into moving walls of bubbly foam, brilliant white against the blue horizon. From there, you could graduate to catching the foam with a board, and finally discover the magic of riding unbroken waves. No teams, no contests; no spectators or umpires or referees. Just the sea and the waves. Pure existence.

Once I got into surfboards, the ocean was an infinitely patient coach pitching up endless waves. No matter how many times I blew it, there was always another one on the way. No hurry, no pressure, no exasperation, no judgmental attitude. Endless calm. And instant feedback: do it right, you stay upright and on your feet. Do it wrong, you fall. It's up to you to figure out what happened, and what to do to fix it

Between waves, and during days with no waves, there were other lessons. Observe the reefs, the sand bars, the currents, the tides. The fish, the birds, the sky, the clouds.

I learned to pay attention to what was going on, and what it meant. Reef boils become active long before any set arrives. Water motion stops as a swell approaches. Offshore wind holds the waves up. Rip currents are great for getting out to the lineup faster. Other useful stuff.

As I muddled along, advancing by trial and error, I made an exciting discovery. Without anyone putting pressure on me, I did a lot better than I expected. Not that I discovered any great gift, or talent, or even moderate aptitude. Far from it. But since I was able to focus on what I was doing, rather than what someone else thought about it, my efforts paid off a lot better than they otherwise would have. At the same time I began to develop more coordination and strength, a process which occurred at about the same rate as sedimentation during the Cretaceous Period. But occur it did.

The ocean had no comment, made no criticism, applied no pressure; it let me make my own mistakes and learn from them as I could. So the ocean and the waves became a place of solace, of refuge, of freedom to be me. A pretty solid foundation for a lifetime love affair.

I wasn't the first person to turn to the ocean and surfing as a refuge. Surf superstar Laird Hamilton, bullied at school and subject to a domineering and sometimes violent father, is said to have sought refuge in the waves. Of course, in his case the end result was far more spectacular. But I did what I could with the hand I had been dealt.

1950s: The road to surferhood

I started on the road to surferhood in 1951. The following year, it was time for junior high school, which was just three blocks from the elementary school.

In elementary school I had been behind most of the other kids in terms of coordination, strength and confidence. In junior high school, as everyone else continued on the road to physical maturity, the gap widened. I was very much the archetypal late bloomer, clumsy, insecure and inarticulate. A total nerd. Which is very bad in the adolescent stage of life, filled with little junior macho competitions. I continued to retreat to the sea.

Throughout the 1940s and 1950s, and even beyond, the Caves and the Slides below the north side of the Point La Jolla cliffs were almost a secret spot. Secluded, and little-known except to locals. A place for constructive solitude. To kids, a place for adventure.

As I gravitated more toward surfing, I used my surfboard for the same sort of exploration we had done at a younger age with fins and masks and snorkels. I paddled from the Shores to the Caves, where I got off my board and explored each cave, green and red and purple mosses and sea grass glowing dimly in the faint light. I paddled beneath a low sandstone arch, not quite a tunnel, not quite a cave, but a great adventure all the same. I surfed – or attempted to surf – every possibly rideable (and unrideable) reef and shallow in the area. My desire to escape or evade was turning into something more positive: the desire to see and try everything that I could in, on and around the sea. The desire to experience the magic of the unknown.

The air above the coast—and especially along a cliff or bluff—is a boulevard for birds. Ospreys, gulls, terns, pelicans, migratory fowl of all types. The beach itself is an avian hangout, bouncy plovers, skeptical curlews, the occasional hysterical-sounding killdeer. A cormorant surfacing just offshore, red of eye and with the suspicious, disapproving glare of a crabby old neighbor. Pedestrian sandpipers milling about and charging the wet sand after every wave, like groupies chasing a rock star, probing for sand crabs. Egrets posing elegantly next to shimmering pools, waiting for a small fish to spear. Further out, over the waves, a superhighway. Migrating ducks and geese, their ragged V formations headed determinedly toward the pole or the tropics.

Whenever a school of fish appears on the surface, the immediate area is instantly converted into a market and dining hall. Service is free-for-all style; hierarchy is thrown to the wind. Diving pelicans slashing down like ballistic missiles. Seagulls and terns screaming at each other and fighting over every silvery catch. Porpoises and sea lions boiling up from below to keep the prey in a state of panic, while nearby a bobbing raft of ducks gapes in amazement. You have to wonder what it's like for the fish.

Spending an afternoon or a Saturday paddling or wandering among all this activity was balm for the soul. With a show like this, who cared about peer pressure and fitting in, all the childish politics of cool and hip, nerd and square? For a skinny misfit it was freedom from unwanted attention, a place to observe without being observed.

1950s: Young surfer dudes

By 1954 I had graduated from the generally mild waves of the beach break at La Jolla Shores to surfing Windansea, the reef break right down the street from the high school, where I was to spend a lot of time during the next few years. This had a major effect on much of the rest of my life.

The surfing industry was still more or less in its infancy, and even more so in San Diego. No surf shops. Imagine that. And no wax, and no leashes, and no wetsuits. We made our own spears. And our own skateboards. Instead of Frisbees, we threw heavy metal pie tins that skimmed through the air like flying saucers and hurt like hell if they hit you or you caught them wrong. To buy fiberglass and resin, we had to go to Kettenburg Boat Works, where the boating types looked at us as if we were retrograde invaders from another planet.

They say you can choose your friends – and not your relatives – but mine were in essence assigned by the accidents of geography and the sea.

La Jolla Junior-Senior High School was only a couple of blocks from Windansea, and once I got into surfing, it was inevitable that I would end up doing it there. And from that fact it followed that my peer group was composed of whoever else was usually surfing there as well. In many respects this group was like a motley extended family, bound not by blood or marriage but by common interests, by being thrown together at the same place and time. Dysfunctional, but a family.

Like a family, the group displayed an incredible tolerance for the extreme range of personalities, backgrounds and behaviors among its members. There were rich kids and poor kids, kids who lived in nice homes and kids who lived in their cars. High-school dropouts and graduates of USC and Stanford. Well-balanced kids and kids who already in high school had tendencies toward drinking or violence or anti-social activities.

There was cooperation and antagonism, generosity and theft, mutual respect and mutual disdain. Good times and laughter could degenerate into squalls of hostility, even violence, without much warning. But somehow within a short time everything was calm again. And there was never any issue of teamwork or second string or bench-warming. You went in the water, and when a wave came, you surfed it.

Without going into burdensome details, it should be noted that my biological family was, shall we say, lacking in warmth and closeness. This made my ersatz surfing foster family more important to me than it might have been otherwise. And since I got plenty of unpredictable and unstable behavior at home the peculiarity and instability of the surf crew seemed normal, even acceptable. A perfect fit, as it were.

So there I was, the former loner, the social reject, all thumbs and two left feet, finally involved in something I enjoyed with a group of people who, if not exactly kind and helpful, at least didn't really give a damn about much besides the ocean.

In junior high school our little group lived for surfing. There were no surf magazines and no surf movies, but we devoured whatever tidbits we could. There were no public buoy reports and no surf forecasts, so we learned to read the weather map printed every day in the local paper, and came to understand where the troughs needed to be to create a solid north swell, and that a high pressure area over Nevada would bring offshore winds to Southern California.

We were fascinated by anything that had some connection to surfing or, by extension, Hawai'i. Someone stumbled across a book by a political scientist named Eugene Burdick, *The Ninth Wave*, which included stuff about bodysurfing and surfing Santa Cruz on big redwood planks. We took turns reading the one copy that was available at the public library. Someone else came across a 33-1/3 RPM record (on red vinyl!) called *Polynesia!* which featured drumming and singing from the South Seas. (Amazingly, that 1954 album can still be found online.) In short, we lived, breathed, slept and dreamed about the ocean and waves and riding those waves. It was all part of the magic.

As far as the rest of the school was concerned, our obsession with surfing set us apart, and not in a good way. At our junior-senior high school (grades 7 through 12) there were only a handful of us. We sat at our own table in the cafeteria. The jocks – football especially –thought we were weird, and from their table they would sometimes try to hit one of us in the head with a thrown apple core or some other bit of garbage if we weren't looking.

Meanwhile, my parents were generally oblivious to whatever I was doing outside the house. For both of them, the ocean was to look at occasionally. My dad had a dim perception that I was involved in something connected with the ocean and some sort of floatation device; he called it "rafting." I supposed he was recalling the days when we used to play on the waves in Navy surplus life rafts; I never asked. Being from the Midwest, they didn't know the ocean and didn't care to. They weren't afraid of it, but they didn't really trust it. To them, it was like the desert, but with salt water instead of sand. Death Valley with waves.

But all this indifference changed when some kid somewhere got hit in the head with a surfboard, or maybe there was just some speculation about the possibility of some kid somewhere getting hit in the head with a surfboard. Whatever the cause, my parents' mental alarms went off. Surfing was dangerous! So my dad told me that I was never to go surfing. Ever.

To me, this was beyond dumb. They would panic about an event that probably never even happened, but thought nothing of letting me wander off and play in the shorebreak – accidentally, but still – at night. I mean, from the age of seven or so we were allowed to go on all-day hikes through the sagebrush- and cactus-covered hills, unsupervised, carrying machetes and hatchets and hunting knives. We had rock fights in which at least one kid had to be taken to the hospital for stitches on his split forehead. We crashed spectacularly on bicycles, and later on skateboards. By junior high school I had a .22 rifle and was allowed to wander around with my similarly-armed little pals shooting at things out in the boonies (which in those days was about a mile or so away from my best buddy's house). I had a lethal pole spear with razor-sharp barbs, and went out with similarly-armed pals in the water. We could have shot or speared each other – or ourselves – and my parents had no worries about any of that.

But suddenly, among all these activities, surfing was dangerous and forbidden. So now I had to start making up stories about where I was going and where I had been, and why my hair was wet and I had sand on my feet. I spent even less time at home and more at the beach and in the water. And in the process I learned to love the ocean even more.

In the '50s, Beatniks used to divide society into themselves (Beatniks) vs. what they called "squares" – normal people. We didn't think in those terms, but if we had it would have been us (surfers) and everyone else. Like my parents.

1950s: Street surfing and more

In junior high, about 1953 or '54, the kids in our little surf group made skateboards. I don't recall who thought to do it; I know that a couple of the Older Guys had already made them but I don't think I ever saw one of them riding until later.

Anyhow, our process was simple. You got a roller skate and removed the trucks (the assembly that included a pair of wheels and their axle). Inside each truck was a block of rubber that acted as a shock absorber and also stabilized the wheels. You had to carve down the sides of the rubber at an angle, to allow the board to tip left and right above the wheels. Then you put the trucks back together and screwed or bolted them onto the bottom of a length of wood. That was it – you then had a skateboard. You could cut out a piece of plywood to a desired shape, but additional width restricted the amount of tilt when you wanted to turn (the rail or edge of the board would drag on the pavement). For this reason (and also because they required no shaping skills) we used 2x4s; we kept them short, just a couple of feet long. The short length gave them a good short turning radius. It also made them unstable and prone to shimmying at high speed, but that just added to the excitement.

The worst thing about our homemade skateboards was the steel wheels: if you hit even a small bit of gravel or a crack in the sidewalk, the wheel would stop and you would go flying. We pretty much had to ride on sidewalks since on a rough street the wheels would find an obstacle every few feet.

One of the crew was Rick Naish. I met Rick right about the time I started junior high school in 1952, and we started a friendship that lasted for decades. Naish, who went on to create Naish sails in Kailua, was a genius. In high school he played the saxophone and clarinet, and could transpose music instantly from its original key to any key he wanted, without faltering or missing a beat. I once asked him how he did it.

"Easy. Just play everything a few steps higher or lower." Right.

He was a great golfer and a fearless skier. On our home-made skateboards he ripped hills and got air off of driveways and humps in the sidewalk. He taught me the trick of shaving down the corners of the rubber cushion in the truck to make turning sharper. And he picked up surfing as if it were nothing and went on to ride epic waves at Waimea. A constant flow of creativity and achievement. Keeping up with Naish was an adventure in itself.

Once Naish and I and a kid named Randy Sweeney were riding our primitive skateboards down Torrey Pines Road, a nice long hill with a pretty good grade. The sidewalk had lots of driveways, and if you stayed fairly close to the curb the curved cut of each driveway was like a little ramp. You would hit the uphill side and feel temporarily weightless, then come down in the driveway. Hit the downhill side with enough speed and you could get an inch or so of air, which to us was quite a feat.

So there we were, skating down that sidewalk, getting more and more air on each driveway as our speed increased. On about the third driveway, just as I went up, I saw motion out of the corner of my eye. It was the front truck of my skateboard, which had detached itself and was headed out into the street. Total disaster! When the front of the board hit the sidewalk it stopped dead, sending me flying.

The detached skate wheels in the busy street were quickly reduced to scrap by the tires of a dozen speeding cars and trucks – even in those days Torrey Pines Road was well-traveled access route into La Jolla – and if I had fallen in that direction I would have been ground up right along with them. But as luck would have it I fell forward.

I landed on my feet, running as fast as I could, but there was no way my feet could keep up with my body and I ended up doing a flat dive onto the sidewalk – just like we used to do in order to bodysurf after falling off a surfboard. Probably not the best move, but I didn't have any really viable options. It was either that or land on my head. So I bodysurfed along the cement, removing large areas of skin in the process. Kids at that age being relatively devoid of empathy, Naish and Sweeney though it was the funniest thing they had ever seen.

We continued on to the Shores to go bodysurfing for real. That salt water really hurt when it touched my raw patches! But it was probably a good thing for healing.

Shortly after our skateboard phase, we got into making our own surfboards. We still weren't old enough to drive, so we would get an Older Guy – usually someone's older brother – who was going up to L.A. for a load of balsa to give a couple of us a ride. These kids then picked up enough balsa for the rest of us. Of course they always kept the best pieces for themselves.

Lacking power tools, we made our boards the old-fashioned way: hand saw, drawknife, carpenter's plane, lots of sandpaper. After going through this twice and ending up with clumsy, ugly boards that were an insult to the waves and to surfing itself, I realized that surfboard making, like team sports, was never going to be my thing. Meanwhile kids like Naish, Carl Ekstrom and Al Nelson kept at it, and went on to create their own surfboard brands.

1950s: Living on the edge

Our outlier status as surfers at La Jolla High was only one small part of a bigger picture. We really didn't fit in anywhere.

Windansea, c. 1957: Young misfits?
L to R: Ronald Patterson (RIP), Randy Sweeney, Bill Kemp, Butch Van Artsdalen
(RIP), the author, David Cheney (RIP), Rob Linden, Mike Tellep (RIP)

1950s America was a weird mix of crew cuts, ducktail haircuts, singing cowboys, R&B, Elvis, the McCarthy hearings, the Cold War, the Korean War, loyalty oaths, J. Edgar Hoover, bikers, pachucos, the House Un-American Activities Committee, spy scares, and the rapid growth of suburbia. There were oil wells next to the beach in the LA area, in some places there were still cowboys within earshot of the surf, and the top tunes on AM radio included numbers like *Ghost Riders in the Sky*. There were films like *The Wild One* (bikers) and *Rebel Without a Cause* (alienated rich kid), *Blackboard Jungle* (urban hooligans) and *The Man with the Golden Arm* (drug addiction). None of this applied to us.

As West Coast surfers we didn't fit any of the stereotypes. We were on the edge: not only on the western edge of the country, but outside the prevailing cultural currents of the US, which tended toward buttoned down, conservative and conformist in urban and suburban areas, and primitive in many rural regions. Our reality was surfing and diving, beach parties and coast trips and expeditions to Hawai'i or deep into Mexico; lost weekends in Tijuana and Ensenada; bullfights and the Long Bar.

As San Diego surfers, we were even farther removed, on the edge of the edge: in the extreme southwestern corner of the United States, with Hawai'i calling from beyond the horizon, Mexico visible from the lineup and the nearest large American city, Los Angeles – including the Malibu-Hollywood surf scene – a vague smog-filled blot far to the north. L.A. was so alien to us that we actually felt closer – culturally if not geographically – to Hawai'i. Our sense of familiarity was reflected in the fact that we always referred to Hawai'i as "the Islands" as if they were just offshore, right over the horizon.

It's all about timing

We were lucky that the times allowed us to afford a free and spontaneous lifestyle. You could live in your car at one point and still end up with a decent life. You could go to Aspen to be a ski bum, arrive with $5 in your pocket, spend a season skiing and leave town with all new equipment, money in your wallet and a full tank of gas.

You could live a surfer's life without permanent employment into your thirties, then get the job with the best pension you could find and stick with it until retirement, surfing all the way.

Earlier eras were even more forgiving. A surfer like Woody Brown could sink into depression, end up homeless on the beach in Hawai'i, and rise up again to become a known and loved figure on the surf scene. Doc Paskowitz is another example of an earlier-era surfer who lived life on his terms – including years of living in a van with his family while surfing all over California and Central America – and made a success of it.

It's quite possible that many of the homeless people one sees today in the beach areas of cities like San Diego would have done much better in an earlier age. The bottom rung of the ladder wasn't so far out of reach, and there were more opportunities for people who marched to the tune of a different drummer. Now the fee to get into – or stay afloat in – the economic mainstream is much higher.

The luck of the draw

I was incredibly lucky to grow up in such a special time and place – the '40s and '50s and early '60s; La Jolla back in the day, Mexico, Japan, Hawai'i, all of it. I might have ended up in Salina, Kansas, my dad's hometown. After the war, we might have moved to L.A. or any one of a thousand other places in California. I might never have surfed, never have fallen in love with Mexico, never lived in Japan. Or Aspen on a shoestring. Or Spain, or Brazil. Even Cody, my boxing nemesis, was a stroke of luck – Pomona College really wasn't a place where I belonged.

And there was my old home break, Windansea. Even within the Southern California surfing subculture, Windansea used to be recognized as unique. For all of its imperfections – and who among us is perfect? – it filled a need. And it gave me some of the tools and attitudes that helped live a life that has been, in retrospect, quite possibly the best one that I might have chosen as the best match for me.

I can't wait to see what happens next.

ABOUT THE AUTHOR

David Rearwin was born in 1941 and spent his early childhood in a mostly Hispanic trailer park, absorbing Spanish. At the age of five he moved to a house a block from the beach in La Jolla where he saw his first surfers. Those two things – Spanish and surfing (and, thanks to a chance encounter with some camouflage netting, curiosity about Japan) – shaped his life. A budding journeyman surfer at the age of ten, he still gets out in the waves in his eighties. He recently embraced stand up paddling and stand up paddle surfing as ways to keep in touch with his beloved ocean. When not surfing or paddling he enjoys shooting photos and videos of other people riding waves, and communing with his inner ten-year-old. He lives with his long-suffering wife in San Diego.

His books include *Surf Better, Spanish for Surfers,* and *The Surfer's Workout.* For details visit his author page (Dave Rearwin) on Amazon.

Scott Darran photo

Made in the USA
Coppell, TX
03 December 2021

66893528R00198